DAVID HUME was born in Edinburgh in 1711. He was educated at Edinburgh University where he matriculated in 1723 and stayed for two or three years. He then spent seven years at home, nominally studying law, but in fact reading voraciously, particularly philosophy and criticism. In 1734, after a brief period as a clerk in Bristol, he went to France for three years, where he composed the *Treatise of Human Nature* which was published in London in 1739. In 1740 he settled at Ninewells and in the following years he produced *Essays Moral and Political* and *Philosophical Essays Concerning Human Understanding* which in subsequent editions became *An Enquiry Concerning Human Understanding*.

In 1744 he failed to obtain the chair of Ethics and Pneumatical Philosophy at Edinburgh University; in 1745-6 he was companion to the Marquess of Annandale, and he then spent two years as secretary to General St Clair. In 1749 he returned to Edinburgh where he became Keeper of the Advocate's Library and began work on his *History of Great Britain*. In 1763-5 he was private secretary to the British Ambassador in Paris, Embassy Secretary and, for a short period, chargé d'affaires. In 1767-8 he was in London as Under-Secretary of State, Northern Department. Then in 1768, he returned to Edinburgh where he settled.

David Hume, described by Adam Smith as 'approaching as nearly to the idea of a perfectly wise and virtuous man, as perhaps the nature of human frailty will admit' died in 1776. His *Dialogues on Natural Religion* were published posthumously in 1779.

A TREATISE
OF HUMAN NATURE

*Being an attempt to introduce
the experimental method of reasoning
into moral subjects*

BOOK I Of The Understanding

DAVID HUME

Edited with an introduction by
D. G. C. MACNABB, M.A.
Fellow of Pembroke College, Oxford

FONTANA/COLLINS

Books I and II of *A Treatise of Human Nature*
were first published in 1739
Book III and the Appendix were first published in 1740
The Abstract was first published in 1740
First issued in the Fontana Library in 1962
Fifth Impression September 1978

© in the editor's introduction and notes:
William Collins Sons & Co. Ltd 1962

Made and printed in Great Britain by
William Collins Sons & Co Ltd, Glasgow

CONTENTS

ADVERTISEMENT
to books I and II

My design in the present work is sufficiently explained in the Introduction. The reader must only observe, that all the subjects I have there planned out to myself are not treated in these two volumes. The subjects of the Understanding and Passions make a complete chain of reasoning by themselves; and I was willing to take advantage of this natural division, in order to try the taste of the public. If I have the good fortune to meet with success, I shall proceed to the examination of Morals, Politics, and Criticism, which will complete this Treatise of Human Nature. The approbation of the public I consider as the greatest reward of my labours; but am determined to regard its judgment, whatever it be, as my best instruction.

EDITOR'S NOTE

The footnotes in roman type are Hume's; those in italic are the editor's. † throughout refers readers to the editor's notes, which begin on p. 357.

INTRODUCTION

by D. G. C. Macnabb

I. THE INSPIRATION

David Hume was born in Edinburgh in 1711. His family, though far from wealthy, was well connected, and his father owned a small estate near Berwick, called "Ninewells". He was educated at Edinburgh University, where he matriculated in 1723 and stayed two or three years. There is no record of his graduation, and some uncertainty as to the subjects he studied, but they probably included Latin, Greek, Logic, Metaphysics, Natural Philosophy, Mathematics and Ethics. After leaving Edinburgh he spent some seven years at home, nominally studying law, in fact reading voraciously on other topics, particularly philosophy and criticism.

Hume was one of the many who in their late teens are convinced that they have obtained a new insight into truth, which they must at all costs make known to the world. He was also one of the few who are right in this conviction. In a letter dated 1734,[1] he tells of his long search for some "new medium, by which truth might be established" and the endless disputes of philosophers and critics resolved. At last, at the age of eighteen, "There seemed to be opened up to me a new Scene of Thought, which transported me beyond measure and made me, with an ardour natural to young men, throw up every other pleasure or business to apply entirely to it." The letter, itself a distinctly pathological document addressed to a Physician, continues to tell at great length of the prolonged struggle with mental and physical ailments which Hume

[1] Greig, letter 3.

7

went through in the effort to think out and express his new system of philosophy. Finally after a brief, disagreeable, but apparently salutary change of scene in a merchant's office in Bristol, Hume retired for three years to La Flèche in Anjou, where he composed the " Treatise of Human Nature", published in London in 1738.

The Treatise is therefore a young man's work, the product of eight years' intense and agonising labour, designed to make as credible as possible a new, revolutionary and paradoxical philosophy. It is packed with the excitement of invention and discovery, and the foreknowledge of an intensely hostile reception.

The reception was in fact distressingly negative. Poor sales and for seven months no review. Then in " The History of the Works of the Learned " appeared a long, unfair, frivolously abusive and patronising review. In desperation Hume wrote and published anonymously an abstract of the Treatise, explaining the central thesis of Book I. This abstract is included in the present edition as Appendix A.

What was " the new Scene of Thought " that seemed to be opened up to Hume at eighteen? What was " the new Medium " by which Truth might be established? We shall never know for certain, for we have no evidence how far the cardinal points of Hume's philosophy had crystallised in his mind at that age. But he does say later on in the same letter, speaking of the moral philosophy " transmitted to us by Antiquity " that it was " entirely hypothetical ", and that " everyone consulted his Fancy in creating schemes of Virtue and Happiness, without regarding human Nature, upon which every conclusion must depend. This therefore I resolved to make my principal study, and the source from which I would derive every Truth in Criticism as well as Morality."

In the Introduction to the Treatise the same point is made and applied generally to all philosophy and the sciences as well. Philosophers start from arbitrarily assumed hypotheses and become entangled in endless disputes. A study of Human Nature is the only thing that can provide a sure foundation for argument, a touchstone by which hypotheses can be tested. It is I think fairly safe to assume that some notion of how the study of Human Nature could be used to settle the age-long disputes of philosophy formed at least the setting of Hume's new scene of thought.

2. THE RESULT

What were the main features of the philosophy which resulted from Hume's adolescent vision?

His system hinges mainly on the notion of cause and effect. This concept had been central in philosophy ever since Plato in the *Phaedo* found it necessary to examine it in order to decide what, if anything, could cause the destruction of a soul.

The context was typical of centuries of metaphysical thinking. Philosophers used the idea of cause to argue entirely *a priori* about the freedom of the will, the immortality of the soul, the existence of God, the relation of mind to matter and the reality or unreality of the physical world. Their arguments were all attempts to demonstrate that one thing x can only be, or cannot be, the cause of or caused by another thing y. All assumed or tried to prove that nothing came into existence without a cause.

The result was endless disputes, wherein the number of conflicting views showed that certainty was unattainable, and the dogmatic tone of each disputant implied that it had been attained.[2] And the rival systems were as crazy as could be. Descartes, finding no intelligible connection between the ideas of the mind and their supposed external causes, invoked the veracity of God to reassure us that the latter are what, in our more scientific moments, we take them to be. His followers, arguing that matter could not affect so different a substance as mind, supposed that God

[2] Treatise, Introduction, p. 39.

intervened continually to establish a regular correspondence between our sensations and external events. Going further, Malebranche denied any power to material things, ascribing this attribute to God alone. Leibnitz avoided the difficulties of the infinite divisibility of matter by supposing a world consisting wholly of souls, whose thoughts, unrolling in a pre-established harmony with one another, presented the appearance of a material world in Space and Time. For Berkeley matter was an unintelligible assumption, which, since it confessedly could not cause the ideas in our minds, explains nothing; God is the only intelligible cause of experience, and, since to be is to be perceived, all things exist only in the minds of God and his creature spirits.

Metaphysicians and theologians were not the only offenders. Natural scientists and mathematicians allowed themselves to be embroiled in strange disputes about the possibility of a void, the infinite divisibility of space and matter, and the inter-relation of mind and body. Moralists tried to demonstrate our duties by purely theoretical arguments.

Hume has a cure for all this. It arises, he thinks, from certain mistakes.

(1) The first mistake is to suppose that matters of fact, e.g. the existence of God, or the immortality of the soul, can be *demonstrated* deductively. Demonstrations depend on the relations of ideas, not of things, and prove only what is conceivable or inconceivable, not what is in fact the case.

(2) The second mistake is to think that demonstrations can be carried out without analysing the origins in experience of the ideas employed. Failure so to analyse the ideas of space and time, existence and mind led to most of the absurd disputes about infinite divisibility, and to the fantastic systems of Leibnitz, Malebranche and Berkeley. Failure so to analyse the idea of cause led to the third mistake.

(3) The third mistake is the idea that causation is a real bond between things, which can be either demonstrated *a priori,* or inferred from observations.

(4) The fourth mistake is to suppose that demonstrative reasoning is the only valid kind of reasoning. This can only lead to scepticism, and arises from regarding *belief* as a voluntary act of the mind, owing allegiance to logic alone. Hume attempts to show that on the contrary it is a feeling with which we are forced to regard some ideas rather than others, because they represent what we have been accustomed to find in past experience. It is this " customary determination of the mind " that we refer to when we talk of the " necessary connection " between cause and effect, and it is this special " manner of conception " that differentiates what we call " realities " from figments of the imagination. Empirical reasoning concerning matters of fact is therefore governed by instinct and habit, not by logic, and is none the worse for that.

In parallel fashion Hume in Book III of the Treatise exposes the error of regarding moral goodness and badness as demonstrable and intrinsic properties of men and actions. On the contrary, he says, these terms express only those feelings of approval and disapproval which we feel when we consider human behaviour in the light of the pleasant and unpleasant consequences which experience shows it to be likely to produce for all concerned.

Hume thought that the case for this view depended on an elaborate theory of the psychological machinery of the " passions ", which he elaborates in Book II.

The strength and the consequences of this philosophy were totally unrecognised by almost all Hume's contemporaries and immediate successors. Only Kant saw the importance of his account of causation, and Jeremy Bentham found in Hume's moral theory the inspiration for his doctrine of Utilitarianism.

The consequences of Hume's philosophy are no less than the death of all rationalistic metaphysics and ethics, the acceptance of a purely descriptive role for natural science, and the inclusion of human thought and action as natural processes within the province of biology and psychology.

3. THE METHOD

Hume thought that he reached these conclusions by applying to the human mind the experimental method used by the natural sciences. This claim appears in the sub-title of the Treatise. He realised that there are special difficulties. If experiments are made with human subjects, their knowledge or suspicion of what is going on is likely to affect the results. Therefore, he says, " we must glean up our experiments from a cautious observation of human life ".[3] One wonders whether Ninewells and La Flèche were really favourably situated man-watching stations.

It is probable that Hume's enthusiasm for the experimental method was inspired mainly by Sir Isaac Newton's work. James Gregory, who was Professor of Mathematics at Edinburgh till 1725, was, according to Reid, the first professor who taught the doctrines of Newton in a Scotch university, and he was succeeded by a notable Newtonian, Colin Maclaurin. Hume may also have read Francis Bacon's remark, that his inductive method applied not only to the natural, but to all the sciences (*Novum Organum,* 1 Aph. 79).

Sometimes Hume speaks of the science of man, the foundation of his philosophy, as something entirely new.[4] Sometimes, in more conciliatory mood, he represents himself as following in the footsteps of the English philosophers Locke, Shaftesbury, Mandeville, Hutcheson and

[3] Introduction, p. 44. This sentence shows that Hume did not use the word " experiment " in its modern sense of a *contrived* appeal to experience. It covered any kind of empirical observation.

[4] *ibid.,* p. 41. For the influence of Newton, see Part 1, Sect. IV, p. 56.

Butler.[5] His opinion probably was that though these philosophers, in opposition to continental rationalists, had made some attempt to base their theories on empirical facts about human beings, none had made a systematic attempt to work out an empirical science of man, and none had found any general principles by which the subject could be unified, as Mechanics had been unified by Newton's Laws of Motion, and the science of mind was going to be unified by Hume's application of the Association of Ideas.[6]

It is noteworthy that Hume does not include Berkeley in his list of " British Empiricists ". He is often represented as carrying on that development of the implications of Locke's philosophy which Berkeley began. In fact, apart from his acceptance of Berkeley's views on abstract ideas, he seems to have worked out a philosophy quite independent of Berkeley's, resembling it in some respects, differing in others.

Like Berkeley, Hume tried to get behind the customary associations of words with one another to the impressions of sense (" ideas " in Berkeley's terminology) that gave the words meaning. Hence both of them rejected Locke's account of substance. Both philosophers inherited from Locke the false picture of sense perception as the awareness of a kind of mosaic of simple impressions of sense, mirrored by images in memory and imagination. Hence both ended up with chimerical accounts of our knowledge of the physical world. But Berkeley believed in the power of reason, given concrete ideas to think with, to construct a rational picture of the universe. He was at heart a metaphysician and a theologian, out to put natural science and empirical reasoning in their proper inferior place. Hume's programme, to be the Newton of the human mind, was quite different. Berkeley did not even profess to be trying

[5] *ibid.*, p. 42. For the opinions of these authors, consult L. A. Selby-Bigge, *The British Moralists.*
[6] Abstract, p. 352.

to work out a system of true empirical generalisations about the human mind. His object was to prove the nonsensicality of all materialistic, and the rationality of theistic, explanations. Hume rightly regarded him as a sceptic and a metaphysician, not as an empirical philosopher.

Of the philosophers Hume does mention, he probably owed most to Locke and Hutcheson. Hutcheson maintained that nature has endowed men with more senses than five. Among them is a moral sense. Just as fresh milk has a sweet smell to him that smells it, and stale milk a sour smell, so have actions tending to happiness one feeling, and those tending to unhappiness an opposite feeling to the mind that considers them. These feelings we express by calling the actions " good " and " bad ". Hume's moral theory was similar, and Kemp Smith (*The Philosophy of David Hume*) has argued that it was from his moral theory that Hume got the analogous idea that belief is a feeling we have when we consider what is usual, expressed by such phrases as " I believe . . .", " It must be that . . .", " It is probable that . . .". Ideas that represent what we have been accustomed to find have the smell of truth.

It is generally admitted that Hume did not in fact do what he set out to do. There is perhaps one passage in the Treatise which records a genuine experiment with a spot of ink upon paper. (Part II, Sects. I & IV.) There are no no careful compilations of actual observations of human behaviour, subjected to statistical analysis. Hume could not have carried out his project, first because he had no idea how to conduct a scientific investigation, and secondly because, if he had conducted one, the result would have been empirical psychology, which by itself settles no philosophical problems.

How then did so intelligent a man think that he was doing something which he was not doing? And how did he nevertheless achieve such important results?

The answer, I suggest, is that he was doing something that badly needed doing, and which is in certain ways like conducting an unprejudiced experimental investigation. He threw aside (to a large extent) preconceived theories, and took a new look at the facts. That sounds like a description of sound scientific method. But there is a difference. The natural scientists look at *things,* often with the aid of optical and other instruments. Facts cannot be looked at with a microscope. Scientific facts are often established by looking at things through a microscope. But there are facts of a kind that cannot be established by looking at things through a microscope, but rather by reflection. For instance the fact that facts cannot be looked at through a microscope.

It is surprising how difficult it is to see these facts of reflection clearly, and how startlingly decisive they can be in philosophy. A classical case of this is Aristotle's refutation of Plato's theory of pleasure. Plato said pleasure is the replenishment of a deficiency, e.g. satisfying thirst. Aristotle replied that deficiencies can be replenished quickly or slowly, but that we cannot enjoy ourselves quickly or slowly.

The freshness and vigour of Hume's philosophy arises from this. He uses his own exceptional powers of reflection to take a new look at the facts, and even his more fantastic theories are for the most part designed to accommodate the facts he had discovered. For instance his theory that the mind (or " self ") is only a series of perceptions, and that our belief in independently existing physical things consists only in there being in the mind sub-series of interrupted impressions of sense padded out with lively images to form a coherent picture, is forced on him by his discovery that we have no impression of the mind or self. (Part IV, Section 11, para 6). The disingenuousness of regarding this last proposition as a finding of empirical psychology comes out clearly in Section VI, para 3. Hume here pretends to admit that other people may have impressions of *their* selves but he has none of his. But if this were a properly empirical enquiry he should have issued a questionnaire to a selected cross sec-

tion of subjects and collated the findings of their introspective observations on this point. The fact Hume clearly
perceived is that the mind is not the sort of thing that
could be seen, heard, smelt, tasted, or even felt, as a pain
or a passion is felt.

The analogy between philosophical and empirical investigations can be taken further. Empirical facts are discovered by examining things; facts of reflection are discovered by examining " ideas ". To call them facts is
indeed to depart from Hume's terminology, in which they
should be classed as " relations of ideas." Chemists analyse
actual specimens of water, and find that it is H_2O. Hume
analyses the " idea " of cause and effect, and finds that it
implies contiguity, succession, and a necessary connection
which can neither be perceived by sense in any single case,
nor deductively inferred from any collection of cases.

Hume constantly uses the language of empirical investigation to describe his philosophical investigations. " Let us
therefore cast our eye on any two objects, which we call
cause and effect, and turn them on all sides, in order to
find that impression, which produces an idea of such prodigious consequence " (Part III, Section II). " Take any
action allowed to be vicious; wilful murder for instance.
Examine it in all lights, and see if you can find that matter
of fact . . ., which you call *vice* . . . The vice entirely
escapes you as long as you consider the object. You can
never find it till you turn your reflection into your own
breast and find a sentiment of disapprobation " (Book III,
Part I, Section II).

To what extent was Hume misled by this analogy? Certainly we may write off such expressions as " cast our eye
on," " turn on all sides," " examine in every light " as
metaphorical. For he is talking of imaginary or remembered cases considered in the study, not actual things
observed in the laboratory. But when he speaks of " finding a sentiment of disapprobation in our own breasts," or
finding an impression from which an idea is derived, he is
not speaking metaphorically. This kind of finding he

does, I think, regard as a genuine empirical discovery, an observation in the field of introspective psychology.

Hume appears to have had a picture of his method of philosophical investigation based on his theory of impressions and ideas. An idea, he thought, was a mental picture. However fantastic the idea, the elements (" simple ideas ") of which it was composed were copies of actual impressions of the senses or of feeling. The analysis of an idea then consisted of two stages. First the breaking down of the complex idea into its simple constituents, and second the identification of the simple impressions of which the simple ideas are copies. Hume was convinced of the great value of this method. " It is impossible perfectly to understand any idea, without tracing it up to its origin and examining that primary impression from which it arises. The examination of the impression bestows a clearness on the idea; and the examination of the idea bestows a like clearness on all our reasoning." (Part III, Section II p. 121.) " And by this means, we may, perhaps, attain a new microscope, or species of optics, by which, in the moral sciences the most minute, and most simple ideas may be so enlarged as to fall readily under our observation." (Enquiry, Section VII, Part I, para. 49).

It is of some interest to enquire how Hume's " microscope " was supposed to work. For many philosophers would say he was right in thinking that the analysis of ideas is an important part of philosophical method, and that by it new facts of reflection can be established, against which philosophical theories can be tested. The misconceptions he entertained about his microscope, and the results he achieved by it, cannot but throw light on the vexed question of the nature of philosophical method.

It is of course *general* ideas that Hume analyses, e.g. the ideas of cause, of vice, of existence. Now Hume follows Berkeley in rejecting Locke's doctrine of Abstract General Ideas. We have no single idea or picture in our mind of vice in general. To have a general idea, e.g. of vice, is to be able to form an indefinite number of partic-

ular pictures of particular actions, associated one with
another because of their resemblance, and all associated
by custom with the word *vice*. To analyse a complex
general idea we must therefore call up and compare
specimens of the appropriate range of particular complex
ideas and see what constituent ideas they all have in
common. This procedure has a formal similarity to the
method of empirical enquiry which J. S. Mill called the
" Method of Agreement ". Alternatively we may find that
there is just one simple idea or group of ideas, the exclusion
of which from a complex picture prevents it being an idea
of a vicious action, and the inclusion of which would make
it such. This is the counterpart of Mill's " Method of
Difference ".

Hence we find Hume constantly philosophising by the
use of imaginary cases, or more often asking the reader to
consider any case he pleases of a vicious action, of cause
and effect and so on. The admissibility of imaginary cases
plainly differentiates philosophical analysis from scientific
analysis. Imaginary drops of water are quite useless to the
chemical analyst.

If we ask how Hume decides that imaginary cases (a),
(b), (c), which all contain a certain element (x), are all
instances of a certain concept (C), and that imaginary case
(d), from which (x) is omitted, is not an instance of the
concept (C), how does he answer? In fact, as far as I
know, he does not tell us. The only answer he *could* give,
so far as I can see, is that (a), (b), (c) are all associated by
custom with the word " C " and case (d) is not. If this is
his implicit answer, then what he is doing is analysing the
meanings of words. He is not just classifying the innumerable complex pictures that throng his fancy according
to the elements they happen to have in common, as an
entomologist might do with butterflies. He is rather examining ranges of cases already classified by our habits of
speech, to discover the criteria by which the classification
was made, and he usually sees very clearly for what purposes the classifications he investigates are used. Causal

connections and coincidences are distinguished for the purposes of prediction and practical control, vicious and unfortunate actions for purposes of corrective treatment. It is this sort of interest that makes him a philosopher and not just an unconscious philologist.

But so far we do not seem to have explained the actual use of the microscope, rather the method of selecting and preparing the slides. For Hume is very definite that the illumination he seeks is got by producing and examining not the simple ideas of which complex ideas are composed, but the " primary impressions " from which those simple ideas are derived. Now it would seem that in order to examine an impression we must actually have it; and to have it we must, except in certain cases of feelings, excited merely by our own thoughts, face ourselves with a real case. Did Hume ever actually proceed in this way? Unfortunately it is difficult to tell. His language is often such as might be used either to describe an imaginary experiment or report an actual one. Take the case of the discovery of the crucial impression on which the idea of necessary connection is founded. (Part III, Section XIV, para 1). Hume may be reporting his observations of actual experiments with his own finger and a candle flame, and describing the actual *feeling* he gets when the same thing constantly happens. Let us charitably suppose that he is.

His view appears to be this. We have an idea of cause and effect, of which the idea of flame producing heat is an example. This idea or picture represents a flame and a feeling of heat in the finger immediately following the application of the flame, *and something more*. The content of this extra feature is obscure and evanescent. Introspection of the idea fails to reveal its character, though its verbal associate " necessary connection " is certain. So we have the word for the idea, the context of the idea but not the content of the idea. So we do an experiment. We know from experience that if we burn our finger in the candle flame again and again we shall think of flame and heat as not only regularly connected but *necessarily* so.

The idea of necessity must have some counterpart in the actual experiences. So we give ourselves the actual experience and *find* the missing counterpart—a feeling in the mind. It is not the pain in the finger, which is already represented in the picture by other features; for the same reason, it is not the juxtaposition of flame and finger, the brightness of the flame. The necessary connection eludes us till we find it in our own minds. So this alone can be the source of the elusive idea. In this way we can see of what impression the obscure and puzzling idea of necessary connection is a copy; somewhat as a physiologist, noticing in a blood smear a faint whitish streak, might by using a microscope see that it was the appearance of a concentration of white cells.

Hume's microscope seems therefore to be like a real microscope in its effect. It brings into clear view something obscurely seen. But it is not like a microscope in the way it works. For the clearer view is obtained by conducting an experiment by the use of our unaided natural faculties, without any artificial aid to observation.

4. CRITICISMS AND ASSESSMENT

We all feel, on reading Hume, that something is wrong with his internal impression of necessity. How does he know that others have the *same* feeling as he finds in himself? Would it affect his general position if it were shown experimentally that many people get a feeling of inevitability the very first time they observe certain types of causal process, say communication of motion by impulse?[7] Would this be an *a priori* knowledge of causal powers? And suppose some people felt such an impression in cases where there was in fact no causal connection? As when Siegfried cleaves the already cloven stage anvil?

Surely the proper thing to say of these cases is that

[7] cf. Michotte " *La perception de la causalité* ".

whatever the conditions in which the feeling occurs, and whatever the feeling may be like, if and only if the person who has it confidently expects the correlation to be repeated in other similar cases does he believe there is a causal connection, and if and only if experience in fact shows it to be repeated is there really a causal connection. And these conditions might be fulfilled even if the person in question had no *feeling* of inevitability at all.

The conclusion I wish to suggest is that Hume had indeed made important discoveries about cause and effect; that it is the only relation on which inferences to unobserved matters of fact can be based, that it cannot be established by *a priori* reasoning, that the only kind of empirical evidence for it is constant correlation, that constant correlation is evidence[8] of nothing but further constant correlation, and that the notion of a secret power behind the correlation is logically superfluous and incoherent. These are facts of reflection. But the use of the microscope to detect the impression from which the idea of necessary connection is derived is a misguided exercise designed to save the hypothesis of impressions and ideas.

In two respects perhaps this criticism is too harsh. First, there is a grain of truth in the identification of necessity with an *internal* impression, something in the *mind*. If we say that something has always, often, or sometimes happened, or that something will always, often or sometimes happen, we are describing the world, saying something that can be falsified by the course of events. But if we say that it *must* happen, will *probably* happen, or for that matter *ought* to happen or be done, we are not adding to the previous description any extra features that can be independently falsified by the course of events. These terms are not descriptive. Roughly speaking their function is to express our attitude of mind towards the course of events whatever it may be. This Hume put crudely by saying they are the names of *feelings*.

Secondly, there is some value in the maxim that bids us

[8] and not logically conclusive evidence at that.

trace up our ideas to those original impressions from which they are derived. The celebrated " verification " principle of the earlier logical positivists is in essence Hume's " microscope " turned to the future rather than the past, and fitted with a logical instead of a psychological lens. For them the meaning of a term is not the past impressions from which the idea was associatively built up, but the experiences whose prediction is logically implied by the use of the term, and which verify the statements in which it occurs. A safer, if vaguer, reinterpretation of Hume's maxim would be simply, " Think concretely ". And by thinking concretely about, say, the concept of cause, I mean reflecting on what we actually do and say, and the conditions under which we do it, when we decide that one thing is the cause of another. It will be found, I think, that this is what Hume does. Finding causal connections and using them to extend our knowledge of the course of events and the way things happen, is something we all do, and as he points out, must all have learned to do at a very early age. To say clearly just what we do is to elucidate the concept of cause, and surely it should be possible to say just what we are doing when we are performing some familiar exercise, without delving into the dark abysses of metaphysics.

Looking at Hume's philosophy in this light we can also see where one of its most often cited weaknesses lies (cf. Lindsay, Introduction to Everyman edition of the Treatise). There are some early learned exercises, and corresponding to them some features of our language, which are neither things we just happen to do and ways we just happen to talk, nor things which conceivably might have been otherwise. I mean, for example, identifying permanent objects in space, tracing their changes in time and looking for their causes and effects. For such procedures are presupposed by everything we do and say, and a world with no time order, no persistent identities, no regular connections would be one which we could neither perceive by our senses, nor remember, nor learn to adapt ourselves to, nor describe in any language. This is what philosophers (following Kant) have meant by calling substance and cause "categories". And Hume does appear to be relatively unaware of this distinction and to treat all our concepts as on an equal footing, all a matter of what we as a matter of empirical fact just happen to do.

This mistake gives to Hume's treatment of empirical reasoning, of what other philosophers called Induction, an air of sceptical paradox which the topic need not have. Hume speaks as if we might conceivably be in possession of a normal stock of presently observed and remembered facts, but at a loss for a way of deciding what to expect next, and no grounds for assuming that the course of events would display any regularities at all, let alone regularities of this or that sort. But in fact the truth of the assumptions which make induction reasonable, is also the necessary presupposition of observation and memory being possible. Hence the imaginary sceptic who refuses to believe in the regularity of nature would be compelled to jettison not only his inferences about the unremembered past, the unobserved present, and the not yet observed future, but also the evidence of sense, memory, testimony and the use of significant speech. His proper attitude would be that of the ancient Greek sceptic Cratylus, who when asked a question merely wagged his finger.

Not that Hume was averse to stretching the sceptical bow to its limits when he saw the chance. In his eagerness to limit the province of demonstrative reasoning and enlarge that of customary belief, he sought to represent reason as self-destructive in a way in which it is not. Hume was not content to deny any demonstrative justification of judgments of perception and inductive inferences, and leave them to feeling and habit. He must needs try to show that commonsense and natural science, each using its proper form of inference, were inevitably at loggerheads; the former insists on a real world of coloured noisy smelly objects, the latter, on the best possible empirical evidence, demands a world of objects with only spatio-temporal dimensions and no sensible qualities at all. Instead of treating this as an unsolved problem in the philosophy of perception, Hume simply laughs it off as the sort of thing that happens if you think too much.[9]

Even more perspicuously mistaken is the sceptical argument of Part IV, Section I. Hume's point here appears to be that as a matter of psychological fact we usually check up on our calculations and reasonings, or have them checked by others, and that every confirmation so received increases our confidence in our original conclusion. But as a matter of logic, Hume argues, the reverse should be the case. Each successive act of reasoning carries its own risk of error, and these risks, superimposed one on another, progressively diminish the probability of the original conclusion, and eventually reduce it to nothing. This again is what happens if you think too much and too logically.

This argument entirely misrepresents the logic of corroboration. Corroboration may be of either of two kinds :—

(1) Where the same process, e.g. the addition of a row of figures, is repeated several times by one or more persons and the same result reached each time. Here the perfectly respectable logical principle involved is that the chances of the same (or an equivalent) mistake being made a number of times is the product of the chances of its being made each time; just as the chances of throwing three heads running with a penny are $\frac{1}{2} \times \frac{1}{2} \times \frac{1}{2}$, i.e. $\frac{1}{8}$.

(2) Where further evidence is used at each stage, as when a statistical calculation is checked against a wider range of samples. Here the strength of the evidence is increased, even if the probability fraction remains the same.

The legitimate basis in his philosophy for Hume's repeated professions of scepticism would appear to be this. There are indeed procedures of calculation and deduction which cannot lead to error, if correctly applied. But they

[9] See Part IV, Sect. IV, final para., and Part IV, Sect. VII, p. 318.

are powerless to decide questions of fact. And it is a question of fact whether on any particular occasion they have been correctly applied. The procedures for deciding questions of fact yield only probability, and are liable to the same doubt whether they have been correctly applied. There is therefore no royal road to certainty, however circumscribed. The utmost we can do is to arrive at a cautiously formed but not infallible state of confidence.

Hume's two main unsolved problems, that of personal identity and that of sense perception, are the outcome of the doctrine of impressions and ideas. For concretely as Hume thought on many topics he never did so with regard to impressions and ideas. What do we actually mean by, say, " an impression of cold "? Can it possibly be less than John Doe, a flesh and blood human being, identifiable by many familiar criteria, feeling as he usually feels when the temperature falls? Much less, is Hume's unreflective answer; just a specific kind of event, characterised only by the quality " coldness ", which could conceivably occur, all by itself, at any time, nowhere. Whence did Hume get this curious notion of atomic events, which happen to fall into the " bundles " we call minds? In this way, I think. He was presented by the Cartesians with the mind as an incorporeal substance, whose modifications are " ideas ", logically independent of any thing in the universe except the mind that has them. Hume, brash and concrete, says, " What is a 'substance'? Show me this incorporeal thing having ideas." It cannot be found. Only the ideas can, and they are now logically independent of *everything* in the universe. Out of them, using the association of ideas as " cement ",[10] Hume has to build his world-picture.

Hume's impressions and ideas are the ghostly fragments of an exploded ghost, the incorporeal mind substance, the " ghost in the machine ". They should have been swept away after the explosion and the philosophical laboratory adapted to the study of flesh and blood human beings.

[10] Abstract, p. 353.

Hume's philosophy has often been described as the *reductio ad absurdum* of empiricism. This is not true. That in it which is due to his empiricism is not absurd but true, and that in it which is absurd is due, not to empiricism, but either to the doctrine of impressions and ideas, or to plain mistakes.

5. THE LESSON

The important lesson of Hume is the threefold distinction between questions of logic, questions of fact and questions of value. The first are settled by tracing the logical relations of ideas, and the answers are analytical propositions. The second are settled by experience and inductive inference therefrom, which has no logical justification, and the answers are synthetic propositions. The third are settled by considering how we feel about things. No question of any one of these three kinds can be settled by the methods appropriate to questions of either of the other two kinds. Two and two *must* make four. Heated metals *must* expand. Promises *must* be kept. These are respectively instances of logical, causal and moral necessity. And these three things must not be confused, (which is perhaps a fourth kind of necessity?) This lesson has nothing to do with impressions and ideas.

Of Hume's more immediate successors only Kant understood this lesson, though he did not accept it. For he claimed to find a way of establishing synthetic propositions *a priori,* by showing them to be presuppositions either of empirical knowledge, or of self-consciousness, or of practical choice. In his account of practical reason as issuing in imperatives rather than statements, he answers Hume's arguments for the impotence of reason in morals, by showing them to apply only to theoretical reason. But Kant followed Hume in denying that metaphysics can demonstrate truths about the universe, and confining it to a critical examination of our intellectual powers. Only

Thomas Reid began to see what was wrong with the doctrine of impressions and ideas. And only Bentham saw the possibilities of Hume's Moral Philosophy, as a foundation for Utilitarianism.

6. LATER YEARS

Hume never developed his epistemology any further except in minor respects. His second main work on the theory of knowledge, the *Enquiry Concerning the Human Understanding*, published 10 years later, was expressly designed to remedy the defects in presentation and style of the Treatise, to which he attributed the failure of that work with the public. The distinction of Relations of Ideas and Matters of Fact is far more clearly put,[11] and the treatment of causation remodelled on the lines of the exposition in the Abstract. The subtle sophistries of Parts II and IV of the Treatise, concerned with space and time, sense perception and personal identity, are drastically cut down or completely omitted. But no considerable additions were made to the epistemology of the Treatise.

The same is not true of Hume's moral and religious philosophy. The *Enquiry concerning the principles of Morals* (1751) modified the contentions of the Treatise Book III in several substantial respects, and the *Dialogues concerning Natural Religion,* published posthumously and probably written in the 1750s, is a work of the highest art and originality. Moreover, the *Enquiry Concerning Human Understanding* contains the celebrated chapter on miracles, which was absent from the Treatise.

The remainder of his life has been often described. Apart from a single bid for a Chair at Edinburgh in 1745, Hume never attempted the academic life. He was a man of letters and, in a mild way, a man of affairs. Though he had a lively appreciation of female company he never

---

[11] See Appendix B. On the relation between the two works consult Flew, *Hume's Philosophy of Belief.*

married, and, like other good philosophers, in his latter days he lived with his sister and his cat.

But before that time came he had some adventures. In 1746 he went as Secretary to General St. Clair on an unsuccessful expedition to the coast of Brittany, and later on a diplomatic visit to Vienna and Turin. In 1752 he was appointed Librarian to the faculty of advocates in Edinburgh, and he availed himself of the opportunities afforded by this post to write his Histories of England. Throughout this time he had also been publishing Essays on Moral and Political, including Economic topics. These books earned him the literary fame which his major philosophical works never brought him.

In 1763 he had perhaps his greatest adventure. He accompanied the Earl of Hertford, the British Ambassador, to Paris and was appointed Secretary to the Embassy. Here he met all the great figures of the intellectual and social world of the pre-revolutionary Paris. His love affair with the Comtesse de Boufflers is a favourite topic of his biographers, and opinions differ on the merits of his achievements as a diplomatist when he was left Chargé d'Affaires in 1765.

In 1769, resolved to roam no more, he returned to Edinburgh, and built himself a house in an as yet unnamed side street off St. Andrew Square. But his friend Miss Nancy Orde soon altered that. " St. David Street," she chalked on the walls of the philosopher's house, and in due course that became the street's official name, a fitting, if ironic, tribute to the personal regard and affection in which the infidel philosopher was held. One personal enemy he did however make—Jean Jacques Rousseau. The kindly Hume conceived the idea of offering an asylum in England to the homeless philosopher, exiled from Switzerland, outlawed in France, suspicious of the proffered protection of the King of Prussia. Incited by French Countesses, heedless of warnings, Hume in 1766 imported Rousseau to England, established him complete with mistress and dog in a house in Staffordshire, and obtained for

him a pension from the King. But nothing would persuade
Rousseau that Hume was not secretly plotting his ridicule
and humiliation, and the relationship ended in a spec-
tacular quarrel. In self-justification Hume was forced to
publish the correspondence, from which it is abundantly
clear that the only man who ever hated Hume personally
was mad.

In the spring of 1775 Hume, suffering from cancer of the
bowels, realised that his end was near. He continued to
the last making corrections for future editions of his
works, writing to and seeing his friends. His cheerful
attitude to his approaching death, and, as he firmly believed, total extinction, was clearly modelled on the pagan
philosophers of antiquity, but, according to Adam Smith,
he made no " parade of his magnanimity ". He died on the
29th August at his home in Edinburgh.

Hume was buried in the cemetery at Calton Crags,
Edinburgh, and a monument designed by Robert Adam
was erected over his grave.

7. THE APPENDIX TO THE TREATISE

By the time Book III of the Treatise went to press (1740)
Hume had had second thoughts on some aspects of Book I.
These he published as an appendix to the whole work. As
they concern Book I, the Appendix is included in this
edition.

Its main topics are belief and personal identity. With
regard to the former there is no explicit change of Hume's
view, only an attempt to make his meaning clearer. Nor
has he anything to add to his theory of personal identity,
except an expression of despairing dissatisfaction with it.
A completely new argument is offered against the view
that our own wills provide us with the idea of power (Part
III, Sect. XIV, p. 211) and a few minor mistakes and mis-
prints corrected. The corrections and additions which
Hume tells us in the Appendix he would have liked to

make, are incorporated in the text of this edition in square brackets. In this respect the present text differs both from that of Selby-Bigge, who prints them in their original place in the Appendix, and from the Everyman edition, where they are incorporated without any distinction in the main text, and the references to them in the Appendix omitted.

Hume's problem concerning personal identity has been expressed in the following mnemonic hexameter: "How can a series of conscious states be aware of itself as a series?"

No satisfactory elucidation of the concept of consciousness has yet been produced. I do not know what Hume means when he says that "consciousness is nothing but a reflected thought or perception."

Upon the whole (as Hume would say) four propositions seem to me to be true:

(1) People, men and women, are substances, if anything is. A person acts and is acted upon, and could conceivably exist, if only for a very short time, though everything else in the universe ceased to exist.

(2) Minds are not substances. They are modes. The word "mind" is a handy term for abbreviating talk about people's beliefs, feelings, decisions, intentions etc.

(3) The names of states of mind, e.g. "joy", "belief", "intention" etc. have public meanings, without which they would be no use for communication. These public meanings depend on criteria relating to public phenomena, i.e. bodily behaviour.

(4) States of mind cannot be analysed without remainder in terms of bodily behaviour and behavioural tendencies. (For the nature of the remainder see notes to pages 146 and 240. Hume recognised the truth of propositions (2) and (4) but not the truth of (1) and (3).

8. THE AUTHORSHIP OF THE ABSTRACT

David Hume to Henry Home.

(Greig, *Letters*, Vol. 1, p. 23)

I am sorry I am not able to satisfy your curiosity, by giving you some general notion of the plan upon which I proceed. But my opinions are so new, and even some terms I am obliged to make use of, that I could not propose, by any abridgement, to give my system an air of likelihood, or so much as make it intelligible. It is a thing I have in vain attempted already, at a gentleman's request in this place, who thought it would help him to comprehend and judge of my notions, if he saw them all at once before him.

(London, December 2, 1737)

David Hume to Francis Hutcheson.

(Greig, *Letters*, Vol. 1, p. 37)

My bookseller has sent to Mr. Smith a copy of my book, which I hope he has received, as well as your letter. I have not yet heard what he has done with the Abstract. Perhaps you have. I have got it printed in London; but not in *The Works of the Learned*; there having been an article with regard to my book, somewhat abusive, printed in that work, before I sent up the Abstract.

(Ninewells, March 4, 1740)

Until about 1933 the above passages from Hume's letters were the only evidence of the existence of the Abstract. No copy of it had been traced. The theory accepted by most of the biographers[12] of the men concerned was as follows. Hume tried to write an Abstract of the Treatise in 1737 and failed. In 1739 Hutcheson, Professor of Philosophy at Glasgow, set as an exercise to his 17 year old pupil Adam

---

[12] John Hill Burton, *Life of Hume*. John Rae, *Life of Adam Smith*. Leslie Stephen, *Dict. of National Biography* s.v. David Hume. W. R. Scott, *Francis Hutcheson*. Greig, *David Hume*.

Smith (author-to-be of *The Wealth of Nations*) the task of epitomising the Treatise, Books I and II. He sent the result to Hume, who was so pleased with it that he had it printed in London, and sent Adam Smith a presentation copy of the Treatise.

In 1933 a copy of the Abstract was discovered. Two other copies were traced later. The text was edited by J. M. Keynes (who purchased the first-discovered copy) and P. Sraffa in 1938.[13] In their introduction the editors give the following reasons for ascribing the Abstract to Hume.

(1) The style and way of arguing are strikingly Humean.

(2) Many passages correspond closely with arguments which occur, not in the then published text of the Treatise, Books I and II, but in the Appendix, which appeared later with Book III of the Treatise. The corresponding passages are listed at the end of this note.

(3) The Adam Smith theory did not in any case fit the passage in Hume's letter to Hutcheson very well.

    (a) Hume mentions a letter from Hutcheson to Smith. But both men, as far as is known, were in Glasgow at the time. This does not seem a very strong argument.

    (b) What could Hume have meant by saying that he did not know what he (presumably Smith) had done with the Abstract?

(4) The editors were able to offer a better explanation of the passage about "Smith" in Hume's letter. There was in Dublin at the time a publisher called John Smith, in partnership with a cousin of Hutcheson, who in fact published Irish

---

[13] *An Abstract of a Treatise of Human Nature* 1740 *by David Hume.* Cambridge University Press 1938. (Out of print and scarce.)

editions of Hutcheson's books. We know that Hume was very impatient for a second edition of the Treatise, because he wished to make some corrections and improvements.[14] But he was embarrassed by an agreement with his London publisher, John Noon, "that on printing a second edition, I (sc. Hume) shall take up all copies (sc. of the first edition) remaining on hand at the bookseller's price at the time."

Now publications in Ireland were not at that time subject to the English Copyright Act. Irish publishers could therefore, and often did, produce pirate editions, known as "Dublin Editions", sometimes with the author's approval. By this means Hume might hope to circumvent the obstacles to a second and improved edition. We know that he did in fact consider such a step later with regard to his *History of England*.

I assure you if Mr. Millar were now alive, I should be tempted to go over to Dublin, and to publish there an edition which I hope would entirely discredit the present one.[15]

The editors therefore suggest that Hume, disappointed at the reception of the Treatise (Books I and II) and impatient for a corrected edition, wrote the Abstract himself for anonymous publication, in order to explain and draw attention to the Treatise; obtained from Hutcheson an introduction to John Smith; and sent him copies both of the Treatise and the Abstract. Meanwhile he had the Abstract printed by C. Corbet[16] in London. John Smith must have declined Hume's suggestion, for no second edition of the Treatise appeared in English until 1817.

---

[14] Letter to Hutcheson, 16th March, 1740. Greig, Letters, Vol. I., p. 38.
[15] Letter to William Strahan, 11th March, 1771. Greig, Letters, Vol. II, p. 235.
[16] Corbet made the odd mistake of mis-spelling his own name as "Borbet" on the title page.

The case is a strong but not conclusive one. It remains just possible that Adam Smith wrote the Abstract, and that the improvements suggested in the Appendix to the Treatise were derived from the passages in the Abstract and not *vice versa*. But anyone who adheres to this theory must accept the following unlikely consequences.

(1) Adam Smith, aged 17, thoroughly understood a book which baffled all his elders.

(2) Adam Smith not only understood it, but suggested valuable improvements.

(3) Hume, with uncharacteristic ungraciousness, used these suggestions without ever acknowledging their source, even in his letters to Hutcheson, who must have known the authorship and contents of the Abstract. Adam Smith became one of Hume's closest friends.

(4) Adam Smith succeeded, where Hume failed, in epitomising the central argument of Treatise, Book 1.

Whoever wrote it, there is nothing better for a student to read before retiring on the eve of an examination on Hume.

Parallel passages in the Abstract and the Appendix to the Treatise—

(1) *Abstract*, p. 344   "To account for this" to
          (K & S)   "which we can con-
                                ceive"

    Appendix, p. 313   from "That it is not a
                                new idea" to "believe
                                what he pleased"

(2) *Abstract*, p. 345   "But feels something dif-
                                ferent in the concep-
                                tion of it from a mere
                                reverie of the imagina-
                                tion."

Appendix, p. 325	"But conceives it, along with a certain feeling, different from what attends the mere reveries of the imagination."
(3) *Abstract,* p. 345	from "Our Author proceeds" to "command our belief and opinion."
Treatise Part III, Sect. VII pp. 144-6	from "This operation of the mind" to "governing principles of all our actions."
and *Treatise,* Part III, Sect. X, pp. 124, 125, Ev.	from "We may observe the same effects of poetry" to "one of the same dimensions at ten"
(4) *Abstract,* p. 348	from "Now our own minds afford" to "constantly conjoined"
Treatise, Part III, Sect. XIV pp. 211-12	from "Some have asserted" to "by consulting our own minds"
(5) *Abstract,* p. 350	"The greatest part" to "imagination a n d senses"
Treatise, Part II, Sect. IV, pp. 91-2	"There are many" to "particular objects"

(6) The intriguing fable of Adam and the billiard

balls (*Abstract*, p. 342 ff. does not occur in the Treatise, but is echoed in the *Enquiry Concerning Human Understanding* (Sect. IV, Part I, para. 23 in Selby-Bigge's edition).

9. THE TEXT

The text in this edition follows that of the original edition, except that certain archaisms of spelling, punctuation and the use of capital letters have been corrected. The passages enclosed in square brackets are those of which Hume, in the Appendix, says that his reasoning would have been more convincing had they been inserted in the places he directed. The footnotes in roman type are Hume's; those in italic are the editor's.

My thanks are due to Professor H. H. Price, who made several valuable suggestions for the editor's introduction, and also to all other scholars who have preceded me in writing on Hume.

A TREATISE OF
HUMAN NATURE

INTRODUCTION

Nothing is more usual and more natural for those, who pretend to discover anything new to the world in philosophy and the sciences, than to insinuate the praises of their own systems, by decrying all those which have been advanced before them. And indeed were they content with lamenting that ignorance, which we still lie under in the most important questions that can come before the tribunal of human reason, there are few, who have an acquaintance with the sciences, that would not readily agree with them. It is easy for one of judgment and learning, to perceive the weak foundation even of those systems, which have obtained the greatest credit, and have carried their pretensions highest to accurate and profound reasoning. Principles taken upon trust, consequences lamely deduced from them, want of coherence in the parts, and of evidence in the whole, these are everywhere to be met with in the systems of the most eminent philosophers, and seem to have drawn disgrace upon philosophy itself.

Nor is there required such profound knowledge to discover the present imperfect condition of the sciences, but even the rabble without doors may judge from the noise and clamour which they hear, that all goes not well within. There is nothing which is not the subject of debate, and in which men of learning are not of contrary opinions. The most trivial question escapes not our controversy, and in the most momentous we are not able to give any certain decision. Disputes are multiplied, as if everything was uncertain, and these disputes are managed with the greatest warmth, as if everything was certain. Amidst all this bustle, it is not reason which carries the prize, but eloquence; and no man needs ever despair of gaining proselytes to the most extravagant hypothesis, who has art enough to represent it in any favourable colours. The victory is not gained by the men at arms, who manage the pike and the sword, but by the trumpeters, drummers, and musicians of the army.

From hence in my opinion arises that common prejudice against metaphysical reasonings of all kinds, even amongst those who profess themselves scholars, and have a just value for every other part of literature. By metaphysical reasonings, they do not understand those on any particular branch of science, but every kind of argument which is any way abstruse, and requires some attention to be comprehended. We have so often lost our labour in such researches, that we commonly reject them without hesitation, and resolve, if we must for ever be a prey to errors and delusions, that they shall at least be natural and entertaining. And indeed nothing but the most determined scepticism, along with a great degree of indolence, can justify this aversion to metaphysics. For if truth be at all within the reach of human capacity, it is certain it must lie very deep and abstruse; and to hope we shall arrive at it without pains, while the greatest geniuses have failed with the utmost pains, must certainly be esteemed sufficiently vain and presumptuous. I pretend to no such advantage in the philosophy I am going to unfold, and would esteem it a strong presumption against it, were it so very easy and obvious.

It is evident, that all the sciences have a relation, greater or less, to human nature; and that, however wide any of them may seem to run from it, they still return back by one passage or another. Even *Mathematics, Natural Philosophy,* and *Natural Religion,* are in some measure dependent on the science of MAN; since they lie under the cognisance of men, and are judged of by their powers and faculties. It is impossible to tell what changes and improvements we might make in these sciences were we thoroughly acquainted with the extent and force of human understanding, and could explain the nature of the ideas we employ, and of the operations we perform in our reasonings. And these improvements are the more to be hoped for in natural religion, as it is not content with instructing us in the nature of superior powers, but carries its views further, to their disposition towards us, and our duties towards them; and consequently we ourselves are not only the beings that reason, but also one of the objects concerning which we reason.

If therefore the sciences of Mathematics, Natural Philosophy, and Natural Religion, have such a dependence on the knowledge of man, what may be expected in the other sciences, whose connection with human nature is more close and intimate? The sole end of logic is to explain the principles and operations of our reasoning faculty, and the nature of our ideas; morals and criticism regard our tastes and sentiments; and politics consider men as united in society, and dependent on each other. In these four sciences of *Logic, Morals, Criticism,* and *Politics,* is comprehended almost everything which it can anyway import us to be acquainted with, or which can tend either to the improvement or ornament of the human mind.

Here then is the only expedient, from which we can hope for success in our philosophical researches, to leave the tedious lingering method, which we have hitherto followed, and instead of taking now and then a castle or village on the frontier, to march up directly to the capital or centre of these sciences, to human nature itself; which being once masters of, we may everywhere else hope for an easy victory. From this station we may extend our conquests over all those sciences, which more intimately concern human life, and may afterwards proceed at leisure, to discover more fully those which are the objects of pure curiosity. There is no question of importance, whose decision is not comprised in the science of man; and there is none, which can be decided with any certainty, before we become acquainted with that science. In pretending, therefore, to explain the principles of human nature, we in effect propose a complete system of the sciences, built on a foundation almost entirely new, and the only one upon which they can stand with any security.

And as the science of man is the only solid foundation for the other sciences, so the only solid foundation we can give to this science itself must be laid on experience and observation. It is no astonishing reflection to consider, that the application of experimental philosophy to moral subjects should come after that to natural, at the distance of above a whole century; since we find in fact, that there was about the same interval betwixt the origins of these sciences; and that, reckoning from Thales to Socrates, the space of time is nearly equal to that betwixt my Lord Bacon and some late philosophers[1] in England, who have begun to put the science of man on a new footing, and have engaged the attention, and excited the curiosity of the public. So true it is, that however other nations may rival us in poetry, and excel us in some other agreeable arts, the improvements in reason and philosophy can only be owing to a land of toleration and of liberty.

Nor ought we to think, that this latter improvement in the science of man will do less honour to our native country than the former in natural philosophy, but ought rather to esteem it a greater glory, upon account of the greater importance of that science, as well as the necessity it lay under of such a reformation. For to me it seems evident, that the essence of the mind being equally unknown to us with that of external bodies, it must be equally impossible to form any notion of its powers and qualities otherwise than from careful and exact experiments, and the observation of those particular effects, which result from its different circumstances and situations. And though we must endeavour to render all our principles as universal as possible, by tracing up our experiments to the utmost, and explaining all effects from the simplest and fewest causes, it is still certain we cannot go beyond experience; and any hypothesis, that pretends to discover the ultimate original qualities of human nature, ought at first to be rejected as presumptuous and chimerical.

[1] Mr. Locke, my Lord Shaftesbury, Dr. Mandeville, Mr. Hutchinson, Dr. Butler, etc.

I do not think a philosopher, who would apply himself so earnestly to the explaining the ultimate principles of the soul, would show himself a great master in that very science of human nature, which he pretends to explain, or very knowing in what is naturally satisfactory to the mind of man. For nothing is more certain, than that despair has almost the same effect upon us with enjoyment, and that we are no sooner acquainted with the impossibility of satisfying any desire, than the desire itself vanishes. When we see, that we have arrived at the utmost extent of human reason, we sit down contented; though we be perfectly satisfied in the main of our ignorance, and perceive that we can give no reason for our most general and most refined principles, beside our experience of their reality; which is the reason of the mere vulgar, and what it required no study at first to have discovered for the most particular and most extraordinary phenomenon. And as this impossibility of making any further progress is enough to satisfy the reader, so the writer may derive a more delicate satisfaction from the free confession of his ignorance, and from his prudence in avoiding that error, into which so many have fallen, of imposing their conjectures and hypotheses on the world for the most certain principles. When this mutual contentment and satisfaction can be obtained betwixt the master and scholar, I know not what more we can require of our philosophy.

But if this impossibility of explaining ultimate principles should be esteemed a defect in the science of man, I will venture to affirm, that it is a defect common to it with all the sciences, and all the arts, in which we can employ ourselves, whether they be such as are cultivated in the schools of the philosophers, or practised in the shops of the meanest artisans. None of them can go beyond experience, or establish any principles which are not founded on that authority. Moral philosophy has, indeed, this peculiar disadvantage, which is not found in natural, that in collecting its experiments, it cannot make them purposely, with premeditation, and after such a manner as to satisfy itself concerning every particular difficulty which may arise. When I am at a loss to know the effects of one body upon another in any situation, I need only put them in that situation, and observe what results from it. But should I endeavour to clear up after the same manner any doubt in moral philosophy, by placing myself in the same case with that which I consider, it is evident this reflection and premeditation would so disturb the operation of my natural principles, as must render it impossible to form any just conclusion from the phenomenon. We must therefore glean up our experiments in this science from a cautious observation of human life, and take them as they appear in the common course of the world, by men's behaviour in company, in affairs, and in their pleasures. Where experiments of this kind are judiciously collected and compared, we may hope to establish on them a science which will not be inferior in certainty, and will be much superior in utility, to any other of human comprehension.

OF IDEAS, THEIR ORIGIN, COMPOSITION CONNECTION, ABSTRACTION Etc.

SECTION I

OF THE ORIGIN OF OUR IDEAS

All the perceptions of the human mind resolve themselves into two distinct kinds, which I shall call *impressions* and *ideas*. The difference betwixt these consists in the degrees of force and liveliness, with which they strike upon the mind, and make their way into our thought or consciousness. Those perceptions which enter with most force and violence, we may name *impressions*; and under this name I comprehend all our sensations, passions, and emotions, as they make their first appearance in the soul. By *ideas* I mean the faint images of these in thinking and reasoning; such as, for instance, are all the perceptions excited by the present discourse, excepting only those which arise from the sight and touch, and excepting the immediate pleasure or uneasiness it may occasion. I believe it will not be very necessary to employ many words in explaining this distinction. Every one of himself will readily perceive the difference betwixt feeling and thinking. The common degrees of these are easily distinguished; though it is not impossible but in particular instances they may very nearly approach to each other. Thus, in sleep, in a fever, in madness, or in any very violent emotions of soul, our ideas may approach to our impressions: as on the other hand it sometimes happens, that our impressions are so faint and low, that we cannot distinguish them from our ideas. But notwithstanding this near resemblance in a few instances, they are in general so very different, that no one can make a scruple to rank them under distinct heads, and assign to each a peculiar name to mark the difference.[1]

There is another division of our perceptions, which it will be convenient to observe, and which extends itself both to our impressions and ideas. This division is into *simple* and *complex*. Simple perceptions, or impressions and ideas, are such as admit of no distinction nor separation. The complex are the contrary to these, and may be distinguished into parts. Though a particular colour, taste, and smell, are qualities all united together in this apple, it is easy to perceive they are not the same, but are at least distinguishable from each other.

Having by these divisions given an order and arrangement to our objects, we may now apply ourselves to consider with the more accuracy their qualities and relations. The first circumstance that strikes my eye, is the great resemblance betwixt our impressions and ideas in every other particular, except their degree of force and vivacity. The one seems to be, in a manner, the reflection of the other; so that all the perceptions of the mind are double, and appear both as impressions and ideas. When I shut my eyes and think of my chamber, the ideas I form are exact representations of the impressions I felt; nor is there any circumstance of the one, which is not to be found in the other. In running over my other perceptions, I find still the same resemblance and representation. Ideas and impressions appear always to correspond to each other. This circumstance seems to me remarkable, and engages my attention for a moment.

Upon a more accurate survey I find I have been carried away too far by the first appearance, and that I must make

[1] I here make use of these terms, *impression* and *idea,* in a sense different from what is usual, and I hope this liberty will be allowed me. Perhaps I rather restore the word idea to its original sense, from which Mr. Locke had perverted it, in making it stand for all our perceptions. By the term of impression, I would not be understood to express the manner in which our lively perceptions are produced in the soul, but merely the perceptions themselves; for which there is no particular name, either in the English or any other language that I know of.

use of the distinction of perceptions into *simple* and *complex*, to limit this general decision, *that all our ideas and impressions are resembling*. I observe that many of our complex ideas never had impressions that corresponded to them, and that many of our complex impressions never are exactly copied in ideas. I can imagine to myself such a city as the New Jerusalem, whose pavement is gold, and walls are rubies, though I never saw any such. I have seen Paris; but shall I affirm I can form such an idea of that city, as will perfectly represent all its streets and houses in their real and just proportions?

I perceive, therefore, that though there is, in general, a great resemblance betwixt our *complex* impressions and ideas, yet the rule is not universally true, that they are exact copies of each other. We may next consider, how the case stands with our *simple* perceptions. After the most accurate examination of which I am capable, I venture to affirm, that the rule here holds without any exception, and that every simple idea has a simple impression, which resembles it, and every simple impression a correspondent idea. That idea of red, which we form in the dark, and that impression which strikes our eyes in sunshine, differ only in degree, not in nature. That the case is the same with all our simple impressions and ideas, it is impossible to prove by a particular enumeration of them. Every one may satisfy himself in this point by running over as many as he pleases. But if any one should deny this universal resemblance, I know no way of convincing him, but by desiring him to show a simple impression that has not a correspondent idea, or a simple idea that has not a correspondent impression. If he does not answer this challenge, as it is certain he cannot, we may, from his silence and our own observation, establish our conclusion.

Thus we find, that all simple ideas and impressions resemble each other; and as the complex are formed from them, we may affirm in general, that these two species of perception are exactly correspondent. Having discovered this relation, which requires no further examination, I am curious to find some other of their qualities. Let us consider how they stand with regard to their existence, and which of the impressions and ideas are causes, and which effects.

The full examination of this question is the subject of the present treatise; and therefore we shall here content ourselves with establishing one general proposition, *That all our simple ideas in their first appearance are derived from simple impressions, which are correspondent to them, and which they exactly represent.*

In seeking for phenomena to prove this proposition, I find only those of two kinds; but in each kind the phenomena are obvious, numerous, and conclusive. I first make myself certain, by a new review, of what I have already asserted, that every simple impression is attended with a correspondent idea, and every simple idea with a correspondent impression. From this constant conjunction of resembling perceptions I immediately conclude, that there is a great connection betwixt our correspondent impressions and ideas, and that the existence of the one has a considerable influence upon that of the other. Such a constant conjunction, in such an infinite number of instances, can never arise from chance; but clearly proves a dependence of the impressions on the ideas, or of the ideas on the impressions. That I may know on which side this dependence lies, I consider the order of their *first appearance*; and find by constant experience that the simple impressions always take the precedence of their correspondent ideas, but never appear in the contrary order. To give a child an idea of scarlet or orange, of sweet or bitter, I present the objects, or in other words, convey to him these impressions; but proceed not so absurdly, as to endeavour to produce the impressions by exciting the ideas. Our ideas, upon their appearance, produce not their correspondent impressions, nor do we perceive any colour, or feel any sensation merely upon thinking of them. On the other hand we find, that any impression either of the mind or body is constantly followed by an idea, which resembles it, and is only different in the degrees of force and liveliness. The constant conjunction of our resembling perceptions, is a convincing proof, that the one are the causes of the other; and this priority of the impressions is an equal proof, that our impressions are the causes of our ideas, not our ideas of our impressions.

To confirm this I consider another plain and convincing phenomenon; which is, that wherever by any accident the faculties which give rise to any impression are obstructed in their operations, as when one is born blind or deaf, not only the impressions are lost, but also their correspondent ideas; so that there never appear in the mind the least trace of either of them. Nor is this only true, where the organs of sensation are entirely destroyed, but likewise where they have never been put in action to produce a particular impression. We cannot form to ourselves a just idea of the taste of a pineapple, without having actually tasted it.

There is, however, one contradictory phenomenon, which may prove, that it is not absolutely impossible for ideas to go before their correspondent impressions. I believe it will readily be allowed, that the several distinct ideas of colours, which enter by the eyes, or those of sounds, which are conveyed by the hearing, are really different from each other, though at the same time resembling. Now if this be true of different colours, it must be no less so of the different shades of the same colour, that each of them produces a distinct idea, independent of the rest. For if this should be denied, it is possible, by the continual gradation of shades, to run a colour insensibly into what is most remote from it; and if you will not allow any of the means to be different, you cannot without absurdity deny the extremes to be the same. Suppose therefore a person to have enjoyed his sight for thirty years, and to have become perfectly well acquainted with colours of all kinds, excepting one particular shade of blue, for instance, which it never has been his fortune to meet with. Let all the different shades of that colour, except that single one, be placed before him, descending gradually from the deepest to the lightest; it is plain, that he will perceive a blank, where that shade is wanting, and will be sensible that there is a greater distance in that place betwixt the contiguous colours, than in any other. Now I ask, whether it is possible for him, from his own imagination, to supply this deficiency, and raise up to himself the idea of that particular shade, though it had never been conveyed to him by his senses? I believe there are few but will be of opinion that he can; and this may serve as a proof, that the simple ideas are not always derived from the correspondent impressions; though the instance is so particular and singular, that it is scarce worth our observing, and does not merit that for it alone we should alter our general maxim.

But besides this exception it may not be amiss to remark, on this head, that the principle of the priority of impressions to ideas, must be understood with another limitation, viz. that as our ideas are images of our impressions, so we can form secondary ideas, which are images of the primary, as appears from this very reasoning concerning them. This is not, properly speaking, an exception to the rule so much as an explanation of it. Ideas produce the images of themselves in new ideas; but as the first ideas are supposed to be derived from impressions, it still remains true, that all our simple ideas proceed either mediately or immediately from their correspondent impressions.[2]

This then is the first principle I establish in the science of human nature; nor ought we to despise it because of the simplicity of its appearance. For it is remarkable, that the present question concerning the precedency of our impressions or ideas, is the same with what has made so much noise in other terms, when it has been disputed whether there be any *innate ideas*, or whether all ideas be derived from sensation and reflection.[3] We may observe, that in

---

[2] *Compare Part* III, *Sect.* VIII, *concluding paragraphs.*
[3] *Compare Locke, Essay Conc. Human Understanding, Book* I.

order to prove the ideas of extension and colour not to be innate, philosophers do nothing but show that they are conveyed by our senses. To prove the ideas of passion and desire not to be innate, they observe that we have a preceding experience of these emotions in ourselves. Now if we carefully examine these arguments, we shall find that they prove nothing but that ideas are preceded by other more lively perceptions, from which they are derived, and which they represent. I hope this clear stating of the question will remove all disputes concerning it, and will render this principle of more use in our reasonings, than it seems hitherto to have been.

SECTION II

DIVISION OF THE SUBJECT

Since it appears that our simple impressions are prior to their correspondent ideas, and that the exceptions are very rare, method seems to require we should examine our impressions before we consider our ideas. Impressions may be divided into two kinds, those of *sensation,* and those of *reflection*. The first kind arises in the soul originally, from unknown causes. The second is derived in a great measure from our ideas, and that in the following order. An impression first strikes upon the senses, and makes us perceive heat or cold, thirst or hunger, pleasure or pain, of some kind or other. Of this impression there is a copy taken by the mind, which remains after the impression ceases; and this we call an idea. This idea of pleasure or pain, when it returns upon the soul, produces the new impressions of desire and aversion, hope and fear, which may properly be called impressions of reflection, because derived from it. These again are copied by the memory and imagination, and become ideas; which, perhaps in their turn give rise to other impressions and ideas; so that the impressions of reflection are not only antecedent to their correspondent ideas, but posterior to those of sensation, and derived from them. The examination of our sensations belongs more to anatomists and natural philosophers than to moral; and therefore shall not at present be entered upon. And as the impressions of reflection, viz. passions, desires, and emotions, which principally deserve our attention, arise mostly from ideas, it will be necessary to reverse that method, which at first sight seems most natural; and in order to explain the nature and principles of the human mind, give a particular account of ideas, before we proceed to impressions. For this reason, I have here chosen to begin with ideas.

SECTION III

OF THE IDEAS OF THE MEMORY AND IMAGINATION

We find by experience that when any impression has been present with the mind, it again makes its appearance there as an idea; and this it may do after two different ways: either when, in its new appearance, it retains a considerable degree of its first vivacity, and is somewhat intermediate betwixt an impression and an idea; or when it entirely loses that vivacity, and is a perfect idea. The faculty by which we repeat our impressions in the first manner, is called the *memory,* and the other the *imagination.* It is evident at first sight, that the ideas of the memory are much more lively and strong than those of the imagination, and that the former faculty paints its objects in more distinct colours than any which are employed by the latter. When we remember any past event, the idea of it flows in upon the mind in a forcible manner; whereas in the imagination the perception is faint and languid, and cannot without difficulty be preserved by the mind steady and uniform for any considerable time. Here then is a sensible difference betwixt one species of ideas and another. But of this more fully hereafter.[4]

There is another difference betwixt these two kinds of ideas, which is no less evident, namely that though neither the ideas of the memory nor imagination, neither the lively nor faint ideas, can make their appearance in the mind, unless their correspondent impressions have gone before to prepare the way for them, yet the imagination is not restrained to the same order and form with the original impressions; while the memory is in a manner tied down in that respect, without any power of variation.

It is evident, that the memory preserves the original form in which its objects were presented, and that wherever we depart from it in recollecting anything, it proceeds from some defect or imperfection in that faculty. An historian may, perhaps, for the more convenient carrying on of his narration, relate an event before another to which it was in fact posterior; but then he takes notice of this disorder, if he be exact; and by that means replaces the idea in its due position. It is the same case in our recollection of those places and persons, with which we were formerly acquainted. The chief exercise of the memory is not to preserve the simple ideas, but their order and position. In short, this principle is supported by such a number of common and vulgar phenomena, that we may spare ourselves the trouble of insisting on it any further.

The same evidence follows us in our second principle, *of the liberty of the imagination to transpose and change its ideas.* The fables we meet with in poems and romances put this entirely out of question. Nature there is totally confounded, and nothing mentioned but winged horses, fiery dragons, and monstrous giants. Nor will this liberty of the fancy appear strange, when we consider that all our ideas are copied from our impressions, and that there are not any two impressions which are perfectly inseparable.

[4] Part III, Sect. 5.

Not to mention, that this is an evident consequence of the division of ideas into simple and complex. Wherever the imagination perceives a difference among ideas, it can easily produce a separation.

SECTION IV

OF THE CONNECTION OR ASSOCIATION OF IDEAS

As all simple ideas may be separated by the imagination, and may be united again in what form it pleases, nothing would be more unaccountable than the operations of that faculty, were it not guided by some universal principles, which render it, in some measure, uniform with itself in all times and places. Were ideas entirely loose and unconnected, chance alone would join them; and it is impossible the same simple ideas should fall regularly into complex ones (as they commonly do) without some bond of union among them, some associating quality, by which one idea naturally introduces another. This uniting principle among ideas is not to be considered as an inseparable connection; for that has been already excluded from the imagination : nor yet are we to conclude, that without it the mind cannot join two ideas; for nothing is more free than that faculty : but we are only to regard it as a gentle force, which commonly prevails, and is the cause why, among other things, languages so nearly correspond to each other; Nature, in a manner, pointing out to every one those simple ideas, which are most proper to be united into a complex one. The qualities, from which this association arises, and by which the mind is after this manner conveyed from one idea to another, are three, viz. *resemblance*, *contiguity* in time or place, and *cause* and *effect*.

I believe it will not be very necessary to prove, that these qualities produce an association among ideas, and upon the appearance of one idea naturally introduce another. It is plain, that in the course of our thinking, and in the constant revolution of our ideas, our imagination runs easily from one idea to any other that *resembles* it, and that this quality alone is to the fancy a sufficient bond and association. It is likewise evident,[5] that as the senses, in changing their objects, are necessitated to change them regularly, and take them as they lie *contiguous* to each other, the imagination must by long custom acquire the same method of thinking, and run along the parts of space and time in conceiving its objects. As to the connection that is made by the relation of *cause* and *effect*, we shall have occasion afterwards to examine it to the bottom, and therefore shall not at present insist upon it. It is sufficient to observe, that there is no relation, which produces a stronger connection in the fancy, and makes one idea more readily recall another, than the relation of cause and effect betwixt their objects.

That we may understand the full extent of these relations, we must consider, that two objects are connected together in the imagination, not only when the one is immediately resembling, contiguous to, or the cause of the other, but also when there is interposed betwixt them a third object, which bears to both of them any of these relations. This may be carried on to a great length; though at the same time we may observe, that each remove considerably weakens the relation. Cousins in the fourth degree are connected by *causation,* if I may be allowed to use that term; but not so closely as brothers, much less as child and parent. In general, we may observe, that all the relations of blood depend upon cause and effect, and are esteemed near or remote, according to the number of connecting causes interposed betwixt the persons.

Of the three relations above mentioned, this of causation is the most extensive. Two objects may be considered as placed in this relation, as well when one is the cause of any of the actions or motions of the other, as when the former is the cause of the existence of the latter. For as that

[5] *See Part* iv, *Sect.* vii, *last paragraph.*

action or motion is nothing but the object itself, considered in a certain light, and as the object continues the same in all its different situations, it is easy to imagine how such an influence of objects upon one another may connect them in the imagination.

We may carry this further, and remark, not only that two objects are connected by the relation of cause and effect, when the one produces a motion or any action in the other, but also when it has a power of producing it. And this we may observe to be the source of all the relations of interest and duty, by which men influence each other in society, and are placed in the ties of government and subordination. A master is such a one as by his situation, arising either from force or agreement, has a power of directing in certain particulars the actions of another, whom we call servant. A judge is one, who in all disputed cases can fix by his opinion the possession or property of anything betwixt any members of the society. When a person is possessed of any power, there is no more required to convert it into action, but the exertion of the will; and *that* in every case is considered as possible, and in many as probable; especially in the case of authority, where the obedience of the subject is a pleasure and advantage to the superior.

These are, therefore, the principles of union or cohesion among our simple ideas, and in the imagination supply the place of that inseparable connection, by which they are united in our memory. Here is a kind of *attraction,* which in the mental world will be found to have as extraordinary effects as in the natural, and to show itself in as many and as various forms. Its effects are everywhere conspicuous; but as to its causes, they are mostly unknown, and must be resolved into *original* qualities of human nature, which I pretend not to explain. Nothing is more requisite for a true philosopher, than to restrain the intemperate desire of searching into causes; and having established any doctrine upon a sufficient number of experiments, rest contented with that, when he sees a further examination would lead him into obscure and uncertain speculations. In that case his inquiry would be much better employed in examining the effects than the causes of his principle.

Amongst the effects of this union or association of ideas, there are none more remarkable than those complex ideas, which are the common subjects of our thoughts and reasoning, and generally arise from some principle of union among our simple ideas. These complex ideas may be divided into *relations, modes,* and *substances.* We shall briefly examine each of these in order, and shall subjoin some considerations concerning our *general* and *particular ideas,* before we leave the present subject, which may be considered as the elements of this philosophy.

SECTION V

OF RELATIONS

The word *relation* is commonly used in two senses considerably different from each other. Either for that quality, by which two ideas are connected together in the imagination, and the one naturally introduces the other, after the manner above explained; or for that particular circumstance, in which, even upon the arbitrary union of two ideas in the fancy, we may think proper to compare them. In common language, the former is always the sense in which we use the word relation; and it is only in philosophy that we extend it to mean any particular subject of comparison, without a connecting principle. Thus, distance will be allowed by philosophers to be a true relation, because we acquire an idea of it by the comparing of objects: but in a common way we say, *that nothing can be more distant than such or such things from each other, nothing can have less relation;* as if distance and relation were incompatible.

It may, perhaps, be esteemed an endless task to enumerate all those qualities, which make objects admit of comparison, and by which the ideas of *philosophical* relation are produced. But if we diligently consider them we shall find, that without difficulty they may be comprised under seven general heads, which may be considered as the sources of all philosophical relation.

1. The first is *resemblance:*[6] and this is a relation, without which no philosophical relation can exist, since no objects will admit of comparison, but what have some degree of resemblance. But though resemblance be necessary to all philosophical relation, it does not follow that it always produces a connection or association of ideas. When a quality becomes very general, and is common to a great many individuals, it leads not the mind directly to any one of them; but, by presenting at once too great a choice, does thereby prevent the imagination from fixing on any single object.

2. *Identity* may be esteemed a second species of relation. This relation I here consider as applied in its strictest sense to constant and unchangeable objects; without examining the nature and foundation of personal identity, which shall find its place afterwards. Of all relations the most universal is that of identity, being common to every being, whose existence has any duration.

3. After identity the most universal and comprehensive relations are those of *space* and *time,* which are the sources of an infinite number of comparisons, such as *distant, contiguous, above, below, before, after,* etc.

4. All those objects, which admit of *quantity* or *number,* may be compared in that particular, which is another very fertile source of relation.

5. When any two objects possess the same *quality* in common, the *degrees* in which they possess it form a fifth species of relation. Thus of two objects which are both heavy, the one may be either of greater or less weight than the other. Two colours, that are of the same kind, may yet be of different shades, and in that respect admit of comparison.

[6] *Compare Part i, Sect. VII, p. 64 (footnote).*

6. The relation of *contrariety* may at first sight be regarded as an exception to the rule, *that no relation of any kind can subsist without some degree of resemblance.* But let us consider that no two ideas are in themselves contrary, except those of existence and non-existence, which are plainly resembling, as implying both of them an idea of the object; though the latter excludes the object from all times and places, in which it is supposed not to exist.[7]

7. All other objects, such as fire and water, heat and cold, are only found to be contrary from experience, and from the contrariety of their *causes* or *effects;* which relation of cause and effect is a seventh philosophical relation, as well as a natural one. The resemblance implied in this relation shall be explained afterwards.

It might naturally be expected that I should join *difference* to the other relations; but that I consider rather as a negation of relation than as anything real or positive. Difference is of two kinds, as opposed either to identity or resemblance. The first is called a difference of *number;* the other of *kind.*

SECTION VI

OF MODES AND SUBSTANCES

I would fain ask those philosophers, who found so much of their reasonings on the distinction of substance and accident, and imagine we have clear ideas of each, whether the idea of *substance* be derived from the impressions of sensation or reflection? If it be conveyed to us by our senses, I ask, which of them, and after what manner? If it be perceived by the eyes, it must be a colour; if by the ears, a sound; if by the palate, a taste; and so of the other senses. But I believe none will assert, that substance is either a colour, a sound, or a taste. The idea of sub-

[7]*Compare Part* II, *Sect.* VI.

stance must, therefore, be derived from an impression of reflection, if it really exist. But the impressions of reflection resolve themselves into our passions and emotions; none of which can possibly represent a substance. We have therefore no idea of substance, distinct from that of a collection of particular qualities, nor have we any other meaning when we either talk or reason concerning it.

The idea of a substance as well as that of a mode, is nothing but a collection of simple ideas, that are united by the imagination, and have a particular name assigned them, by which we are able to recall, either to ourselves or others, that collection. But the difference betwixt these ideas consists in this, that the particular qualities which form a substance, are commonly referred to an unknown *something*,[8] in which they are supposed to inhere; or granting this fiction should not take place, are at least supposed to be closely and inseparably connected by the relations of contiguity and causation. The effect of this is, that whatever new simple quality we discover to have the same connection with the rest, we immediately comprehend it among them, even though it did not enter into the first conception of the substance. Thus our idea of gold may at first be a yellow colour, weight, malleableness, fusibility; but upon the discovery of its dissolubility in *aqua regia,* we join that to the other qualities, and suppose it to belong to the substance as much as if its idea had from the beginning made a part of a compound one. The principle of union being regarded as the chief part of the complex idea, gives entrance to whatever quality afterwards occurs, and is equally comprehended by it, as are the others, which first presented themselves.

That this cannot take place in modes, is evident from considering their nature. The simple ideas of which modes are formed, either represent qualities, which are not united by contiguity and causation, but are dispersed in different subjects; or if they be all united together, the

[8] *Compare Locke, Essay Concerning Human Understanding, Book* II, *ch.* 23.

uniting principle is not regarded as the foundation of the complex idea. The idea of a dance is an instance of the first kind of modes; that of beauty of the second. The reason is obvious, why such complex ideas cannot receive any new idea, without changing the name, which distinguishes the mode.

SECTION VII

OF ABSTRACT IDEAS

A very material question has been started concerning *abstract* or *general* ideas, *whether they be general or particular in the mind's conception of them.* A great philosopher[9] has disputed the received opinion in this particular, and has asserted, that all general ideas are nothing but particular ones annexed to a certain term, which gives them a more extensive signification, and makes them recall upon occasion other individuals, which are similar to them. As I look upon this to be one of the greatest and most valuable discoveries that has been made of late years in the republic of letters, I shall here endeavour to confirm it by some arguments, which I hope will put it beyond all doubt and controversy.

It is evident, that in forming most of our general ideas, if not all of them, we abstract from every particular degree of quantity and quality, and that an object ceases not to be of any particular species on account of every small alteration in its extension, duration, and other properties. It may, therefore, be thought, that here is a plain dilemma, that decides concerning the nature of those abstract ideas, which have afforded so much speculation to philosophers. The abstract idea of a man represents men of all sizes and all qualities, which it is concluded it cannot do, but either by representing at once all possible sizes and all possible qualities, or by representing no particular one at all. Now,

[9] Dr. Berkeley.

it having been esteemed absurd to defend the former proposition, as implying an infinite capacity in the mind, it
has been commonly inferred in favour of the latter; and
our abstract ideas have been supposed to represent no
particular degree either of quantity or quality. But that
this inference is erroneous, I shall endeavour to make
appear, *first*, by proving, that it is utterly impossible to
conceive any quantity or quality, without forming a precise notion of its degrees; and, *secondly,* by showing, that
though the capacity of the mind be not infinite, yet we can
at once form a notion of all possible degrees of quantity
and quality, in such a manner at least, as, however imperfect, may serve all the purposes of reflection and conversation.

To begin with the first proposition, *that the mind cannot
form any notion of quantity or quality without forming a
precise notion of degrees of each,* we may prove this by
the three following arguments. First, we have observed,
that whatever objects are different are distinguishable, and
that whatever objects are distinguishable are separable by
the thought and imagination. And we may here add, that
these propositions are equally true in the *inverse,* and that
whatever objects are separable are also distinguishable,
and that whatever objects are distinguishable are also different. For how is it possible we can separate what is not
distinguishable, or distinguish what is not different? In
order therefore to know whether abstraction implies a
separation, we need only consider it in this view, and
examine, whether all the circumstances, which we abstract
from in our general ideas, be such as are distinguishable
and different from those, which we retain as essential parts
of them. But it is evident at first sight, that the precise
length of a line is not different nor distinguishable from
the line itself; nor the precise degree of any quality from
the quality. These ideas therefore admit no more of separation than they do of distinction and difference. They
are consequently conjoined with each other in the conception; and the general idea of a line, notwithstanding all

our abstractions and refinements, has in its appearance in the mind a precise degree of quantity and quality; however it may be made to represent others which have different degrees of both.

Secondly, it is confessed, that no object can appear to the senses; or in other words, that no impression can become present to the mind, without being determined in its degrees both of quantity and quality. The confusion, in which impressions are sometimes involved, proceeds only from their faintness and unsteadiness, not from any capacity in the mind to receive any impression, which in its real existence has no particular degree nor proportion. That is a contradiction in terms; and even implies the flattest of all contradictions, viz. that it is possible for the same thing both to be and not to be.[10]

Now since all ideas are derived from impressions, and are nothing but copies and representations of them, whatever is true of the one must be acknowledged concerning the other. Impressions and ideas differ only in their strength and vivacity. The foregoing conclusion is not founded on any particular degree of vivacity. It cannot, therefore, be affected by any variation in that particular. An idea is a weaker impression; and as a strong impression must necessarily have a determinate quantity and quality, the case must be the same with its copy or representative.

Thirdly, it is a principle generally received in philosophy, that everything in nature is individual, and that it is utterly absurd to suppose a triangle really existent, which has no precise proportion of sides and angles. If this, therefore, be absurd in *fact and reality*, it must also be absurd *in idea*; since nothing of which we can form a clear and distinct idea is absurd and impossible. But to form the idea of an object, and to form an idea simply, is the same thing; the reference of the idea to an object being an extraneous denomination, of which in itself it bears no

[10] *Hume means, e.g., that a thing that had warmth, but no particular degree of warmth, would both have* some *warmth and* no *warmth.*

mark or character. Now as it is impossible to form an idea of an object that is possessed of quantity and quality, and yet is possessed of no precise degree of either, it follows, that there is an equal impossibility of forming an idea, that is not limited and confined in both these particulars. Abstract ideas are therefore in themselves individual, however they may become general in their representation. The image in the mind is only that of a particular object, though the application of it in our reasoning be the same as if it were universal.

This application of ideas, beyond their nature, proceeds from our collecting all their possible degrees of quantity and quality in such an imperfect manner as may serve the purposes of life, which is the second proposition I proposed to explain. When we have found a resemblance[11] among several objects, that often occur to us, we apply the same name to all of them, whatever differences we may observe in the degrees of their quantity and quality, and whatever other differences may appear among them. After we have acquired a custom of this kind, the hearing of that name revives the idea of one of these objects, and makes the imagination conceive it with all its particular circumstances and proportions. But as the same word is supposed to have been frequently applied to other individuals, that are

[11] It is evident, that even different simple ideas may have a similarity or resemblance to each other; nor is it necessary, that the point or circumstance of resemblance should be distinct or separable from that in which they differ. *Blue* and *green* are different simple ideas, but are more resembling than *blue* and *scarlet*; though their perfect simplicity excludes all possibility of separation or distinction. It is the same case with particular sounds, and tastes, and smells. These admit of infinite resemblances upon the general appearance and comparison, without having any common circumstance the same. And of this we may be certain, even from the very abstract terms *simple idea*. They comprehend all simple ideas under them. These resemble each other in their simplicity. And yet from their very nature, which excludes all composition, this circumstance, in which they resemble, is not distinguishable or separable from the rest. It is the same case with all the degrees in any quality. They are all resembling, and yet the quality, in any individual, is not distinct from the degree.

different in many respects from that idea, which is immediately present to the mind; the word not being able to revive the idea of all these individuals, only touches the soul, if I may be allowed so to speak, and revives that custom, which we have acquired by surveying them. They are not really and in fact present to the mind, but only in power;[12] nor do we draw them all out distinctly in the imagination, but keep ourselves in a readiness to survey any of them, as we may be prompted by a present design or necessity. The word raises up an individual idea, along with a certain custom, and that custom produces any other individual one, for which we may have occasion. But as the production of all the ideas, to which the name may be applied, is in most cases impossible, we abridge that work by a more partial consideration, and find but few inconveniences to arise in our reasoning from that abridgment.

For this is one of the most extraordinary circumstances in the present affair, that after the mind has produced an individual idea, upon which we reason, the attendant custom, revived by the general or abstract term, readily suggests any other individual, if by chance we form any reasoning that agrees not with it. Thus, should we mention the word triangle, and form the idea of a particular equilateral one to correspond to it, and should we afterwards assert, *that the three angles of a triangle are equal to each other,* the other individuals of a scalenum and isosceles, which we overlooked at first, immediately crowd in upon us, and make us perceive the falsehood of this proposition, though it be true with relation to that idea which we had formed. If the mind suggests not always these ideas upon occasion, it proceeds from some imperfection in its faculties; and such a one as is often the source of false reasoning and sophistry. But this is principally the case with those ideas which are abstruse and compounded. On other occasions the custom is more entire, and it is seldom we run into such errors.

[12] *Compare Part* I, *Sect.* IV, *p.* 56.

Nay so entire is the custom, that the very same idea may be annexed to several different words, and may be employed in different reasonings, without any danger of mistake. Thus the idea of an equilateral triangle of an inch perpendicular may serve us in talking of a figure, of a rectilineal figure, of a regular figure, of a triangle, and of an equilateral triangle. All these terms, therefore, are in this case attended with the same idea; but as they are wont to be applied in a greater or lesser compass, they excite their particular habits, and thereby keep the mind in a readiness to observe, that no conclusion be formed contrary to any ideas, which are usually comprised under them.

Before those habits have become entirely perfect, perhaps the mind may not be content with forming the idea of only one individual, but may run over several, in order to make itself comprehend its own meaning, and the compass of that collection, which it intends to express by the general term. That we may fix the meaning of the word, figure, we may revolve in our minds the ideas of circles, squares, parallelograms, triangles of different sizes and proportions, and may not rest on one image or idea. However this may be, it is certain *that* we form the idea of individuals whenever we use any general term; *that* we seldom or never can exhaust these individuals; and *that* those which remain, are only represented by means of that habit by which we recall them, whenever any present occasion requires it. This then is the nature of our abstract ideas and general terms; and it is after this manner we account for the foregoing paradox, *that some ideas are particular in their nature, but general in their representation*. A particular idea becomes general by being annexed to a general term; that is, to a term which, from a customary conjunction, has a relation to many other particular ideas, and readily recalls them in the imagination.

The only difficulty that can remain on this subject, must be with regard to that custom, which so readily recalls every particular idea for which we may have occasion, and

is excited by any word or sound to which we commonly
annex it. The most proper method, in my opinion, of
giving a satisfactory explication of this act of the mind, is
by producing other instances which are analogous to it,
and other principles which facilitate its operation. To
explain the ultimate causes of our mental actions is impossible. It is sufficient if we can give any satisfactory
account of them from experience and analogy.

First then I observe, that when we mention any great
number, such as a thousand, the mind has generally no
adequate idea of it, but only a power of producing such
an idea, by its adequate idea of the decimals under which
the number is comprehended. This imperfection, however, in our ideas, is never felt in our reasonings, which
seems to be an instance parallel to the present one of
universal ideas.

Secondly, we have several instances of habits which may
be revived by one single word; as when a person who has
by rote any periods of a discourse, or any number of
verses, will be put in remembrance of the whole, which he
is at a loss to recollect, by that single word or expression
with which they begin.

Thirdly, I believe every one who examines the situation
of his mind in reasoning, will agree with me, that we do
not annex distinct and complete ideas to every term we
make use of, and that in talking of *government, church,
negotiation, conquest,* we seldom spread out in our minds
all the simple ideas of which these complex ones are composed. It is however observable, that notwithstanding this
imperfection, we may avoid talking nonsense on these
subjects, and may perceive any repugnance among the
ideas as well as if we had a full comprehension of them.
Thus if instead of saying, *that in war the weaker have
always recourse to negotiations,* we should say, *that they
have always recourse to conquest,* the custom which we
have acquired of attributing certain relations to ideas,
still follows the words, and makes us immediately perceive
the absurdity of that proposition; in the same manner as

one particular idea may serve us in reasoning concerning other ideas, however different from it in several circumstances.

Fourthly, as the individuals are collected together, and placed under a general term with a view to that resemblance which they bear to each other, this relation must facilitate their entrance in the imagination, and make them be suggested more readily upon occasion. And indeed if we consider the common progress of the thought, either in reflection or conversation, we shall find great reason to be satisfied in this particular. Nothing is more admirable than the readiness with which the imagination suggests its ideas, and presents them at the very instant in which they become necessary or useful. The fancy runs from one end of the universe to the other, in collecting those ideas which belong to any subject. One would think the whole intellectual world of ideas was at once subjected to our view, and that we did nothing but pick out such as were most proper for our purpose. There may not, however, be any present, beside those very ideas, that are thus collected by a kind of magical faculty in the soul, which, though it be always most perfect in the greatest geniuses, and is properly what we call a genius, is however inexplicable by the utmost efforts of human understanding.

Perhaps these four reflections may help to remove all difficulties to the hypothesis I have proposed concerning abstract ideas, so contrary to that which has hitherto prevailed in philosophy. But to tell the truth, I place my chief confidence in what I have already proved concerning the impossibility of general ideas, according to the common method of explaining them. We must certainly seek some new system on this head, and there plainly is none beside what I have proposed. If ideas be particular in their nature, and at the same time finite in their number, it is only by custom they can become general in their representation, and contain an infinite number of other ideas under them.

Before I leave this subject, I shall employ the same

principles to explain that *distinction of reason,* which is so much talked of, and is so little understood in the schools. Of this kind is the distinction betwixt figure and the body figured; motion and the body moved. The difficulty of explaining this distinction arises from the principle above explained, *that all ideas which are different are separable.* For it follows from thence, that if the figure be different from the body, their ideas must be separable as well as distinguishable; if they be not different, their ideas can neither be separable nor distinguishable. What then is meant by a distinction of reason, since it implies neither a difference nor separation?

To remove this difficulty, we must have recourse to the foregoing explication of abstract ideas. It is certain that the mind would never have dreamed of distinguishing a figure from the body figured, as being in reality neither distinguishable, nor different, nor separable, did it not observe, that even in this simplicity there might be contained many different resemblances and relations. Thus, when a globe of white marble is presented, we receive only the impression of a white colour disposed in a certain form, nor are we able to separate and distinguish the colour from the form. But observing afterwards a globe of black marble and a cube of white, and comparing them with our former object, we find two separate resemblances, in what formerly seemed, and really is, perfectly inseparable. After a little more practice of this kind, we begin to distinguish the figure from the colour by a *distinction of reason;* that is, we consider the figure and colour together, since they are, in effect, the same and undistinguishable; but still view them in different aspects, according to the resemblances of which they are susceptible. When we would consider only the figure of the globe of white marble we form in reality an idea both of the figure and colour, but tacitly carry our eye to its resemblance with the globe of black marble : and in the same manner, when we would consider its colour only, we turn our view to its resemblance with the cube of white marble. By this means we accompany our ideas with a kind of reflection, of which custom renders us, in a great measure, insensible. A person who desires us to consider the figure of a globe of white marble without thinking on its colour, desires an impossibility; but his meaning is, that we should consider the colour and figure together, but still keep in our eye the resemblance to the globe of black marble, or that to any other globe of whatever colour or substance.

PART II

OF THE IDEAS OF SPACE AND TIME

SECTION I

OF THE INFINITE DIVISIBILITY OF OUR IDEAS OF SPACE AND TIME

Whatever has the air of a paradox, and is contrary to the first and most unprejudiced notion of mankind, is often greedily embraced by philosophers, as showing the superiority of their science, which could discover opinions so remote from vulgar conception. On the other hand, anything proposed to us, which causes surprise and admiration, gives such a satisfaction to the mind, that it indulges itself in those agreeable emotions, and will never be persuaded that its pleasure is entirely without foundation. From these dispositions in philosophers and their disciples, arises that mutual complaisance betwixt them; while the former furnish such plenty of strange and unaccountable opinions, and the latter so readily believe them. Of this mutual complaisance I cannot give a more evident instance than in the doctrine of infinite divisibility, with the examination of which I shall begin this subject of the ideas of space and time.

It is universally allowed, that the capacity of the mind is limited, and can never attain a full and adequate conception of infinity : and though it were not allowed, it would be sufficiently evident from the plainest observation and experience. It is also obvious, that whatever is capable of being divided *in infinitum,* must consist of an infinite number of parts, and that it is impossible to set any bounds to the number of parts, without setting bounds at the same time to the division. It requires scarce any induction to conclude from hence, that the *idea* which we form of any finite quality, is not infinitely divisible, but that by proper distinctions and separations we may run up this idea to inferior ones, which will be perfectly simple and indivisible. In rejecting the infinite capacity of the mind, we suppose it may arrive at an end in the division of its ideas; nor are there any possible means of evading the evidence of this conclusion.

It is therefore certain, that the imagination reaches a *minimum,* and may raise up to itself an idea, of which it cannot conceive any subdivision, and which cannot be diminished without a total annihilation. When you tell me of the thousandth and ten thousandth part of a grain of sand, I have a distinct idea of these numbers and of their different proportions; but the images which I form in my mind to represent the things themselves, are nothing different from each other, nor inferior to that image, by which I represent the grain of sand itself, which is supposed so vastly to exceed them. What consists of parts is distinguishable into them, and what is distinguishable is separable. But, whatever we may imagine of the thing, the idea of a grain of sand is not distinguishable nor separable into twenty, much less into a thousand, ten thousand, or an infinite number of different ideas.†[1]

It is the same case with the impressions of the senses, as with the ideas of the imagination. Put a spot of ink upon paper, fix your eye upon that spot, and retire to such a distance that at last you lose sight of it; it is plain, that the moment before it vanished, the image, or impression, was perfectly indivisible. It is not for want of rays of light striking on our eyes, that the minute parts of distant bodies convey not any sensible impression; but because they are removed beyond that distance, at which their impressions were reduced to a *minimum,* and were incapable of any further diminution. A microscope or telescope, which render them visible, produces not any new rays of light,

[1] Throughout, this symbol † refers readers to the editor's notes, which begin on p. 357.

but only spreads those which always flowed from them; and by that means both gives parts to impressions, which to the naked eye appear simple and uncompounded, and advances to a *minimum* what was formerly imperceptible.

We may hence discover the error of the common opinion, that the capacity of the mind is limited on both sides, and that it is impossible for the imagination to form an adequate idea of what goes beyond a certain degree of minuteness as well as of greatness. Nothing can be more minute than some ideas which we form in the fancy, and images which appear to the senses; since there are ideas and images perfectly simple and indivisible. The only defect of our senses is, that they give us disproportionate images of things, and represent as minute and uncompounded what is really great and composed of a vast number of parts. This mistake we are not sensible of; but, taking the impressions of those minute objects, which appear to the senses, to be equal, or nearly equal to the objects, and finding by reason, that there are other objects vastly more minute, we too hastily conclude, that these are inferior to any idea of our imagination or impression of our senses. This however is certain, that we can form ideas, which shall be no greater than the smallest atom of the animal spirits of an insect a thousand times less than a mite : † and we ought rather to conclude, that the difficulty lies in enlarging our conceptions so much as to form a just notion of a mite, or even of an insect a thousand times less than a mite. For, in order to form a just notion of these animals, we must have a distinct idea representing every part of them; which, according to the system of infinite divisibility, is utterly impossible, and according to that of indivisible parts or atoms, is extremely difficult, by reason of the vast number and multiplicity of these parts.

OF THE INFINITE DIVISIBILITY OF SPACE AND TIME†

Wherever ideas are adequate representations of objects, the relations, contradictions, and agreements of the ideas are all applicable to the objects; and this we may, in general, observe to be the foundation of all human knowledge. But our ideas are adequate representations of the most minute parts of extension; and, through whatever divisions and subdivisions we may suppose these parts to be arrived at, they can never become inferior to some ideas which we form. The plain consequence is, that whatever *appears* impossible and contradictory upon the comparison of these ideas, must be *really* impossible and contradictory, without any further excuse or evasion.

Everything capable of being infinitely divided contains an infinite number of parts; otherwise the division would be stopped short by the indivisible parts, which we should immediately arrive at. If therefore any finite extension be infinitely divisible, it can be no contradiction to suppose that a finite extension contains an infinite number of parts : and *vice versa,* if it be a contradiction to suppose, that a finite extension contains an infinite number of parts, no finite extension can be infinitely divisible. But that this latter supposition is absurd, I easily convince myself by the consideration of my clear ideas. I first take the least idea I can form of a part of extension, and being certain that there is nothing more minute than this idea, I conclude, that whatever I discover by its means must be a real quality of extension. I then repeat this idea once, twice, thrice, etc., and find the compound idea of extension, arising from its repetition, always to augment, and become double, triple, quadruple, etc., till at last it swells up to a considerable bulk, greater or smaller, in proportion as I repeat more or less the same idea. When I stop in the addition of parts, the idea of extension ceases to augment; and were I to carry on the addition *in infinitum,* I clearly perceive, that the idea of extension must also become infinite. Upon the whole, I conclude, that the idea of an infinite number of parts is individually the same idea with that of an infinite extension; that no finite extension is capable of containing an infinite number of parts; and, consequently, that no finite extension is infinitely divisible.[2]

I may subjoin another argument proposed by a noted author,[3] which seems to me very strong and beautiful. It is evident, that existence in itself belongs only to unity, and is never applicable to number, but on account of the units of which the number is composed. Twenty men may be said to exist; but it is only because one, two, three, four, etc. are existent; and if you deny the existence of the latter, that of the former falls of course. It is therefore utterly absurd to suppose any number to exist, and yet deny the existence of units; and as extension is always a number, according to the common sentiment of metaphysicians, and never dissolves itself into any unit or indivisible quantity, it follows that extension can never at all exist. It is in vain to reply, that any determinate quantity of extension is a unit; but such a one as admits of an infinite number of fractions, and is inexhaustible in its subdivisions. For by the same rule these twenty men *may be considered as a unit.* The whole globe of the earth, nay the whole universe *may be considered as a unit.* That term of unity is merely a fictitious denomination, which the mind may apply to any quantity of objects it collects together; nor can such a unity any more exist alone than number can, as being in reality a true number. But the

---

[2] It has been objected to me, that infinite divisibility supposes only an infinite number of *proportional* not of *aliquot* parts, and that an infinite number of proportional parts does not form an infinite extension. But this distinction is entirely frivolous. Whether these parts be called *aliquot* or *proportional,* they cannot be inferior to those minute parts, we conceive; and therefore, cannot form a less extension by their conjunction.

[3] Mons. Malezieu.

unity, which can exist alone, and whose existence is necessary to that of all number, is of another kind, and must be perfectly indivisible, and incapable of being resolved into any lesser unity.†

All this reasoning takes place with regard to time; along with an additional argument, which it may be proper to take notice of. It is a property inseparable from time, and which in a manner constitutes its essence, that each of its parts succeeds another, and that none of them, however contiguous, can ever be coexistent. For the same reason that the year 1737 cannot concur with the present year 1738, every moment must be distinct from, and posterior or antecedent to another. It is certain then, that time, as it exists, must be composed of indivisible moments. For if in time we could never arrive at an end of division, and if each moment, as it succeeds another, were not perfectly single and indivisible, there would be an infinite number of coexistent moments, or parts of time; which I believe will be allowed to be an arrant contradiction.

The infinite divisibility of space implies that of time, as is evident from the nature of motion. If the latter, therefore, be impossible, the former must be equally so.

I doubt not but it will readily be allowed by the most obstinate defender of the doctrine of infinite divisibility, that these arguments are difficulties, and that it is impossible to give any answer to them which will be perfectly clear and satisfactory. But here we may observe, that nothing can be more absurd than this custom of calling a *difficulty* what pretends to be a *demonstration*, and endeavouring by that means to elude its force and evidence. It is not in demonstrations, as in probabilities, that difficulties can take place, and one argument counterbalance another, and diminish its authority. A demonstration, if just, admits of no opposite difficulty; and if not just, it is a mere sophism, and consequently can never be a difficulty. It is either irresistible, or has no manner of force. To talk therefore of objections and replies, and balancing of arguments in such a question as this, is to confess, either that human reason is nothing but a play of words, or that the person himself, who talks so, has not a capacity equal to such subjects. Demonstrations may be difficult to be comprehended, because of the abstractedness of the subject; but can never have any such difficulties as will weaken their authority, when once they are comprehended.[4]

It is true, mathematicians are wont to say, that there are here equally strong arguments on the other side of the question, and that the doctrine of indivisible points is also liable to unanswerable objections. Before I examine these arguments and objections in detail, I will here take them in a body, and endeavour by a short and decisive reason to prove at once, that it is utterly impossible they can have any just foundation.

It is an established maxim in metaphysics, *That whatever the mind clearly conceives includes the idea of possible existence,* or in other words *that nothing we imagine is absolutely impossible.* We can form the idea of a golden mountain, and from thence conclude, that such a mountain may actually exist. We can form no idea of a mountain without a valley, and therefore regard it as impossible.

Now it is certain we have an idea of extension; for otherwise, why do we talk and reason concerning it? It is likewise certain, that this idea, as conceived by the imagination, though divisible into parts or inferior ideas, is not infinitely divisible, nor consists of an infinite number of parts : for that exceeds the comprehension of our limited capacities. Here then is an idea of extension, which consists of parts or inferior ideas, that are perfectly indivisible : consequently this idea implies no contradiction : consequently it is possible for extension really to exist conformable to it : and consequently, all the arguments employed against the possibility of mathematical points are mere scholastic quibbles, and unworthy of our attention.

These consequences we may carry one step further, and conclude that all the pretended demonstrations for the

[4] *Contrast Part* iv, *Section* 1: "*All knowledge resolves itself into probability.*"

infinite divisibility of extension are equally sophistical; since it is certain these demonstrations cannot be just without proving the impossibility of mathematical points; which it is an evident absurdity to pretend to.

SECTION III

OF THE OTHER QUALITIES OF OUR IDEAS OF SPACE AND TIME

No discovery could have been made more happily for deciding all controversies concerning ideas, than that above mentioned, that impressions always take the precedency of them, and that every idea, with which the imagination is furnished, first makes its appearance in a correspondent impression. These latter perceptions are all so clear and evident, that they admit of no controversy; though many of our ideas are so obscure, that it is almost impossible even for the mind, which forms them, to tell exactly their nature and composition. Let us apply this principle, in order to discover further the nature of our ideas of space and time.

Upon opening my eyes and turning them to the surrounding objects, I perceive many visible bodies; and upon shutting them again, and considering the distance betwixt these bodies, I acquire the idea of extension. As every idea is derived from some impression which is exactly similar to it, the impressions similar to this idea of extension, must either be some sensations derived from the sight, or some internal impressions arising from these sensations.

Our internal impressions are our passions, emotions, desires, and aversions; none of which, I believe, will ever be asserted to be the model from which the idea of space is derived. There remains therefore nothing but the senses which can convey to us this original impression. Now, what impression do our senses here convey to us? This is the principal question, and decides without appeal concerning the nature of the idea.

The table before me is alone sufficient by its view to give me the idea of extension. This idea, then, is borrowed from, and represents some impression which this moment appears to the senses. But my senses convey to me only the impressions of coloured points, disposed in a certain manner.† If the eye is sensible of anything further, I desire it may be pointed out to me. But, if it be impossible to show anything further, we may conclude with certainty, that the idea of extension is nothing but a copy of these coloured points, and of the manner of their appearance.

Suppose that, in the extended object, or composition of coloured points, from which we first received the idea of extension, the points were of a purple colour; it follows, that in every repetition of that idea we would not only place the points in the same order with respect to each other, but also bestow on them that precise colour with which alone we are acquainted. But afterwards, having experience of the other colours of violet, green, red, white, black, and of all the different compositions of these, and finding a resemblance in the disposition of coloured points, of which they are composed, we omit the peculiarities of colour, as far as possible, and found an abstract idea merely on that disposition of points, or manner of appearance, in which they agree. Nay, even when the resemblance is carried beyond the objects of one sense, and the impressions of touch are found to be similar to those of sight in the disposition of their parts; this does not hinder the abstract idea from representing both, upon account of their resemblance. All abstract ideas are really nothing but particular ones, considered in a certain light; but being annexed to general terms, they are able to represent a vast variety, and to comprehend objects, which, as they are alike in some particulars, are in others vastly wide of each other.[5]

The idea of time, being derived from the succession of

[5] *Compare Part* I, *Section* VII.

our perceptions of every kind, ideas as well as impressions, and impressions of reflection as well as of sensation, will afford us an instance of an abstract idea, which comprehends a still greater variety than that of space, and yet is represented in the fancy by some particular individual idea of a determined quantity and quality.

As it is from the disposition of visible and tangible objects we receive the idea of space, so from the succession of ideas and impressions we form the idea of time; nor is it possible for time alone ever to make its appearance, or be taken notice of by the mind. A man in a sound sleep, or strongly occupied with one thought, is insensible of time; and according as his perceptions succeed each other with greater or less rapidity, the same duration appears longer or shorter to his imagination. It has been remarked by a great philosopher,[6] that our perceptions have certain bounds in this particular, which are fixed by the original nature and constitution of the mind, and beyond which no influence of external objects on the senses is ever able to hasten or retard our thought. If you wheel about a burning coal with rapidity, it will present to the senses an image of a circle of fire; nor will there seem to be any interval of time betwixt its revolutions; merely because it is impossible for our perceptions to succeed each other, with the same rapidity that motion may be communicated to external objects. Wherever we have no successive perceptions, we have no notion of time, even though there be a real succession in the objects. From these phenomena, as well as from many others, we may conclude, that time cannot make its appearance to the mind, either alone or attended with a steady unchangeable object, but is always discovered by some *perceivable* succession of changeable objects.

To confirm this we may add the following argument, which to me seems perfectly decisive and convincing. It is evident, that time or duration consists of different parts: for otherwise, we could not conceive a longer or shorter

6 Mr. Locke.

duration. It is also evident, that these parts are not coexistent : for that quality of the coexistence of parts belongs to extension, and is what distinguishes it from duration. Now as time is composed of parts that are not coexistent, an unchangeable object, since it produces none but coexistent impressions, produces none that can give us the idea of time; and, consequently, that idea must be derived from a succession of changeable objects, and time in its first appearance can never be severed from such a succession.

Having therefore found, that time in its first appearance to the mind is always conjoined with a succession of changeable objects, and that otherwise it can never fall under our notice, we must now examine, whether it can be *conceived* without our conceiving any succession of objects, and whether it can alone form a distinct idea in the imagination.

In order to know whether any objects, which are joined in impression, be separable in idea, we need only consider if they be different from each other; in which case it is plain they may be conceived apart. Everything that is different is distinguishable, and everything that is distinguishable may be separated, according to the maxims above explained. If, on the contrary, they be not different they are not distinguishable; and if they be not distinguishable, they cannot be separated. But this is precisely the case with respect to time, compared with our successive perceptions. The idea of time is not derived from a particular impression mixed up with others, and plainly distinguishable from them, but arises altogether from the manner in which impressions appear to the mind, without making one of the number. Five notes played on a flute give us the impression and idea of time, though time be not a sixth impression which presents itself to the hearing or any other of the senses. Nor is it a sixth impression which the mind by reflection finds in itself. These five sounds making their appearance in this particular manner, excite no emotion in the mind, nor produce an affection of any kind,

which being observed by it can give rise to a new idea.
For *that* is necessary to produce a new idea of reflection;
nor can the mind, by revolving over a thousand times all
its ideas of sensation, ever extract from them any new
original idea, unless nature has so framed its faculties, that
it feels some new original impression arise from such a contemplation. But here it only takes notice of the *manner* in
which the different sounds make their appearance, and
that it may afterwards consider without considering these
particular sounds, but may conjoin it with any other objects. The ideas of some objects it certainly must have, nor
is it possible for it without these ideas ever to arrive at any
conception of time; which, since it appears not as any
primary distinct impression, can plainly be nothing but
different ideas, or impressions, or objects disposed in a
certain manner, that is, succeeding each other.

I know there are some who pretend that the idea of
duration is applicable in a proper sense to objects which
are perfectly unchangeable; and this I take to be the
common opinion of philosophers as well as of the vulgar.
But to be convinced of its falsehood, we need but reflect on
the foregoing conclusion, that the idea of duration is always derived from a succession of changeable objects, and
can never be conveyed to the mind by anything steadfast
and unchangeable. For it inevitably follows from thence,
that since the idea of duration cannot be derived from
such an object, it can never in any propriety or exactness
be applied to it, nor can anything unchangeable be ever
said to have duration. Ideas always represent the objects
or impressions from which they are derived, and can
never without a fiction represent or be applied to any
other. By what fiction we apply the idea of time, even to
what is unchangeable, and suppose, as is common, that
duration is a measure of rest as well as of motion, we shall
consider afterwards.[7]

There is another very decisive argument, which establishes the present doctrine concerning our ideas of space

[7] Sect. 5.

and time, and is founded only on that simple principle, *that our ideas of them are compounded of parts, which are indivisible.* This argument may be worth the examining.

Every idea that is distinguishable being also separable, let us take one of those simple indivisible ideas, of which the compound one of *extension* is formed, and separating it from all others, and considering it apart, let us form a judgment of its nature and qualities.

It is plain it is not the idea of extension. For the idea of extension consists of parts; and this idea, according to the supposition, is perfectly simple and indivisible. Is it, therefore, nothing? That is absolutely impossible. For as the compound idea of extension, which is real, is composed of such ideas, were these so many nonentities, there would be a real existence composed of nonentities, which is absurd. Here, therefore, I must ask, *What is our idea of a simple and indivisible point?* No wonder if my answer appear somewhat new, since the question itself has scarce ever yet been thought of. We are wont to dispute concerning the nature of mathematical points, but seldom concerning the nature of their ideas.

The idea of space is conveyed to the mind by two senses, the sight and touch; nor does anything ever appear extended, that is not either visible or tangible. That compound impression, which represents extension, consists of several lesser impressions, that are indivisible to the eye or feeling, and may be called impressions of atoms or corpuscles endowed with colour and solidity. But this is not all. It is not only requisite that these atoms should be coloured or tangible, in order to discover themselves to our senses; it is also necessary we should preserve the idea of their colour or tangibility, in order to comprehend them by our imagination. There is nothing but the idea of their colour or tangibility which can render them conceivable by the mind. Upon the removal of the ideas of these sensible qualities, they are utterly annihilated to the thought or imagination.

Now, such as the parts are, such is the whole. If a point

be not considered as coloured or tangible, it can convey to us no idea; and consequently the idea of extension, which is composed of the ideas of these points, can never possibly exist : but if the idea of extension really can exist, as we are conscious it does, its parts must also exist; and in order to do that, must be considered as coloured or tangible. We have, therefore, no idea of space or extension, but when we regard it as an object either of our sight or feeling.[8]

The same reasoning will prove, that the indivisible moments of time must be filled with some real object or existence, whose succession forms the duration, and makes it be conceivable by the mind.

SECTION IV

OBJECTIONS ANSWERED

Our system concerning space and time consists of two parts, which are intimately connected together. The first depends on this chain of reasoning. The capacity of the mind is not infinite, consequently no idea of extension or duration consists of an infinite number of parts or inferior ideas, but of a finite number, and these simple and indivisible : it is therefore possible for space and time to exist conformable to this idea : and if it be possible, it is certain they actually do exist conformable to it, since their infinite divisibility is utterly impossible and contradictory.

The other part of our system is a consequence of this. The parts, into which the ideas of space and time resolve themselves, become at last indivisible; and these indivisible parts, being nothing in themselves, are inconceivable when not filled with something real and existent. The ideas of space and time are therefore no separate or distinct ideas, but merely those of the manner or order in which objects exist; or, in other words, it is impossible to conceive either a vacuum and extension without matter, or a time when

[8] *Compare Part IV, Section IV, last paragraph.*

there was no succession or change in any real existence. The intimate connection betwixt these parts of our system is the reason why we shall examine together the objections which have been urged against both of them, beginning with those against the finite divisibility of extension.

I. The first of these objections which I shall take notice of, is more proper to prove this connection and dependence of the one part upon the other than to destroy either of them. It has often been maintained in the schools, that extension must be divisible *in infinitum,* because the system of mathematical points is absurd; and that system is absurd, because a mathematical point is a nonentity, and consequently can never by its conjunction with others form a real existence. This would be perfectly decisive, were there no medium betwixt the infinite divisibility of matter, and the nonentity of mathematical points. But there is evidently a medium, viz. the bestowing a colour or solidity on these points; and the absurdity of both the extremes is a demonstration of the truth and reality of this medium. The system of *physical* points, which is another medium, is too absurd to need a refutation. A real extension, such as a physical point is supposed to be, can never exist without parts different from each other; and wherever objects are different, they are distinguishable and separable by the imagination.

II. The second objection is derived from the necessity there would be of *penetration,* if extension consisted of mathematical points. A simple and indivisible atom that touches another must necessarily penetrate it; for it is impossible it can touch it by its external parts, from the very supposition of its perfect simplicity, which excludes all parts. It must therefore touch it intimately, and in its whole essence, *secundum se, tota, et totaliter;* which is the very definition of penetration. But penetration is impossible: mathematical points are of consequence equally impossible.

I answer this objection by substituting a juster idea of penetration. Suppose two bodies, containing no void within their circumference, to approach each other, and to unite in such a manner that the body, which results from their union, is no more extended than either of them; it is this we must mean when we talk of penetration. But it is evident this penetration is nothing but the annihilation of one of these bodies, and the preservation of the other, without being able to distinguish particularly which is preserved and which annihilated. Before the approach we have the idea of two bodies; after it we have the idea only of one. It is impossible for the mind to preserve any notion of difference betwixt two bodies of the same nature existing in the same place at the same time.†

Taking then penetration in this sense, for the annihilation of one body upon its approach to another, I ask any one if he sees a necessity that a coloured or tangible point should be annihilated upon the approach of another coloured or tangible point? On the contrary, does he not evidently perceive, that from the union of these points there results an object which is compounded and divisible, and may be distinguished into two parts, of which each preserves its existence, distinct and separate, notwithstanding its contiguity to the other? Let him aid his fancy by conceiving these points to be of different colours, the better to prevent their coalition and confusion. A blue and a red point may surely lie contiguous without any penetration or annihilation. For if they cannot, what possibly can become of them? Whether shall the red or the blue be annihilated? Or if these colours unite into one, what new colour will they produce by their union?†

What chiefly gives rise to these objections, and at the same time renders it so difficult to give a satisfactory answer to them, is the natural infirmity and unsteadiness both of our imagination and senses when employed on such minute objects. Put a spot of ink upon paper, and retire to such a distance that the spot becomes altogether invisible; you will find, that upon your return and nearer approach the spot first becomes visible by short intervals, and afterwards becomes always visible; and afterwards acquires only a new force in its colouring, without augmenting its bulk; and afterwards, when it has increased to such a degree as to be really extended, it is still difficult for the imagination to break it into its component parts, because of the uneasiness it finds in the conception of such a minute object as a single point. This infirmity affects most of our reasonings on the present subject, and makes it almost impossible to answer in an intelligible manner, and in proper expressions, many questions which may arise concerning it.

III. There have been many objections drawn from the *mathematics* against the indivisibility of the parts of extension, though at first sight that science seems rather favourable to the present doctrine; and if it be contrary in its *demonstrations,* it is perfectly conformable in its *definitions.* My present business then must be, to defend the definitions and refute the demonstrations.

A surface is *defined* to be length and breadth without depth; a line to be length without breadth or depth; a point to be what has neither length, breadth, nor depth. It is evident that all this is perfectly unintelligible upon any other supposition than that of the composition of extension by indivisible points or atoms. How else could anything exist without length, without breadth, or without depth?

Two different answers, I find, have been made to this argument, neither of which is, in my opinion, satisfactory. The first is, that the objects of geometry, those surfaces, lines, and points, whose proportions and positions it examines, are mere ideas in the mind; and not only never did, but never can exist in nature. They never did exist; for no one will pretend to draw a line or make a surface entirely conformable to the definition : they never can exist; for we may produce demonstrations from these very ideas to prove that they are impossible.

But can anything be imagined more absurd and contradictory than this reasoning? Whatever can be conceived by a clear and distinct idea, necessarily implies the possibility of existence; and he who pretends to prove the impossibility of its existence by any argument derived from the clear idea, in reality asserts that we have no clear idea of it, because we have a clear idea. It is in vain to search for a contradiction in anything that is distinctly conceived by the mind. Did it imply any contradiction, it is impossible it could ever be conceived.[9]

There is therefore no medium betwixt allowing at least the possibility of indivisible points, and denying their ideas; and it is on this latter principle that the second answer to the foregoing argument is founded. It has been pretended,[10] that though it be impossible to conceive a length without any breadth, yet by an abstraction without a separation we can consider the one without regarding the other; in the same manner as we may think of the length of the way betwixt two towns and overlook its breadth. The length is inseparable from the breadth both in nature and in our minds; but this excludes not a partial consideration, and a *distinction of reason*, after the manner above explained.[11]

In refuting this answer I shall not insist on the argument, which I have already sufficiently explained, that if it be impossible for the mind to arrive at a *minimum* in its ideas, its capacity must be infinite in order to comprehend the infinite number of parts, of which its idea of any extension would be composed. I shall here endeavour to find some new absurdities in this reasoning.

A surface terminates a solid; a line terminates a surface; a point terminates a line; but I assert, that if the *ideas* of a point, line, or surface, were not indivisible, it is impossible we should ever conceive these terminations. For let these ideas be supposed infinitely divisible, and then let the fancy endeavour to fix itself on the idea of the last surface, line, or point, it immediately finds this idea to

---

[9] *For a modern solution of these problems see A. N. Whitehead "The Nature of Mathematics," Home University Library Series.*

[10] L'Art de penser. ("*La Logique, ou L'Art de Penser*", Arnauld et Nicole, Paris, 1662, also known as the "*Logique de Port Royal*".)

[11] *Part* I, *Section* VII, *concluding paragraph.*

break into parts; and upon its seizing the last of these parts, it loses its hold by a new division, and so on *in infinitum,* without any possibility of its arriving at a concluding idea. The number of fractions bring it no nearer the last division than the first idea it formed. Every particle eludes the grasp by a new fraction, like quicksilver, when we endeavour to seize it. But as in fact there must be something which terminates the idea of every finite quantity, and as this terminating idea cannot itself consist of parts or inferior ideas, otherwise it would be the last of its parts, which finished the idea, and so on; this is a clear proof, that the ideas of surfaces, lines, and points, admit not of any division; those of surfaces in depth, of lines in breadth and depth, and of points in any dimension.

The *schoolmen* were so sensible of the force of this argument, that some of them maintained that nature has mixed among those particles of matter, which are divisible *in infinitum,* a number of mathematical points in order to give a termination to bodies; and others eluded the force of this reasoning by a heap of unintelligible cavils and distinctions. Both these adversaries equally yield the victory. A man who hides himself confesses as evidently the superiority of his enemy, as another, who fairly delivers his arms.

Thus it appears, that the definitions of mathematics destroy the pretended demonstrations; and that if we have the idea of indivisible points, lines, and surfaces, conformable to the definition, their existence is certainly possible; but if we have no such idea, it is impossible we can ever conceive the termination of any figure, without which conception there can be no geometrical demonstration.

But I go further, and maintain, that none of these demonstrations can have sufficient weight to establish such a principle as this of infinite divisibility; and that because with regard to such minute objects, they are not properly demonstrations, being built on ideas which are not exact, and maxims which are not precisely true. When geometry decides anything concerning the proportions of quantity, we ought not to look for the utmost *precision* and exactness. None of its proofs extend so far; it takes the dimensions and proportions of figures justly; but roughly, and with some liberty. Its errors are never considerable, nor would it err at all, did it not aspire to such an absolute perfection.

I first ask mathematicians what they mean when they say one line or surface is *equal* to, or *greater*, or *less* than another? Let any of them give an answer, to whatever sect he belongs, and whether he maintains the composition of extension by indivisible points, or by quantities divisible *in infinitum*. This question will embarrass both of them.

There are few or no mathematicians who defend the hypothesis of indivisible points, and yet these have the readiest and justest answer to the present question. They need only reply, that lines or surfaces are equal, when the numbers of points in each are equal; and that as the proportion of the numbers varies, the proportion of the lines and surfaces is also varied. But though this answer be *just* as well as obvious, yet I may affirm, that this standard of equality is entirely *useless,* and that it never is from such a comparison we determine objects to be equal or unequal with respect to each other. For as the points which enter into the composition of any line or surface, whether perceived by the sight or touch, are so minute and so confounded with each other that it is utterly impossible for the mind to compute their number, such a computation will never afford us a standard by which we may judge of proportions. No one will ever be able to determine, by an exact enumeration, that an inch has fewer points than a foot, or a foot fewer than an ell, or any greater measure; for which reason, we seldom or never consider this as the standard of equality or inequality.

As to those who imagine that extension is divisible *in infinitum,* it is impossible they can make use of this answer, or fix the equality of any line or surface by a numeration of its component parts. For since, according to their hypothesis, the least as well as greatest figures contain an infinite number of parts, and since infinite numbers, properly speaking, can neither be equal nor unequal with respect to each other, the equality or inequality of any portions of space can never depend on any proportion in the number of their parts. It is true, it may be said, that the inequality of an ell and a yard consists in the different numbers of the feet of which they are composed, and that of a foot and a yard in the number of inches. But as that quantity we call an inch in the one is supposed equal to what we call an inch in the other, and as it is impossible for the mind to find this equality by proceeding *in infinitum* with these references to inferior quantities, it is evident that at last we must fix some standard of equality different from an enumeration of the parts.

There are some who pretend,[12] that equality is best defined by *congruity,* and that any two figures are equal, when upon the placing of one upon the other, all their parts correspond to and touch each other. In order to judge of this definition let us consider, that since equality is a relation, it is not, strictly speaking, a property in the figures themselves, but arises merely from the comparison which the mind makes betwixt them. If it consists, therefore, in this imaginary application and mutual contact of parts, we must, at least, have a distinct notion of these parts, and must conceive their contact. Now it is plain, that in this conception we would run up these parts to the greatest minuteness which can possibly be conceived, since the contact of large parts would never render the figures equal. But the minutest parts we can conceive are mathematical points, and consequently this standard of equality is the same with that derived from the equality of the number of points, which we have already determined to be a just but a useless standard. We must therefore look to some other quarter for a solution of the present difficulty.

[There are many philosophers, who refuse to assign any

[12] See Dr. Barrow's Mathematical Lectures (*Isaac Barrow, Professor of Mathematics at Cambridge immediately before Sir Isaac Newton.*)

standard of *equality,* but assert, that it is sufficient to present two objects, that are equal, in order to give us a just notion of this proportion. All definitions, say they, are fruitless without the perception of such objects; and where we perceive such objects we no longer stand in need of any definition. To this reasoning I entirely agree; and assert, that the only useful notion of equality, or inequality, is derived from the whole united appearance and the comparison of particular objects.]

It is evident that the eye, or rather the mind, is often able at one view to determine the proportions of bodies, and pronounce them equal to, or greater or less than each other, without examining or comparing the number of their minute parts. Such judgments are not only common, but in many cases certain and infallible. When the measure of a yard and that of a foot are presented, the mind can no more question, that the first is longer than the second, than it can doubt of those principles which are the most clear and self-evident.

There are therefore three proportions, which the mind distinguishes in the general appearance of its objects, and calls by the names of *greater, less,* and *equal.* But though its decisions concerning these proportions be sometimes infallible, they are not always so; nor are our judgments of this kind more exempt from doubt and error than those on any other subject. We frequently correct our first opinion by a review and reflection; and pronounce those objects to be equal, which at first we esteemed unequal; and regard an object as less, though before it appeared greater than another. Nor is this the only correction which these judgments of our senses undergo; but we often discover our error by a juxtaposition of the objects; or, where that is impracticable, by the use of some common and invariable measure, which, being successively applied to each, informs us of their different proportions. And even this correction is susceptible of a new correction, and of different degrees of exactness, according to the nature of the instrument by which we measure the bodies, and the care which we employ in the comparison.

When therefore the mind is accustomed to these judgments and their corrections, and finds that the same proportion which makes two figures have in the eye that appearance, which we call *equality,* makes them also correspond to each other, and to any common measure with which they are compared, we form a mixed notion of equality derived both from the looser and stricter methods of comparison. But we are not content with this. For as sound reason convinces us that there are bodies *vastly* more minute than those which appear to the senses; and as a false reason would persuade us, that there are bodies *infinitely* more minute, we clearly perceive that we are not possessed of any instrument or art of measuring which can secure us from all error and uncertainty. We are sensible that the addition or removal of one of these minute parts is not discernible either in the appearance or measuring; and as we imagine that two figures, which were equal before, cannot be equal after this removal or addition, we therefore suppose some imaginary standard of equality, by which the appearances and measuring are exactly corrected, and the figures reduced entirely to that proportion. This standard is plainly imaginary. For as the very idea of equality is that of such a particular appearance, corrected by juxtaposition or a common measure, the notion of any correction beyond what we have instruments and art to make, is a mere fiction of the mind, and useless as well as incomprehensible. But though this standard be only imaginary, the fiction however is very natural; nor is anything more usual, than for the mind to proceed after this manner with any action, even after the reason has ceased, which first determined it to begin. This appears very conspicuously with regard to time; where, though it is evident we have no exact method of determining the proportions of parts, not even so exact as in extension, yet the various corrections of our measures, and their different degrees of exactness, have given us an obscure and implicit notion of a perfect and entire equality. The case is the same in many other subjects. A musician, finding his ear become every day more delicate, and correcting himself by reflection and attention, proceeds with the same act of the mind even when the subject fails him, and entertains a notion of a complete *tierce* or *octavē,* without being able to tell whence he derives his standard. A painter forms the same fiction with regard to colours; a mechanic with regard to motion. To the one *light* and *shade,* to the other *swift* and *slow,* are imagined to be capable of an exact comparison and equality beyond the judgments of the senses.

We may apply the same reasoning to *curve* and *right* lines. Nothing is more apparent to the senses than the distinction betwixt a curve and a right line; nor are there any ideas we more easily form than the ideas of these objects. But however easily we may form these ideas, it is impossible to produce any definition of them, which will fix the precise boundaries betwixt them. When we draw lines upon paper or any continued surface, there is a certain order by which the lines run along from one point to another, that they may produce the entire impression of a curve or right line; but this order is perfectly unknown, and nothing is observed but the united appearance. Thus, even upon the system of indivisible points, we can only form a distant notion of some unknown standard to these objects. Upon that of infinite divisibility we cannot go even this length, but are reduced merely to the general appearance, as the rule by which we determine lines to be either curve or right ones. But though we can give no perfect definition of these lines, nor produce any very exact method of distinguishing the one from the other, yet this hinders us not from correcting the first appearance by a more accurate consideration, and by a comparison with some rule, of whose rectitude, from repeated trials, we have a greater assurance. And it is from these corrections, and by carrying on the same action of the mind, even when its reason fails us, that we form the loose idea of a perfect standard to these figures, without being able to explain or comprehend it.

It is true, mathematicians pretend they give an exact definition of a right line when they say *it is the shortest way betwixt two points.* But in the first place I observe, that this is more properly the discovery of one of the properties of a right line, than a just definition of it. For I ask any one, if, upon mention of a right line, he thinks not immediately on such a particular appearance, and if it is not by accident only that he considers this property? A right line can be comprehended alone; but this definition is unintelligible without a comparison with other lines, which we conceive to be more extended. In common life, it is established as a maxim, that the straightest way is always the shortest; which would be as absurd as to say, the shortest way is always the shortest, if our idea of a right line was not different from that of the shortest way betwixt two points.

Secondly, I repeat, what I have already established, that we have no precise idea of equality and inequality, shorter and longer, more than of a right line or a curve; and consequently that the one can never afford us a perfect standard for the other. An exact idea can never be built on such as are loose and undeterminate.

The idea of a *plain surface* is as little susceptible of a precise standard as that of a right line; nor have we any other means of distinguishing such a surface, than its general appearance. It is in vain that mathematicians represent a plain surface as produced by the flowing of a right line. It will immediately be objected, that our idea of a surface is as independent of this method of forming a surface, as our idea of an ellipse is of that of a cone; that the idea of a right line is no more precise than that of a plain surface; that a right line may flow irregularly, and by that means form a figure quite different from a plane; and that therefore we must suppose it to flow along two right lines parallel to each other, and on the same plane; which is a description that explains a thing by itself, and returns in a circle.

It appears, then, that the ideas which are most essential to geometry, viz. those of equality and inequality, of a right line and a plain surface, are far from being exact and determinate, according to our common method of conceiving them. Not only we are incapable of telling, if the case be in any degree doubtful, when such particular figures are equal; when such a line is a right one, and such a surface a plain one; but we can form no idea of that proportion, or of these figures, which is firm and invariable. Our appeal is still to the weak and fallible judgment, which we make from the appearance of the objects, and correct by a compass, or common measure; and if we join the supposition of any further correction, it is of such a one as is either useless or imaginary. In vain should we have recourse to the common topic, and employ the supposition of a Deity, whose omnipotence may enable him to form a perfect geometrical figure, and describe a right line without any curve or inflection. As the ultimate standard of these figures is derived from nothing but the senses and imagination, it is absurd to talk of any perfection beyond what these faculties can judge of; since the true perfection of anything consists in its conformity to its standard.

Now, since these ideas are so loose and uncertain, I would fain ask any mathematician, what infallible assurance he has, not only of the more intricate and obscure propositions of his science, but of the most vulgar and obvious principles? How can he prove to me, for instance, that two right lines cannot have one common segment? Or that it is impossible to draw more than one right line betwixt any two points? Should he tell me, that these opinions are obviously absurd, and repugnant to our clear ideas; I would answer, that I do not deny, where two right lines incline upon each other with a sensible angle, but it is absurd to imagine them to have a common segment. But supposing these two lines to approach at the rate of an inch in twenty leagues, I perceive no absurdity in asserting, that upon their contact they become one. For, I beseech you, by what rule or standard do you judge, when you assert that the line, in which I have supposed them to concur, cannot make the same right line with those two, that form so small an angle betwixt them? You must surely have some idea of a right line, to which this line does not agree. Do you therefore mean, that it takes not the points in the same order and by the same rule, as is peculiar and essential to a right line? If so, I must inform you, that besides that, in judging after this manner, you allow that extension is composed of indivisible points (which, perhaps, is more than you intend), besides this, I say, I must inform you, that neither is this the standard from which we form the idea of a right line; nor, if it were, is there any such firmness in our senses or imagination, as to determine when such an order is violated or preserved. The original standard of a right line is in reality nothing but a certain general appearance; and it is evident right lines may be made to concur with each other, and yet correspond to this standard, though corrected by all the means either practicable or imaginable.

[To whatever side mathematicians turn, this dilemma still meets them. If they judge of equality, or any other proportion, by the accurate and exact standard, viz. the enumeration of the minute indivisible parts, they both employ a standard, which is useless in practice, and actually establish the indivisibility of extension, which they endeavour to explode. Or if they employ, as is usual, the inaccurate standard, derived from a comparison of objects, upon their general appearance, corrected by measuring and juxtaposition; their first principles, though certain and infallible, are too coarse to afford any such subtile inference as they commonly draw from them. The first principles are founded on the imagination and senses; the conclusion therefore can never go beyond, much less contradict, these faculties.]

This may open our eyes a little, and let us see, that no

geometrical demonstration for the infinite divisibility of extension can have so much force as what we naturally attribute to every argument, which is supported by such magnificent pretensions. At the same time we may learn the reason, why geometry fails of evidence in this single point, while all its other reasonings command our fullest assent and approbation. And indeed it seems more requisite to give the reason of this exception, than to show that we really must make such an exception, and regard all the mathematical arguments for infinite divisibility as utterly sophistical. For it is evident, that as no idea of quantity is infinitely divisible, there cannot be imagined a more glaring absurdity, than to endeavour to prove, that quantity itself admits of such a division; and to prove this by means of ideas, which are directly opposite in that particular. And as this absurdity is very glaring in itself, so there is no argument founded on it, which is not attended with a new absurdity, and involves not an evident contradiction.

I might give as instances those arguments for infinite divisibility, which are derived from the *point of contact*. I know there is no mathematician, who will not refuse to be judged by the diagrams he describes upon paper, these being loose draughts, as he will tell us, and serving only to convey with greater facility certain ideas, which are the true foundation of all our reasoning. This I am satisfied with, and am willing to rest the controversy merely upon these ideas. I desire therefore our mathematician to form, as accurately as possible, the ideas of a circle and a right line; and I then ask, if upon the conception of their contact he can conceive them as touching in a mathematical point, or if he must necessarily imagine them to concur for some space. Whichever side he chooses, he runs himself into equal difficulties. If he affirms, that in tracing these figures in his imagination, he can imagine them to touch only in a point, he allows the possibility of that idea, and consequently of the thing. If he says, that in his conception of the contact of those lines he must make them concur, he thereby acknowledges the fallacy of geometrical demonstrations, when carried beyond a certain degree of minuteness; since it is certain he has such demonstrations against the concurrence of a circle and a right line; that is, in other words, he can prove an idea, viz. that of concurrence, to be *incompatible* with two other ideas, viz. those of a circle and right line; though at the same time he acknowledges these ideas to be *inseparable*.†

SECTION V

THE SAME SUBJECT CONTINUED

If the second part of my system be true, *that the idea of space or extension is nothing but the idea of visible or tangible points distributed in a certain order,* it follows, that we can form no idea of a vacuum, or space, where there is nothing visible or tangible. This gives rise to three objections, which I shall examine together, because the answer I shall give to one is a consequence of that which I shall make use of for the others.

First, it may be said, that men have disputed for many ages concerning a vacuum and a plenum,† without being able to bring the affair to a final decision; and philosophers, even at this day, think themselves at liberty to take party on either side, as their fancy leads them. But whatever foundation there may be for a controversy concerning the things themselves, it may be pretended that the very dispute is decisive concerning the idea, and that it is impossible men could so long reason about a vacuum, and either refute or defend it, without having a notion of what they refuted or defended.

Secondly, if this argument should be contested, the reality, or at least possibility, of the *idea* of a vacuum, may be proved by the following reason. Every idea is possible which is a necessary and infallible consequence of such as are possible. Now though we allow the world to be at present a plenum, we may easily conceive it to be deprived of motion; and this idea will certainly be allowed possible. It must also be allowed possible, to conceive the annihilation of any part of matter by the omnipotence of the Deity, while the other parts remain at rest. For as every idea that is distinguishable is separable by the imagination, and as every idea that is separable by the imagination may be conceived to be separately existent, it is evident, that the existence of one particle of matter no more implies the existence of another, than a square figure in one body implies a square figure in every one. This being granted, I now demand what results from the concurrence of these two possible ideas of *rest* and *annihilation,* and what must we conceive to follow upon the annihilation of all the air and subtile matter in the chamber, supposing the walls to remain the same, without any motion or alteration? There are some metaphysicians who answer, that since matter and extension are the same, the annihilation of the one necessarily implies that of the other; and there being now no distance betwixt the walls of the chamber, they touch each other; in the same manner as my hand touches the paper which is immediately before me. But though this answer be very common, I defy these metaphysicians to conceive the matter according to their hypothesis, or imagine the floor and roof, with all the opposite sides of the chamber, to touch each other, while they continue in rest, and preserve the same position. For how can the two walls, that run from south to north, touch each other, while they touch the opposite ends of two walls that run from east to west? And how can the floor and roof ever meet, while they are separated by the four walls that lie in a contrary position? If you change their position, you suppose a motion. If you conceive anything betwixt them, you suppose a new creation. But keeping strictly to the two ideas of *rest* and *annihilation,* it is evident, that the idea which results from them is not that of a contact of parts, but something else, which is concluded to be the idea of a vacuum.

The third objection carries the matter still further, and not only asserts, that the idea of a vacuum is real and possible, but also necessary and unavoidable. This assertion is founded on the motion we observe in bodies, which, it is maintained, would be impossible and inconceivable without a vacuum, into which one body must move in order to make way for another. I shall not enlarge upon this objection, because it principally belongs to natural philosophy, which lies without our present sphere.

In order to answer these objections, we must take the matter pretty deep, and consider the nature and origin of several ideas, lest we dispute without understanding perfectly the subject of the controversy. It is evident the idea of darkness is no positive idea, but merely the negation of light, or, more properly speaking, of coloured and visible objects. A man who enjoys his sight, receives no other perception from turning his eyes on every side, when entirely deprived of light, than what is common to him with one born blind,† and it is certain such a one has no idea either of light or darkness. The consequence of this is, that it is not from the mere removal of visible objects we receive the impression of extension without matter; and that the idea of utter darkness can never be the same with that of vacuum.

Suppose again a man to be supported in the air, and to be softly conveyed along by some invisible power; it is evident he is sensible of nothing, and never receives the idea of extension, nor indeed any idea, from this invariable motion. Even supposing he moves his limbs to and fro, this cannot convey to him that idea. He feels in that case a certain sensation or impression, the parts of which are successive to each other, and may give him the idea of time, but certainly are not disposed in such a manner as is necessary to convey the idea of space or extension.

Since, then, it appears that darkness and motion, with the utter removal of everything visible and tangible, can never give us the idea of extension without matter, or of a vacuum; the next question is, whether they can convey this idea, when mixed with something visible and tangible?

It is commonly allowed by philosophers, that all bodies which discover themselves to the eye, appear as if painted on a plain surface, and that their different degrees of remoteness from ourselves are discovered more by reason than by the senses.[18] When I hold up my hand before me, and spread my fingers, they are separated as perfectly by the blue colour of the firmament, as they could be by any visible object which I could place betwixt them. In order, therefore, to know whether the sight can convey the impression and idea of a vacuum, we must suppose, that amidst an entire darkness, there are luminous bodies presented to us, whose light discovers only these bodies themselves, without giving us any impression of the surrounding objects.

We must form a parallel supposition concerning the objects of our feeling. It is not proper to suppose a perfect removal of all tangible objects : we must allow something to be perceived by the feeling; and after an interval and motion of the hand or other organ of sensation, another object of the touch to be met with; and upon leaving that, another; and so on, as often as we please. The question is, whether these intervals do not afford us the idea of extension without body?

To begin with the first case; it is evident, that when only two luminous bodies appear to the eye, we can perceive whether they be conjoined or separate; whether they be separated by a great or small distance; and if this distance varies, we can perceive its increase or diminution, with the motion of the bodies. But as the distance is not in this case anything coloured or visible, it may be thought that there is here a vacuum or pure extension, not only intelligible to the mind, but obvious to the very senses.

This is our natural and most familiar way of thinking, but which we shall learn to correct by a little reflection.

[18] *Compare Locke, Essay, Book* ii, *ch.* 9, *Sect.* 8, *and Berkeley,* "*A New Theory of Vision.*"

We may observe, that when two bodies present themselves, where there was formerly an entire darkness, the only change that is discoverable is in the appearance of these two objects, and that all the rest continues to be as before, a perfect negation of light, and of every coloured or visible object. This is not only true of what may be said to be remote from these bodies, but also of the very distance, which is interposed betwixt them; *that* being nothing but darkness, or the negation of light; without parts, without composition, invariable and indivisible. Now, since this distance causes no perception different from what a blind man receives from his eyes, or what is conveyed to us in the darkest night, it must partake of the same properties; and as blindness and darkness afford us no ideas of extension, it is impossible that the dark and undistinguishable distance betwixt two bodies can ever produce that idea.

The sole difference betwixt an absolute darkness and the appearance of two or more visible luminous objects consists, as I said, in the objects themselves, and in the manner they affect our senses. The angles, which the rays of light flowing from them form with each other;[14] the motion that is required in the eye, in its passage from one to the other; and the different parts of the organs which are affected by them; these produce the only perceptions from which we can judge of the distance. But as these perceptions are each of them simple and indivisible, they can never give us the idea of extension.

We may illustrate this by considering the sense of feeling, and the imaginary distance or interval interposed betwixt tangible or solid objects. I suppose two cases, viz. that of a man supported in the air, and moving his limbs to and fro, without meeting anything tangible; and that of a man, who, feeling something tangible, leaves it, and after a motion of which he is sensible, perceives another tangible object; and I then ask, wherein consists the difference betwixt these two cases? No one will make any scruple to affirm, that it consists merely in the perceiving

[14] *See Appendix, final paragraph.*

those objects, and that the sensation, which arises from the motion, is in both cases the same; and as that sensation is not capable of conveying to us an idea of extension, when unaccompanied with some other perception, it can no more give us that idea, when mixed with the impressions of tangible objects, since that mixture produces no alteration upon it.

But though motion and darkness, either alone or attended with tangible and visible objects, convey no idea of a vacuum or extension without matter, yet they are the causes why we falsely imagine we can form such an idea. For there is a close relation betwixt that motion and darkness, and a real extension, or composition of visible and tangible objects.

First, we may observe, that two visible objects, appearing in the midst of utter darkness, affect the senses in the same manner, and form the same angle by the rays which flow from them, and meet in the eye, as if the distance betwixt them were filled with visible objects, that give us a true idea of extension. The sensation of motion is likewise the same, when there is nothing tangible interposed betwixt two bodies, as when we feel a compounded body, whose different parts are placed beyond each other.

Secondly, we find by experience, that two bodies, which are so placed as to effect the senses in the same manner with two others, that have a certain extent of visible objects interposed betwixt them, are capable of receiving the same extent, without any sensible impulse or penetration, and without any change on that angle, under which they appear to the senses. In like manner, where there is one object, which we cannot feel after another without an interval, and the perceiving of that sensation we call motion in our hand or organ of sensation; experience shows us, that it is possible the same object may be felt with the same sensation of motion, along with the interposed impression of solid and tangible objects, attending the sensation. That is, in other words, an invisible and intangible distance may be converted into a visible and tangible one, without any change on the distant objects.

Thirdly, we may observe, as another relation betwixt these two kinds of distance, that they have nearly the same effects on every natural phenomenon. For as all qualities, such as heat, cold, light, attraction, etc., diminish in proportion to the distance; there is but little difference observed, whether this distance be marked out by compounded and sensible objects, or be known only by the manner in which the distant objects affect the senses.

Here then are three relations betwixt that distance, which conveys the idea of extension, and that other, which is not filled with any coloured or solid object. The distant objects affect the senses in the same manner, whether separated by the one distance or the other; the second species of distance is found capable of receiving the first; and they both equally diminish the force of every quality.

These relations betwixt the two kinds of distance, will afford us an easy reason why the one has so often been taken for the other, and why we imagine we have an idea of extension without the idea of any object either of the sight or feeling. For we may establish it as a general maxim in this science of human nature, that wherever there is a close relation betwixt two ideas, the mind is very apt to mistake them, and in all its discourses and reasonings to use the one for the other. This phenomenon occurs on so many occasions, and is of such consequence, that I cannot forbear stopping a moment to examine its causes. I shall only premise, that we must distinguish exactly betwixt the phenomenon itself, and the causes which I shall assign for it; and must not imagine, for any uncertainty in the latter, that the former is also uncertain. The phenomenon may be real, though my explication be chimerical. The falsehood of the one is no consequence of that of the other; though at the same time we may observe, that it is very natural for us to draw such a consequence; which is an evident instance of that very principle, which I endeavour to explain.

When I received the relations of *resemblance, contiguity,* and *causation,* as principles of union among ideas, without examining into their causes, it was more in prosecution of my first maxim, that we must in the end rest contented with experience, than for want of something specious and plausible, which I might have displayed on that subject. It would have been easy to have made an imaginary dissection of the brain, and have shown, why, upon our conception of any idea, the animal spirits run into all the contiguous traces, and rouse up the other ideas that are related to it. But though I have neglected any advantage, which I might have drawn from this topic in explaining the relations of ideas, I am afraid I must here have recourse to it, in order to account for the mistakes that arise from these relations.[15] I shall therefore observe, that as the mind is endowed with a power of exciting any idea it pleases; whenever it despatches the spirits into that region of the brain, in which the idea is placed; these spirits always excite the idea, when they run precisely into the proper traces, and rummage that cell, which belongs to the idea. But as their motion is seldom direct, and naturally turns a little to the one side or the other; for this reason the animal spirits, falling into the contiguous traces, present other related ideas, in lieu of that which the mind desired at first to survey. This change we are not always sensible of; but continuing still the same train of thought, make use of the related idea, which is presented to us, and employ it in our reasoning, as if it were the same with what we demanded. This is the cause of many mistakes and sophisms in philosophy; as will naturally be imagined, and as it would be easy to show, if there was occasion.

Of the three relations above mentioned that of resemblance is the most fertile source of error; and indeed there are few mistakes in reasoning, which do not borrow largely from that origin. Resembling ideas are not only related together, but the actions of the mind, which we employ

[15] *It is not clear why Hume thought that an excursion into physiology was more necessary in this context than in the other.*

in considering them, are so little different, that we are not able to distinguish them. This last circumstance is of great consequence; and we may in general observe, that wherever the actions of the mind in forming any two ideas are the same or resembling, we are very apt to confound these ideas, and take the one for the other. Of this we shall see many instances in the progress of this treatise. But though resemblance be the relation, which most readily produces a mistake in ideas, yet the others of causation and contiguity may also concur in the same influence. We might produce the figures of poets and orators, as sufficient proofs of this, were it as usual as it is reasonable, in metaphysical subjects, to draw our arguments from that quarter. But lest metaphysicians should esteem this below their dignity, I shall borrow a proof from an observation, which may be made on most of their own discourses, viz. that it is usual for men to use words for ideas, and to talk instead of thinking in their reasonings. We use words for ideas, because they are commonly so closely connected, that the mind easily mistakes them. And this likewise is the reason, why we substitute the idea of a distance, which is not considered either as visible or tangible, in the room of extension, which is nothing but a composition of visible or tangible points disposed in a certain order. In causing this mistake there concur both the relations of *causation* and *resemblance*. As the first species of distance is found to be convertible into the second, it is in this respect a kind of cause; and the similarity of their manner of affecting the senses, and diminishing every quality, forms the relation of resemblance.

After this chain of reasoning and explication of my principles, I am now prepared to answer all the objections that have been offered, whether derived from *metaphysics* or *mechanics*. The frequent disputes concerning a vacuum, or extension without matter, prove not the reality of the idea, upon which the dispute turns; there being nothing more common, than to see men deceive themselves in this particular; especially when, by means of any close relation, there is another idea presented, which may be the occasion of their mistake.

We may make almost the same answer to the second objection, derived from the conjunction of the ideas of rest and annihilation. When everything is annihilated in the chamber, and the walls continue immovable, the chamber must be conceived much in the same manner as at present, when the air that fills it is not an object of the senses. This annihilation leaves to the *eye* that fictitious distance, which is discovered by the different parts of the organ that are affected, and by the degrees of light and shade; and to the *feeling,* that which consists in a sensation of motion in the hand, or other member of the body. In vain should we search any further. On whichever side we turn this subject, we shall find that these are the only impressions such an object can produce after the supposed annihilation; and it has already been remarked, that impressions can give rise to no ideas, but to such as resemble them.

Since a body interposed betwixt two others may be supposed to be annihilated, without producing any change upon such as lie on each hand of it, it is easily conceived how it may be created anew, and yet produce as little alteration. Now the motion of a body has much the same effect as its creation. The distant bodies are no more affected in the one case, than in the other. This suffices to satisfy the imagination, and proves there is no repugnance in such a motion. Afterwards experience comes in play to persuade us that two bodies, situated in the manner above described, have really such a capacity of receiving body betwixt them, and that there is no obstacle to the conversion of the invisible and intangible distance into one that is visible and tangible. However natural that conversion may seem, we cannot be sure it is practicable, before we have had experience of it.

Thus I seem to have answered the three objections above mentioned; though at the same time I am sensible, that few will be satisfied with these answers, but will immediately propose new objections and difficulties. It will probably be said, that my reasoning makes nothing to the matter in hand, and that I explain only the manner in which objects affect the senses, without endeavouring to account for their real nature and operations. Though there be nothing visible or tangible interposed betwixt two bodies, yet we find *by experience,* that the bodies may be placed in the same manner, with regard to the eye, and require the same motion of the hand in passing from one to the other, as if divided by something visible and tangible. This invisible and intangible distance is also found *by experience* to contain a capacity of receiving body, or of becoming visible and tangible. Here is the whole of my system; and in no part of it have I endeavoured to explain the cause which separates bodies after this manner, and gives them a capacity of receiving others betwixt them, without any impulse or penetration.

I answer this objection by pleading guilty, and by confessing that my intention never was to penetrate into the nature of bodies, or explain the secret causes of their operations. For, besides that this belongs not to my present purpose, I am afraid, that such an enterprise is beyond the reach of human understanding, and that we can never pretend to know body otherwise than by those external properties, which discover themselves to the senses. As to those who attempt anything further, I cannot approve of their ambition, till I see, in some one instance at least, that they have met with success. But at present I content myself with knowing perfectly the manner in which objects affect my senses, and their connections with each other, as far as experience informs me of them. This suffices for the conduct of life; and this also suffices for my philosophy, which pretends only to explain the nature and causes of our perceptions, or impressions and ideas.[16]

[16] As long as we confine our speculations to *the appearances* of objects to our senses, without entering into disquisitions concerning their real nature and operations, we are safe from all difficulties, and can never be embarrassed by any question. Thus, if it be asked, if the invisible and intangible distance interposed

I shall conclude this subject of extension with a paradox, which will easily be explained from the foregoing reasoning. This paradox is, that if you are pleased to give to the invisible and intangible distance, or, in other words, to the capacity of becoming a visible and tangible distance, the name of a vacuum, extension and matter are the same, and yet there is a vacuum. If you will not give it that name, motion is possible in a plenum, without any impulse *in infinitum,* without returning in a circle, and without penetration. But however we may express ourselves, we must always confess that we have no idea of any real extension without filling it with sensible objects, and conceiving its parts as visible or tangible.

As to the doctrine, that time is nothing but the manner in which some real objects exist, we may observe, that it is liable to the same objections as the similar doctrine with

---

betwixt two objects, be something or nothing: it is easy to answer, that it is *something,* viz. a property of the objects, which affect the *senses* after such a particular manner. If it be asked, whether two objects having such a distance betwixt them, touch or not, it may be answered, that this depends upon the definition of the word *touch.* If objects be said to touch, when there is nothing *sensible* interposed betwixt them, these objects touch. If objects be said to touch, when their *images* strike contiguous parts of the eye, and when the hand *feels* both objects successively, without any interposed motion, these objects do not touch. The appearances of objects to our senses are all consistent; and no difficulties can ever arise, but from the obscurity of the terms we make use of.

If we carry our inquiry beyond the appearances of objects to the senses, I am afraid that most of our conclusions will be full of scepticism and uncertainty. Thus, if it be asked, whether or not the invisible and intangible distance be always full of *body,* or of something that by an improvement of our organs might become visible or tangible, I must acknowledge, that I find no very decisive arguments on either side: though I am inclined to the contrary opinion, as being more suitable to vulgar and popular notions. If *the Newtonian* philosophy be rightly understood, it will be found to mean no more. A vacuum is asserted; that is, bodies are said to be placed after such a manner, as to receive bodies betwixt them, without impulsion or penetration. The real nature of this position of bodies is unknown. We are only acquainted with its effects on the senses, and its power of receiving body. Nothing is more suitable to that philosophy, than a modest scepticism to a certain degree, and a fair confession of ignorance in subjects that exceed all human capacity.

regard to extension. If it be a sufficient proof, that we have the idea of a vacuum, because we dispute and reason concerning it; we must for the same reason have the idea of time without any changeable existence; since there is no subject of dispute more frequent and common. But that we really have no such idea, is certain. For whence should it be derived? Does it arise from an impression of sensation or of reflection? Point it out distinctly to us, that we may know its nature and qualities. But if you cannot point out *any such impression*, you may be certain you are mistaken, when you imagine you have *any such idea*.

But though it be impossible to show the impression, from which the idea of time without a changeable existence is derived, yet we can easily point out those appearances, which make us fancy we have that idea. For we may observe, that there is a continual succession of perceptions in our mind; so that, the idea of time being for ever present with us, when we consider a steadfast object at five o'clock, and regard the same at six, we are apt to apply to it that idea in the same manner as if every moment were distinguished by a different position, or an alteration of the object. The first and second appearances of the object, being compared with the succession of our perceptions, seem equally removed as if the object had really changed. To which we may add, what experience shows us, that the object was susceptible of such a number of changes betwixt these appearances; as also that the unchangeable or rather fictitious duration has the same effect upon every quality, by increasing or diminishing it, as that succession which is obvious to the senses. From these three relations we are apt to confound our ideas, and imagine we can form the idea of a time and duration, without any change or succession.

SECTION VI

OF THE IDEAS OF EXISTENCE, AND OF EXTERNAL EXISTENCE†

It may not be amiss, before we leave this subject, to explain the ideas of *existence* and of *external existence;* which have their difficulties, as well as the ideas of space and time. By this means we shall be the better prepared for the examination of knowledge and probability, when we understand perfectly all those particular ideas, which may enter into our reasoning.

There is no impression nor idea of any kind, of which we have any consciousness or memory, that is not conceived as existent; and it is evident that, from this consciousness, the most perfect idea and assurance of *being* is derived. From hence we may form a dilemma, the most clear and conclusive that can be imagined, viz. that since we never remember any idea or impression without attributing existence to it, the idea of existence must either be derived from a distinct impression, conjoined with every perception or object of our thought, or must be the very same with the idea of the perception or object.

As this dilemma is an evident consequence of the principle, that every idea arises from a similar impression, so our decision betwixt the propositions of the dilemma is no more doubtful. So far from there being any distinct impression attending every impression and every idea, that I do not think there are any two distinct impressions which are inseparably conjoined. Though certain sensations may at one time be united, we quickly find they admit of a separation, and may be presented apart. And thus, though every impression and idea we remember be considered as existent, the idea of existence is not derived from any particular impression.

The idea of existence, then, is the very same with the

idea of what we conceive to be existent. To reflect on anything simply, and to reflect on it as existent, are nothing different from each other. That idea, when conjoined with the idea of any object, makes no addition to it. Whatever we conceive, we conceive to be existent. Any idea we please to form is the idea of a being; and the idea of a being is any idea we please to form.

Whoever opposes this, must necessarily point out that distinct impression, from which the idea of entity is derived, and must prove, that this impression is inseparable from every perception we believe to be existent. This we may without hesitation conclude to be impossible.

Our foregoing reasoning[17] concerning the *distinction* of ideas, without any real *difference,* will not here serve us in any stead. That kind of distinction is founded on the different resemblances, which the same simple idea may have to several different ideas. But no object can be presented resembling some object with respect to its existence, and different from others in the same particular; since every object that is presented, must necessarily be existent.

A like reasoning will account for the idea of *external existence.* We may observe, that it is universally allowed by philosophers, and is besides pretty obvious of itself, that nothing is ever really present with the mind but its perceptions or impressions and ideas, and that external objects become known to us only by those perceptions they occasion. To hate, to love, to think, to feel, to see; all this is nothing but to perceive.

Now since nothing is ever present to the mind but perceptions, and since all ideas are derived from something antecedently present to the mind; it follows, that it is impossible for us so much as to conceive or form an idea of anything specifically different from ideas and impressions. Let us fix our attention out of ourselves as much as possible; let us chase our imagination to the heavens, or to the utmost limits of the universe; we never really advance a step beyond ourselves, nor can conceive any kind of

[17] Part I, Sect. 7.

existence, but those perceptions, which have appeared in that narrow compass. This is the universe of the imagination, nor have we any idea but what is there produced.

The furthest we can go towards a conception of external objects, when supposed *specifically* different from our perceptions, is to form a relative idea of them, without pretending to comprehend the related objects. Generally speaking, we do not suppose them specifically different; but only attribute to them different relations, connections, and durations. But of this more fully hereafter.[18]

[18] Part IV, Sect. 2.

PART III

OF KNOWLEDGE AND PROBABILITY

SECTION I

OF KNOWLEDGE

There are seven different kinds of philosophical relation,[1] viz. *resemblance, identity, relations of time and place, proportion in quantity or number, degrees in any quality, contrariety, and causation.* These relations may be divided into two classes; into such as depend entirely on the ideas, which we compare together, and such as may be changed without any change in the ideas. It is from the idea of a triangle, that we discover the relation of equality, which its three angles bear to two right ones; and this relation is invariable, as long as our idea remains the same. On the contrary, the relations of *contiguity* and *distance* betwixt two objects may be changed merely by an alteration of their place, without any change on the objects themselves or on their ideas; and the place depends on a hundred different accidents, which cannot be foreseen by the mind. It is the same case with *identity* and *causation*. Two objects, though perfectly resembling each other, and even appearing in the same place at different times, may be numerically different : and as the power, by which one object produces another, is never discoverable merely from their idea, it is evident *cause* and *effect* are relations, of which we receive information from experience, and not from any abstract reasoning or reflection. There is no single phenomenon, even the most simple, which can be accounted for from the qualities of the objects, as they

[1] Part I, Sect. 5.

appear to us; or which we could foresee without the help of our memory and experience.[2]

It appears therefore that of these seven philosophical relations, there remain only four, which depending solely upon ideas, can be the objects of knowledge and certainty. These four are *resemblance, contrariety, degrees in quality, and proportions in quantity or number.* Three of these relations are discoverable at first sight, and fall more properly under the province of intuition than demonstration. When any objects *resemble* each other, the resemblance will at first strike the eye, or rather the mind; and seldom requires a second examination. The case is the same with *contrariety,* and with the *degree* of any *quality.* No one can once doubt but existence and non-existence destroy each other, and are perfectly incompatible and contrary. And though it be impossible to judge exactly of the degrees of any quality, such as colour, taste, heat, cold, when the difference betwixt them is very small; yet it is easy to decide, that any of them is superior or inferior to another, when their difference is considerable. And this decision we always pronounce at first sight, without any inquiry or reasoning.

We might proceed, after the same manner, in fixing the *proportions* of *quantity* or *number,* and might at one view observe a superiority or inferiority betwixt any numbers, or figures; especially where the difference is very great and remarkable. As to equality or any exact proportion, we can only guess at it from a single consideration; except in very short numbers, or very limited portions of extension; which are comprehended in an instant, and where we perceive an impossibility of falling into any considerable error. In all other cases we must settle the proportions with some liberty, or proceed in a more *artificial* manner.

I have already observed,[3] that geometry, or the *art* by which we fix the proportions of figures; though it much excels both in universality and exactness, the loose judg-

[2] *For a clearer exposition see Appendix* A.
[3] *Part* II, *Sect.* IV.

ments of the senses and imagination; yet never attains a perfect precision and exactness. Its first principles are still drawn from the general appearance of the objects; and that appearance can never afford us any security, when we examine the prodigious minuteness of which nature is susceptible. Our ideas seem to give a perfect assurance, that no two right lines can have a common segment; but if we consider these ideas, we shall find, that they always suppose a sensible inclination of the two lines, and that where the angle they form is extremely small, we have no standard of a right line so precise as to assure us of the truth of this proposition. It is the same case with most of the primary decisions of the mathematicians.

There remain therefore algebra and arithmetic as the only sciences, in which we can carry on a chain of reasoning to any degree of intricacy, and yet preserve a perfect exactness and certainty. We are possessed of a precise standard, by which we can judge of the equality and proportion of numbers; and according as they correspond or not to that standard, we determine their relations, without any possibility of error. When two numbers are so combined, as that the one has always an unit answering to every unit of the other, we pronounce them equal; and it is for want of such a standard of equality in extension, that geometry can scarce be esteemed a perfect and infallible science.

But here it may not be amiss to obviate a difficulty, which may arise from my asserting, that though geometry falls short of that perfect precision and certainty, which are peculiar to arithmetic and algebra, yet it excels the imperfect judgments of our senses and imagination. The reason why I impute any defect to geometry, is, because its original and fundamental principles are derived merely from appearances; and it may perhaps be imagined, that this defect must always attend it, and keep it from ever reaching a greater exactness in the comparison of objects or ideas, than what our eye or imagination alone is able to attain. I own that this defect so far attends it, as to keep it from ever aspiring to a full certainty: but since these fundamental principles depend on the easiest and least deceitful appearances, they bestow on their consequences a degree of exactness, of which these consequences are singly incapable. It is impossible for the eye to determine the angles of a chiliagon to be equal to 1996 right angles, or make any conjecture, that approaches this proportion; but when it determines, that right lines cannot concur; that we cannot draw more than one right line between two given points; its mistakes can never be of any consequence. And this is the nature and use of geometry, to run us up to such appearances, as, by reason of their simplicity, cannot lead us into any considerable error.

I shall here take occasion to propose a second observation concerning our demonstrative reasonings, which is suggested by the same object of the mathematics. It is usual with mathematicians to pretend, that those ideas, which are their objects, are of so refined and spiritual a nature, that they fall not under the conception of the fancy, but must be comprehended by a pure and intellectual view, of which the superior faculties of the soul are alone capable. The same notion runs through most parts of philosophy, and is principally made use of to explain our abstract ideas, and to show how we can form an idea of a triangle, for instance, which shall neither be an isosceles nor scalenum, nor be confined to any particular length and proportion of sides. It is easy to see why philosophers are so fond of this notion of some spiritual and refined perceptions; since by that means they cover many of their absurdities, and may refuse to submit to the decisions of clear ideas, by appealing to such as are obscure and uncertain. But to destroy this artifice, we need but reflect on that principle so oft insisted on, *that all our ideas are copied from our impressions.* For from thence we may immediately conclude, that since all impressions are clear and precise, the ideas, which are copied from them, must be of the same nature, and can never, but from our fault, contain anything so dark and intricate.

An idea is by its very nature weaker and fainter than an impression; but being in every other respect the same, cannot imply any very great mystery. If its weakness render it obscure, it is our business to remedy that defect, as much as possible, by keeping the idea steady and precise; and till we have done so, it is in vain to pretend to reasoning and philosophy.

SECTION II

OF PROBABILITY, AND OF THE IDEA OF CAUSE AND EFFECT

This is all I think necessary to observe concerning those four relations, which are the foundation of science; but as to the other three, which depend not upon the idea, and may be absent or present even while *that* remains the same, it will be proper to explain them more particularly. These three relations are *identity, the situations in time and place, and causation*.

All kinds of reasoning consist in nothing but a *comparison,* and a discovery of those relations, either constant or inconstant, which two or more objects bear to each other. This comparison we may make, either when both the objects are present to the senses, or when neither of them is present, or when only one. When both the objects are present to the senses along with the relation, we call *this* perception rather than reasoning; nor is there in this case any exercise of the thought, or any action, properly speaking, but a mere passive admission of the impressions through the organs of sensation. According to this way of thinking, we ought not to receive as reasoning any of the observations we may make concerning *identity* and the *relations* of *time* and *place;* since in none of them the mind can go beyond what is immediately present to the senses, either to discover the real existence or the relations of objects. It is only *causation,* which produces such a con-

nection, as to give us assurance from the existence or action
of one object, that it was followed or preceded by any
other existence or action; nor can the other two relations
ever be made use of in reasoning, except so far as they
either affect or are affected by it. There is nothing in any
objects to persuade us, that they are either always *remote*
or always *contiguous;* and when from experience and observation we discover, that their relation in this particular
is invariable, we always conclude there is some secret *cause*
which separates or unites them. The same reasoning extends to *identity.* We readily suppose an object may continue individually the same, though several times absent
from and present to the senses; and ascribe to it an
identity, notwithstanding the interruption of the perception, whenever we conclude, that if we had kept our eye
or hand constantly upon it, it would have conveyed an
invariable and uninterrupted perception. But this conclusion beyond the impression of our senses can be founded
only on the connection of *cause and effect;* nor can we
otherwise have any security that the object is not changed
upon us, however much the new object may resemble that
which was formerly present to the senses. Whenever we
discover such a perfect resemblance, we consider whether
it be common in that species of objects; whether possibly
or probably any cause could operate in producing the
change and resemblance; and according as we determine
concerning these causes and effects, we form our judgment concerning the identity of the object.

Here then it appears, that of those three relations, which
depend not upon the mere ideas, the only one that can be
traced beyond our senses, and informs us of existences and
objects, which we do not see or feel, is *causation.* This
relation therefore we shall endeavour to explain fully
before we leave the subject of the understanding.

To begin regularly, we must consider the idea of *causation,* and see from what origin it is derived. It is impossible to reason justly, without understanding perfectly the
idea concerning which we reason; and it is impossible per-

fectly to understand any idea, without tracing it up to its origin, and examining that primary impression, from which it arises. The examination of the impression bestows a clearness on the idea; and the examination of the idea bestows a like clearness on all our reasoning.

Let us therefore cast our eye on any two objects, which we call cause and effect, and turn them on all sides, in order to find that impression, which produces an idea of such prodigious consequence. At first sight I perceive, that I must not search for it in any of the particular *qualities* of the objects; since, whichever of these qualities I pitch on, I find some object that is not possessed of it, and yet falls under the denomination of cause or effect. And indeed there is nothing existent, either externally or internally, which is not to be considered either as a cause or an effect; though it is plain there is no one quality which universally belongs to all beings, and gives them a title to that denomination.

The idea then of causation must be derived from some *relation* among objects; and that relation we must now endeavour to discover. I find in the first place, that whatever objects are considered as causes or effects, are *contiguous;* and that nothing can operate in a time or place, which is ever so little removed from those of its existence. Though distant objects may sometimes seem productive of each other, they are commonly found upon examination to be linked by a chain of causes, which are contiguous among themselves, and to the distant objects; and when in any particular instance we cannot discover this connection, we still presume it to exist. We may therefore consider the relation of *contiguity* as essential to that of causation; at least may suppose it such, according to the general opinion, till we can find a more proper occasion[4] to clear up this matter, by examining what objects are or are not susceptible of juxtaposition and conjunction.

The second relation I shall observe as essential to causes and effects, is not so universally acknowledged, but is

[4] Part IV, Sect. 5.

liable to some controversy. It is that of *priority* of time in the cause before the effect. Some pretend that it is not absolutely necessary a cause should precede its effect; but that any object or action, in the very first moment of its existence, may exert its productive quality, and give rise to another object or action, perfectly contemporary with itself. But beside that experience in most instances seems to contradict this opinion, we may establish the relation of priority by a kind of inference or reasoning. It is an established maxim, both in natural and moral philosophy, that an object, which exists for any time in its full perfection without producing another, is not its sole cause; but is assisted by some other principle which pushes it from its state of inactivity, and makes it exert that energy, of which it was secretly possessed. Now if any cause may be perfectly contemporary with its effect, it is certain, according to this maxim, that they must all of them be so; since any one of them, which retards its operation for a single moment, exerts not itself at that very individual time, in which it might have operated; and therefore is no proper cause. The consequence of this would be no less than the destruction of that succession of causes, which we observe in the world; and indeed the utter annihilation of time. For if one cause were contemporary with its effect, and this effect with *its* effect, and so on, it is plain there would be no such thing as succession, and all objects must be coexistent.

If this argument appear satisfactory, it is well. If not, I beg the reader to allow me the same liberty, which I have used in the preceding case, of supposing it such. For he shall find, that the affair is of no great importance.†

Having thus discovered or supposed the two relations of *contiguity* and *succession* to be essential to causes and effects, I find I am stopped short, and can proceed no further in considering any single instance of cause and effect. Motion in one body is regarded upon impulse as cause of motion in another. When we consider these objects with the utmost attention, we find only that the one body approaches the other; and that the motion of it precedes that of the other, but without any sensible interval. It is in vain to rack ourselves with *further* thought and reflection upon this subject. We can go no *further* in considering this particular instance.

Should any one leave this instance, and pretend to define a cause, by saying it is something productive of another, it is evident he would say nothing. For what does he mean by *production*? Can he give any definition of it, that will not be the same with that of causation? If he can, I desire it may be produced. If he cannot, he here runs in a circle, and gives a synonymous term instead of a definition.

Shall we then rest contented with these two relations of contiguity and succession, as affording a complete idea of causation? By no means. An object may be contiguous and prior to another, without being considered as its cause. There is a *necessary connection* to be taken into consideration; and that relation is of much greater importance, than any of the other two above mentioned.

Here again I turn the object on all sides, in order to discover the nature of this necessary connection, and find the impression, or impressions, from which its idea may be derived. When I cast my eye on the *known qualities* of objects, I immediately discover that the relation of cause and effect depends not in the least on *them*. When I consider their *relations,* I can find none but those of contiguity and succession; which I have already regarded as imperfect and unsatisfactory. Shall the despair of success make me assert, that I am here possessed of an idea, which is not preceded by any similar impression? This would be too strong a proof of levity and inconstancy; since the contrary principle has been already so firmly established, as to admit of no further doubt; at least, till we have more fully examined the present difficulty.

We must therefore proceed like those who, being in search of anything that lies concealed from them, and not finding it in the place they expected, beat about all the neighbouring fields, without any certain view or design, in hopes their good fortune will at last guide them to what they search for. It is necessary for us to leave the direct survey of this question concerning the nature of that *necessary connection,* which enters into our idea of cause and effect; and endeavour to find some other questions, the examination of which will perhaps afford a hint, that may serve to clear up the present difficulty. Of these questions there occur two, which I shall proceed to examine, viz.

First, for what reason we pronounce it *necessary,* that everything whose existence has a beginning, should also have a cause?

Secondly, why we conclude, that such particular causes must *necessarily* have such particular effects; and what is the nature of that *inference* we draw from the one to the other, and of the *belief* we repose in it?

I shall only observe before I proceed any further, that though the ideas of cause and effect be derived from the impressions of reflection as well as from those of sensation, yet for brevity's sake, I commonly mention only the latter as the origin of these ideas; though I desire that, whatever I say of them, may also extend to the former. Passions are connected with their objects and with one another; no less than external bodies are connected together. The same relation then of cause and effect, which belongs to one, must be common to all of them.

SECTION III

WHY A CAUSE IS ALWAYS NECESSARY

To begin with the first question concerning the necessity of a cause : It is a general maxim in philosophy, that *whatever begins to exist, must have a cause of existence.* This is commonly taken for granted in all reasonings, without any proof given or demanded. It is supposed to be founded on intuition, and to be one of those maxims which, though they may be denied with the lips, it is impossible for men in their hearts really to doubt of. But if we examine this maxim by the idea of knowledge above explained, we shall discover in it no mark of any such intuitive certainty; but on the contrary shall find, that it is of a nature quite foreign to that species of conviction.

All certainty arises from the comparison of ideas, and from the discovery of such relations as are unalterable, so long as the ideas continue the same. These relations are *resemblance, proportions in quantity and number, degrees of any quality, and contrariety;* none of which are implied in this proposition, *Whatever has a beginning has also a cause of existence.* That proposition therefore is not intuitively certain. At least any one, who would assert it to be intuitively certain, must deny these to be the only infallible relations, and must find some other relation of that kind to be implied in it; which it will then be time enough to examine.

But here is an argument, which proves at once, that the foregoing proposition is neither intuitively nor demonstrably certain. We can never demonstrate the necessity of a cause to every new existence, or new modification of existence, without showing at the same time the impossibility there is, that anything can ever begin to exist without some productive principle; and where the latter proposition cannot be proved, we must despair of ever being able to prove the former. Now that the latter proposition is utterly incapable of a demonstrative proof, we may satisfy ourselves by considering, that as all distinct ideas are separable from each other, and as the ideas of cause and effect are evidently distinct, it will be easy for us to conceive any object to be non-existent this moment, and existent the next, without conjoining to it the distinct idea of a cause or productive principle. The separation therefore of the idea of a cause from that of a beginning of existence, is plainly possible for the imagination; and consequently the actual separation of these objects is so far possible, that it implies no contradiction nor absurdity; and is therefore incapable of being refuted by any reasoning from mere ideas, without which it is impossible to demonstrate the necessity of a cause.

Accordingly, we shall find upon examination, that every demonstration, which has been produced for the necessity of a cause, is fallacious and sophistical. All the points of time and place, say some philosophers,[5] in which we can suppose any object to begin to exist, are in themselves equal; and unless there be some cause, which is peculiar to one time and to one place, and which by that means determines and fixes the existence, it must remain in eternal suspense; and the object can never begin to be, for want of something to fix its beginning. But I ask, is there any more difficulty in supposing the time and place to be fixed without a cause, than to suppose the existence to be determined in that manner? The first question that occurs on this subject is always, *whether* the object shall exist or not : the next, *when* and *where* it shall begin to exist. If the removal of a cause be intuitively absurd in the one case, it must be so in the other; and if that absurdity be not clear without a proof in the one case, it will equally require one in the other. The absurdity then of the one supposition can never be a proof of that of the other; since they are both upon the same footing, and must stand or fall by the same reasoning.

The second argument,[6] which I find used on this head, labours under an equal difficulty. Everything, it is said, must have a cause; for if anything wanted a cause, *it* would produce *itself,* that is, exist before it existed, which is impossible. But this reasoning is plainly unconclusive; because it supposes that, in our denial of a cause, we still grant what we expressly deny, viz. that there must be a cause; which therefore is taken to be the object itself; and *that,* no doubt, is an evident contradiction. But to say that anything is produced, or, to express myself more properly, comes into existence, without a cause, is not to

[5] Mr. Hobbes (*see p. 371*). [6] Dr. Clarke and others (*see p. 371*).

affirm that it is itself its own cause; but, on the contrary, in excluding all external causes, excludes *a fortiori* the thing itself which is created. An object that exists absolutely without any cause, certainly is not its own cause; and when you assert, that the one follows from the other, you suppose the very point in question, and take it for granted, that it is utterly impossible anything can ever begin to exist without a cause, but that, under the exclusion of one productive principle, we must still have recourse to another.

It is exactly the same case with the third argument,[7] which has been employed to demonstrate the necessity of a cause. Whatever is produced without any cause, is produced by *nothing;* or, in other words, has nothing for its cause. But nothing can never be a cause, no more than it can be something, or equal to two right angles. By the same intuition, that we perceive nothing not to be equal to two right angles, or not to be something, we perceive, that it can never be a cause; and consequently must perceive, that every object has a real cause of its existence.

I believe it will not be necessary to employ many words in showing the weakness of this argument, after what I have said of the foregoing. They are all of them founded on the same fallacy, and are derived from the same turn of thought. It is sufficient only to observe, that when we exclude all causes we really do exclude them, and neither suppose nothing nor the object itself to be the case of the existence; and consequently can draw no argument from the absurdity of these suppositions to prove the absurdity of that exclusion. If everything must have a cause, it follows, that, upon the exclusion of other causes, we must accept of the object itself or of nothing as causes. But it is the very point in question, whether everything must have a cause or not; and therefore, according to all just reasoning, it ought never to be taken for granted.

They are still more frivolous who say, that every effect must have a cause, because it is implied in the very idea

[7] Mr. Locke (*see p. 371*)

of effect. Every effect necessarily presupposes a cause; effect being a relative term, of which cause is the correlative. But this does not prove that every being must be preceded by a cause; no more than it follows, because every husband must have a wife, that therefore every man must be married. The true state of the question is, whether every object which begins to exist, must owe its existence to a cause; and this I assert neither to be intuitively nor demonstratively certain, and hope to have proved it sufficiently by the foregoing arguments.

Since it is not from knowledge or any scientific reasoning, that we derive the opinion of the necessity of a cause to every new production, that opinion must necessarily arise from observation and experience. The next question, then, should naturally be, *how experience gives rise to such a principle?* But as I find it will be more convenient to sink this question in the following, *why we conclude, that such particular causes must necessarily have such particular effects, and why we form an inference from one to another?* we shall make that the subject of our future inquiry. It will, perhaps, be found in the end, that the same answer will serve for both questions.[8]

SECTION IV

OF THE COMPONENT PARTS OF OUR REASONINGS CONCERNING CAUSE AND EFFECT

Though the mind in its reasonings from causes or effects, carries its view beyond those objects which it sees or remembers, it must never lose sight of them entirely, nor reason merely upon its own ideas, without some mixture of impressions, or at least of ideas of the memory, which are equivalent to impressions. When we infer effects from

[8] *For Hume's answer to the former question see Part* III, *Sect.* XII.

causes, we must establish the existence of these causes; which we have only two ways of doing, either by an immediate perception of our memory or senses, or by an inference from other causes; which causes again we must ascertain in the same manner, either by a present impression or by an inference from *their* causes, and so on, till we arrive at some object, which we see or remember. It is impossible for us to carry on our inferences *ad infinitum;* and the only thing that can stop them, is an impression of the memory or senses, beyond which there is no room for doubt or inquiry.

To give an instance of this, we may choose any point of history, and consider for what reason we either believe or reject it. Thus, we believe that Cæsar was killed in the senate-house on the *ides* of *March*, and that because this fact is established on the unanimous testimony of historians, who agree to assign this precise time and place to that event. Here are certain characters and letters present either to our memory or senses; which characters we likewise remember to have been used as the signs of certain ideas; and these ideas were either in the minds of such as were immediately present at that action, and received the ideas directly from its existence; or they were derived from the testimony of others, and that again from another testimony, by a visible gradation, till we arrive at those who were eye-witnesses and spectators of the event. It is obvious all this chain of argument or connection of causes and effects, is at first founded on those characters or letters, which are seen or remembered, and that without the authority either of the memory or senses, our whole reasoning would be chimerical and without foundation. Every link of the chain would in that case hang upon another; but there would not be anything fixed to one end of it, capable of sustaining the whole; and consequently there would be no belief nor evidence. And this actually is the case with all *hypothetical* arguments, or reasonings upon a supposition; there being in them neither any present impression, nor belief of a real existence.

I need not observe, that it is no just objection to the present doctrine, that we can reason upon our past conclusions or principles, without having recourse to those impressions, from which they first arose. For even supposing these impressions should be entirely effaced from the memory, the conviction they produced may still remain; and it is equally true, that all reasonings concerning causes and effects are originally derived from some impression; in the same manner, as the assurance of a demonstration proceeds always from a comparison of ideas, though it may continue after the comparison is forgot.

SECTION V

OF THE IMPRESSIONS OF THE SENSES AND MEMORY

In this kind of reasoning, then, from causation, we employ materials, which are of a mixed and heterogeneous nature, and which, however connected, are yet essentially different from each other. All our arguments concerning causes and effects consist both of an impression of the memory or senses, and of the idea of that existence, which produces the object of the impression, or is produced by it. Here therefore we have three things to explain, viz. *first,* the original impression. *Secondly,* the transition to the idea of the connected cause or effect. *Thirdly,* the nature and qualities of that idea.

As to those *impressions,* which arise from the *senses,* their ultimate cause is, in my opinion, perfectly inexplicable by human reason, and it will always be impossible to decide with certainty, whether they arise immediately from the object, or are produced by the creative power of the mind, or are derived from the Author of our being. Nor is such a question any way material to our present purpose. We may draw inferences from the coherence of our perceptions, whether they be true or false; whether they represent nature justly, or be mere illusions of the senses.†

When we search for the characteristic, which distinguishes the *memory* from the imagination, we must immediately perceive, that it cannot lie in the simple ideas it presents to us; since both these faculties borrow their simple ideas from the impressions, and can never go beyond these original perceptions. These faculties are as little distinguished from each other by the arrangement of their complex ideas. For, though it be a peculiar property of the memory to preserve the original order and position of its ideas, while the imagination transposes and changes them as it pleases; yet this difference is not sufficient to distinguish them in their operation, or make us know the one from the other; it being impossible to recall the past impressions, in order to compare them with our present ideas, and see whether their arrangement be exactly similar. Since therefore the memory is known, neither by the order of its *complex* ideas, nor the nature of its *simple* ones; it follows, that the difference betwixt it and the imagination lies in its superior force and vivacity. A man may indulge his fancy in feigning any past scene of adventures; nor would there be any possibility of distinguishing this from a remembrance of a like kind, were not the ideas of the imagination fainter and more obscure.

[It frequently happens, that when two men have been engaged in any scene of action, the one shall remember it much better than the other, and shall have all the difficulty in the world to make his companion recollect it. He runs over several circumstances in vain; mentions the time, the place, the company, what was said, what was done on all sides; till at last he hits on some lucky circumstance, that revives the whole, and gives his friend a perfect memory of everything. Here the person that forgets, receives at first all the ideas from the discourse of the other, with the same circumstances of time and place; though he considers them as mere fictions of the imagination. But as soon as the circumstance is mentioned that touches the memory, the very same ideas now appear in a new light, and have, in a manner, a different feeling from what they had before. Without any other alteration, beside that of the feeling, they become immediately ideas of the memory, and are assented to.

Since therefore the imagination can represent all the same objects that the memory can offer to us, and since those faculties are only distinguished by the different *feeling* of the ideas they present, it may be proper to consider what is the nature of that feeling. And here I believe every one will readily agree with me, that the ideas of the memory are more *strong* and *lively* than those of the fancy.]

A painter, who intended to represent a passion or emotion of any kind, would endeavour to get a sight of a person actuated by a like emotion, in order to enliven his ideas, and give them a force and vivacity superior to what is found in those, which are mere fictions of the imagination. The more recent this memory is, the clearer is the idea; and when, after a long interval, he would return to the contemplation of his object, he always finds its idea to be much decayed, if not wholly obliterated. We are frequently in doubt concerning the ideas of the memory, as they become very weak and feeble; and are at a loss to determine whether any image proceeds from the fancy or the memory, when it is not drawn in such lively colours as distinguish that latter faculty. I think I remember such an event, says one; but am not sure. A long tract of time has almost worn it out of my memory, and leaves me uncertain whether or not it be the pure offspring of my fancy.

And as an idea of the memory, by losing its force and vivacity, may degenerate to such a degree, as to be taken for an idea of the imagination; so on the other hand an idea of the imagination may acquire such a force and vivacity, as to pass for an idea of the memory, and counterfeit its effects on the belief and judgment. This is noted in the case of liars; who by the frequent repetition of their lies, come at last to believe and remember them, as realities; custom and habit having, in this case, as in many others, the same influence on the mind as nature, and infixing the idea with equal force and vigour.

Thus it appears, that the *belief* or *assent*, which always attends the memory and senses, is nothing but the vivacity of those perceptions they present; and that this alone distinguishes them from the imagination.† To believe is in this case to feel an immediate impression of the senses, or a repetition of that impression in the memory. It is merely the force and liveliness of the perception, which constitutes the first act of the judgment, and lays the foundation of that reasoning, which we build upon it, when we trace the relation of cause and effect.

SECTION VI

OF THE INFERENCE FROM THE IMPRESSION TO THE IDEA

It is easy to observe, that in tracing this relation, the inference we draw from cause to effect is not derived merely from a survey of these particular objects, and from such a penetration into their essences as may discover the dependence of the one upon the other. There is no object which implies the existence of any other, if we consider these objects in themselves, and never look beyond the ideas which we form of them. Such an inference would amount to knowledge, and would imply the absolute contradiction and impossibility of conceiving anything different. But as all distinct ideas are separable, it is evident there can be no impossibility of that kind. When we pass from a present impression to the idea of any object, we might possibly have separated the idea from the impression, and have substituted any other idea in its room.

It is therefore by *experience* only that we can infer the

existence of one object from that of another. The nature of experience is this. We remember to have had frequent instances of the existence of one species of objects; and also remember,[9] that the individuals of another species of objects have always attended them, and have existed in a regular order of contiguity and succession with regard to them. Thus we remember to have seen that species of object we call *flame,* and to have felt that species of sensation we call *heat.* We likewise call to mind their constant conjunction in all past instances. Without any further ceremony, we call the one *cause,* and the other *effect,* and infer the existence of the one from that of the other. In all those instances from which we learn the conjunction of particular causes and effects, both the causes and effects have been perceived by the senses, and are remembered: but in all cases, wherein we reason concerning them, there is only one perceived or remembered, and the other is supplied in conformity to our past experience.

Thus in advancing we have insensibly discovered a new relation betwixt cause and effect when we least expected it, and were entirely employed upon another subject. This relation is their *constant conjunction.* Contiguity and succession are not sufficient to make us pronounce any two objects to be cause and effect, unless we perceive that these two relations are preserved in several instances. We may now see the advantage of quitting the direct survey of this relation, in order to discover the nature of that *necessary connection* which makes so essential a part of it. There are hopes, that by this means we may at last arrive at our proposed end; though to tell the truth, this new-discovered relation of a constant conjunction seems to advance us but very little in our way. For it implies no more than this, that like objects have always been placed in like relations of contiguity and succession; and it seems evident, at least at first sight, that by this means we can never discover any new idea, and can only multiply, but

[9] *For a qualification of this view see end of this section and Part* III, *Sect.* VIII.

not enlarge, the objects of our mind. It may be thought, that what we learn not from one object, we can never learn from a hundred, which are all of the same kind, and are perfectly resembling in every circumstance. As our senses show us in one instance two bodies, or motions, or qualities, in certain relations of succession and contiguity, so our memory presents us only with a multitude of instances wherein we always find like bodies, motions, or qualities, in like relations. From the mere repetition of any past impression, even to infinity, there never will arise any new original idea, such as that of a necessary connection; and the number of impressions has in this case no more effect than if we confined ourselves to one only. But though this reasoning seems just and obvious, yet, as it would be folly to despair too soon, we shall continue the thread of our discourse; and having found, that after the discovery of the constant conjunction of any objects, we always draw an inference from one object to another, we shall now examine the nature of that inference, and of the transition from the impression to the idea. Perhaps it will appear in the end, that the necessary connection depends on the inference, instead of the inference's depending on the necessary connection.

Since it appears, that the transition from an impression present to the memory or senses to the idea of an object, which we call cause or effect, is founded on past *experience,* and on our remembrance of their *constant conjunction,* the next question is, whether experience produces the idea by means of the understanding or imagination; whether we are determined by reason to make the transition, or by a certain association and relation of perceptions. If reason determined us, it would proceed upon that principle, *that instances, of which we have had no experience, must resemble those of which we have had experience, and that the course of nature continues always uniformly the same.* In order, therefore, to clear up this matter, let us consider all the arguments upon which such a proposition may be supposed to be founded; and as these must be derived either from *knowledge* or *probability*, let us cast our eye on each of these degrees of evidence, and see whether they afford any just conclusion of this nature.

Our foregoing method of reasoning will easily convince us, that there can be no *demonstrative* arguments to prove, *that those instances of which we have had no experience resemble those of which we have had experience*. We can at least conceive a change in the course of nature; which sufficiently proves that such a change is not absolutely impossible. To form a clear idea of anything is an undeniable argument for its possibility, and is alone a refutation of any pretended demonstration against it.

Probability, as it discovers not the relations of ideas, considered as such, but only those of objects, must, in some respects, be founded on the impressions of our memory and senses, and in some respects on our ideas. Were there no mixture of any impression in our probable reasonings, the conclusion would be entirely chimerical : and were there no mixture of ideas, the action of the mind, in observing the relation, would, properly speaking, be sensation, not reasoning. It is, therefore, necessary, that in all probable reasonings there be something present to the mind, either seen or remembered; and that from this we infer something connected with it, which is not seen nor remembered.

The only connection or relation of objects, which can lead us beyond the immediate impressions of our memory and senses, is that of cause and effect; and that because it is the only one, on which we can found a just inference from one object to another. The idea of cause and effect is derived from *experience*, which informs us, that such particular objects, in all past instances, have been constantly conjoined with each other : and as an object similar to one of these is supposed to be immediately present in its impression, we thence presume on the existence of one similar to its usual attendant. According to this account of things, which is, I think, in every point unquestionable, probability is founded on the presumption of a resemblance betwixt those objects of which we have had experience, and those of which we have had none; and, therefore, it is impossible this presumption can arise from probability. The same principle cannot be both the cause and effect of another; and this is, perhaps, the only proposition concerning that relation, which is either intuitively or demonstratively certain.

Should any one think to elude this argument; and without determining whether our reasoning on this subject be derived from demonstration or probability, pretend that all conclusions from causes and effects are built on solid reasoning: I can only desire that this reasoning may be produced, in order to be exposed to our examination. It may perhaps be said, that after experience of the constant conjunction of certain objects, we reason in the following manner. Such an object is always found to produce another. It is impossible it could have this effect, if it was not endowed with a power of production. The power necessarily implies the effect; and therefore there is a just foundation for drawing a conclusion from the existence of one object to that of its usual attendant. The past production implies a power: the power implies a new production: and the new production is what we infer from the power and the past production.

It were easy for me to show the weakness of this reasoning, were I willing to make use of those observations I have already made, that the idea of *production* is the same with that of *causation,* and that no existence certainly and demonstratively implies a power in any other object; or were it proper to anticipate what I shall have occasion to remark afterwards concerning the idea we form of *power* and *efficacy.* But as such a method of proceeding may seem either to weaken my system, by resting one part of it on another, or to breed a confusion in my reasoning, I shall endeavour to maintain my present assertion without any such assistance.

It shall therefore be allowed for a moment, that the production of one object by another in any one instance implies a power; and that this power is connected with its effect. But it having been already proved, that the power lies not in the sensible qualities of the cause; and there being nothing but the sensible qualities present to us; I ask, why in other instances you presume that the same power still exists, merely upon the appearance of these qualities? Your appeal to past experience decides nothing in the present case; and at the utmost can only prove, that the very object, which produced any other, was at that very instant endowed with such a power; but can never prove, that the same power must continue in the same object or collection of sensible qualities; much less, that a like power is always conjoined with like sensible qualities. Should it be said, that we have experience, that the same power continues united with the same object, and that like objects are endowed with like powers, I would renew my question, *why from this experience we form any conclusion beyond those past instances, of which we have had experience?* If you answer this question in the same manner as the preceding, your answer gives still occasion to a new question of the same kind, even *in infinitum;* which clearly proves, that the foregoing reasoning had no just foundation.

Thus, not only our reason fails us in the discovery of the *ultimate connection*† of causes and effects, but even after experience has informed us of their *constant conjunction,* it is impossible for us to satisfy ourselves by our reason, why we should extend that experience beyond those particular instances which have fallen under our observation. We suppose, but are never able to prove, that there must be a resemblance betwixt those objects, of which we have had experience, and those which lie beyond the reach of our discovery.

We have already[10] taken notice of certain relations, which make us pass from one object to another, even though there be no reason to determine us to that transition; and this we may establish for a general rule, that

[10] *Part I, Sect. IV.*

wherever the mind constantly and uniformly makes a transition without any reason, it is influenced by these relations. Now, this is exactly the present case. Reason can never show us the connection of one object with another, though aided by experience, and the observation of their constant conjunction in all past instances. When the mind therefore passes from the idea or impression of one object to the idea or belief of another, it is not determined by reason, but by certain principles, which associate together the ideas of these objects, and unite them in the imagination. Had ideas no more union in the fancy, than objects seem to have to the understanding, we could never draw any inference from causes to effects, nor repose belief in any matter of fact. The inference therefore depends solely on the union of ideas.

The principles of union among ideas, I have reduced to three general ones, and have asserted, that the idea or impression of any object naturally introduces the idea of any other object, that is resembling, contiguous to, or connected with it. These principles I allow to be neither the *infallible* nor the *sole* causes of a union among ideas. They are not the infallible causes. For one may fix his attention during some time on any one object without looking further. They are not the sole causes. For the thought has evidently a very irregular motion in running along its objects, and may leap from the heavens to the earth, from one end of the creation to the other, without any certain method or order. But though I allow this weakness in these three relations, and this irregularity in the imagination; yet I assert, that the only *general* principles which associate ideas, are resemblance, contiguity, and causation.

There is indeed a principle of union among ideas, which at first sight may be esteemed different from any of these, but will be found at the bottom to depend on the same origin. When every individual of any species of objects is found by experience to be constantly united with an individual of another species, the appearance of any new individual of either species naturally conveys the thought to its usual attendant. Thus, because such a particular idea is commonly annexed to such a particular word, nothing is required but the hearing of that word to produce the correspondent idea; and it will scarce be possible for the mind, by its utmost efforts, to prevent that transition. In this case it is not absolutely necessary, that upon hearing such a particular sound, we should reflect on any past experience, and consider what idea has been usually connected with the sound. The imagination of itself supplies the place of this reflection, and is so accustomed to pass from the word to the idea, that it interposes not a moment's delay betwixt the hearing of the one, and the conception of the other.

But though I acknowledge this to be a true principle of association among ideas, I assert it to be the very same with that betwixt the ideas of cause and effect, and to be an essential part in all our reasonings from that relation. We have no other notion of cause and effect, but that of certain objects, which have been *always conjoined* together, and which in all past instances have been found inseparable. We cannot penetrate into the reason of the conjunction. We only observe the thing itself, and always find that, from the constant conjunction, the objects require a union in the imagination. When the impression of one becomes present to us, we immediately form an idea of its usual attendant; and consequently we may establish this as one part of the definition of an opinion or belief, that it is *an idea related to or associated with a present impression*.

Thus, though causation be a *philosophical* relation, as implying contiguity, succession, and constant conjunction, yet it is only so far as it is a *natural* relation, and produces a union among our ideas, that we are able to reason upon it, or draw any inference from it.

OF THE NATURE OF THE IDEA OR BELIEF

The idea of an object is an essential part of the belief of it, but not the whole. We conceive many things which we do not believe. In order, then, to discover more fully the nature of belief, or the qualities of those ideas we assent to, let us weigh the following considerations.

It is evident, that all reasonings from causes or effects terminate in conclusions concerning matter of fact; that is, concerning the existence of objects or of their qualities. It is also evident, that the idea of existence is nothing different from the idea of any object, and that when after the simple conception of anything we would conceive it as existent, we in reality make no addition to or alteration on our first idea.[11] Thus, when we affirm that God is existent, we simply form the idea of such a Being as he is represented to us; nor is the existence, which we attribute to him, conceived by a particular idea, which we join to the idea of his other qualities, and can again separate and distinguish from them. But I go further; and, not content with asserting, that the conception of the existence of any object is no addition to the simple conception of it, I likewise maintain, that the belief of the existence joins no new ideas to those, which compose the idea of the object. When I think of God, when I think of him as existent, and when I believe him to be existent, my idea of him neither increases nor diminishes. But as it is certain there is a great difference betwixt the simple conception of the existence of an object, and the belief of it, and as this difference lies not in the parts or composition of the idea which we conceive; it follows, that it must lie in the *manner* in which we conceive it.

[11] *Compare Part* II, *Sect.* VI.

Suppose a person present with me, who advances propositions, to which I do not assent, *that Cæsar died in his bed, that silver is more fusible than lead, or mercury heavier than gold;* it is evident, that, notwithstanding my incredulity, I clearly understand his meaning, and form all the same ideas which he forms. My imagination is endowed with the same powers as his; nor is it possible for him to conceive any idea, which I cannot conceive; or conjoin any, which I cannot conjoin. I therefore ask, wherein consists the difference betwixt believing and disbelieving any proposition? The answer is easy with regard to propositions, that are proved by intuition or demonstration. In that case, the person who assents not only conceives the ideas according to the proposition, but is necessarily determined to conceive them in that particular manner, either immediately, or by the interposition of other ideas. Whatever is absurd is unintelligible; nor is it possible for the imagination to conceive anything contrary to a demonstration. But as, in reasoning from causation, and concerning matters of fact, this absolute necessity cannot take place, and the imagination is free to conceive both sides of the question, I still ask, *wherein consists the difference betwixt incredulity and belief?* since, in both cases the conception of the idea is equally possible and requisite.

It will not be a satisfactory answer to say, that a person who does not assent to a proposition you advance; after having conceived the object in the same manner with you, immediately conceives it in a different manner, and has different ideas of it. This answer is unsatisfactory; not because it contains any falsehood, but because it discovers not all the truth. It is confessed that, in all cases wherein we dissent from any person, we conceive both sides of the question; but as we can believe only one, it evidently follows, that the belief must make some difference betwixt that conception to which we assent, and that from which we dissent. We may mingle, and unite, and separate, and confound, and vary our ideas in a hundred different ways;

but until there appears some principle, which fixes one of these different situations, we have in reality no opinion : and this principle, as it plainly makes no addition to our precedent ideas, can only change the *manner* of our conceiving them.

All the perceptions of the mind are of two kinds, viz. impressions and ideas, which differ from each other only in their different degrees of force and vivacity. Our ideas are copied from our impressions, and represent them in all their parts. When you would any way vary the idea of a particular object, you can only increase or diminish its force and vivacity.[12] If you make any other change on it, it represents a different object or impression. The case is the same as in colours. A particular shade of any colour may acquire a new degree of liveliness or brightness without any other variation. But when you produce any other variation, it is no longer the same shade or colour; so that as belief does nothing but vary the manner in which we conceive any object, it can only bestow on our ideas an additional force and vivacity. An opinion, therefore, or belief, may be most accurately defined, *a lively idea related to or associated with a present impression.*[13]

[12] *Hume qualifies this remark in his Appendix, final paragraph.*

[13] We may here take occasion to observe a very remarkable error, which, being frequently inculcated in the schools, has become a kind of established maxim, and is universally received by all logicians. This error consists in the vulgar division of the acts of the understanding into *conception, judgment,* and *reasoning,* and in the definitions we give of them. Conception is defined to be the simple survey of one or more ideas : judgment to be the separating or uniting of different ideas : reasoning to be the separating or uniting of different ideas by the interposition of others, which show the relation they bear to each other. But these distinctions and definitions are faulty in very considerable articles. For, *first,* it is far from being true, that, in every judgment which we form, we unite two different ideas; since in that proposition, *God is,* or indeed, any other, which regards existence, the idea of existence is no distinct idea, which we unite with that of the object, and which is capable of forming a compound idea by the union. *Secondly,* as we can thus form a proposition, which contains only one idea, so we may exert our reason without employing more than two ideas and without having recourse to a

Here are the heads of those arguments, which lead us to this conclusion. When we infer the existence of an object from that of others, some object must always be present either to the memory or senses, in order to be the foundation of our reasoning; since the mind cannot run up with its inferences *in infinitum.* Reason can never satisfy us that the existence of any one object does ever imply that of another; so that when we pass from the impression of one to the idea or belief of another, we are not determined by reason, but by custom, or a principle of association. But belief is somewhat more than a simple idea. It is a particular manner of forming an idea; and as the same idea can only be varied by a variation of its degrees of force and vivacity; it follows upon the whole, that belief is a lively idea produced by a relation to a present impression, according to the foregoing definition.

[This operation of the mind, which forms the belief of any matter of fact, seems hitherto to have been one of the greatest mysteries of philosophy; though no one has so much as suspected, that there was any difficulty in explaining it. For my part I must own, that I find a considerable difficulty in the case; and that even when I think

---

third to serve as a medium betwixt them. We infer a cause immediately from its effect; and this inference is not only a true species of reasoning, but the strongest of all others, and more convincing than when we interpose another idea to connect the two extremes. What we may in general affirm concerning these three acts of the understanding is, that taking them in a proper light, they all resolve themselves into the first, and are nothing but particular ways of conceiving our objects. Whether we consider a single object, or several; whether we dwell on these objects, or run from them to others; and in whatever form or order we survey them, the act of the mind exceeds not a simple conception; and the only remarkable difference, which occurs on this occasion, is, when we join belief to the conception, and are persuaded of the truth of what we conceive. This act of the mind has never yet been explained by any philosopher; and therefore I am at liberty to propose my hypothesis concerning it which is, that it is only a strong and steady conception of any idea, and such as approaches in some measure to an immediate impression.

I understand the subject perfectly, I am at a loss for terms to express my meaning. I conclude, by an induction which seems to me very evident, that an opinion or belief is nothing but an idea, that is different from a fiction, not in the nature, or the order of its parts, but in the *manner* of its being conceived. But when I would explain this *manner,* I scarce find any word that fully answers the case, but am obliged to have recourse to every one's feeling, in order to give him a perfect notion of this operation of the mind. An idea assented to *feels* different from a fictitious idea, that the fancy alone presents to us : and this different feeling I endeavour to explain by calling it a superior *force,* or *vivacity,* or *solidity,* or *firmness,* or *steadiness.* This variety of terms, which may seem so un-philosophical, is intended only to express that act of the mind, which renders realities more present to us than fictions, causes them to weigh more in the thought, and gives them a superior influence on the passions and imagination. Provided we agree about the thing, it is needless to dispute about the terms. The imagination has the command over all its ideas, and can join, and mix, and vary them in all the ways possible. It may conceive objects with all the circumstances of place and time. It may set them, in a manner, before our eyes in their true colours, just as they might have existed. But as it is impossible that that faculty can ever of itself reach belief, it is evident, that belief consists not in the nature and order of our ideas, but in the manner of their conception, and in their feeling to the mind. I confess, that it is impossible to explain perfectly this feeling or manner of conception. We may make use of words that express something near it. But its true and proper name is *belief,* which is a term that every one sufficiently understands in common life. And in philosophy, we can go no further than assert, that it is something *felt* by the mind, which distinguishes the ideas of the judgment from the fictions of the imagination. It gives them more force and influence;

makes them appear of greater importance; infixes them in the mind; and renders them the governing principles of all our actions.]†

This definition will also be found to be entirely conformable to every one's feeling and experience. Nothing is more evident, than that those ideas, to which we assent, are more strong, firm, and vivid, than the loose reveries of a castle-builder. If one person sits down to read a book as a romance, and another as a true history, they plainly receive the same ideas, and in the same order; nor does the incredulity of the one, and the belief of the other, hinder them from putting the very same sense upon their author. His words produce the same ideas in both; though his testimony has not the same influence on them. The latter has a more lively conception of all the incidents. He enters deeper into the concerns of the persons : represents to himself their actions, and characters, and friendships, and enmities : he even goes so far as to form a notion of their features, and air, and person. While the former, who gives no credit to the testimony of the author, has a more faint and languid conception of all these particulars, and, except on account of the style and ingenuity of the composition, can receive little entertainment from it.

SECTION VIII

OF THE CAUSES OF BELIEF†

Having thus explained the nature of belief, and shown that it consists in a lively idea related to a present impression; let us now proceed to examine from what principles it is derived, and what bestows the vivacity on the idea.

I would willingly establish it as a general maxim in the science of human nature, *that when any impression becomes present to us, it not only transports the mind to such ideas as are related to it; but likewise communicates to them a share of its force and vivacity.* All the operations of the mind depend, in a great measure, on its disposition when it performs them; and according as the spirits are more or less elevated, and the attention more or less fixed, the action will always have more or less vigour and vivacity. When therefore any object is presented which elevates and enlivens the thought, every action, to which the mind applies itself, will be more strong and vivid, as long as that disposition continues. Now it is evident the continuance of the disposition depends entirely on the objects about which the mind is employed; and that any new object naturally gives a new direction to the spirits, and changes the disposition; as on the contrary, when the mind fixes constantly on the same object, or passes easily and insensibly along related objects, the disposition has a much longer duration. Hence it happens, that when the mind is once enlivened by a present impression, it proceeds to form a more lively idea of the related objects, by a natural transition of the disposition from the one to the other. The change of the objects is so easy, that the mind is scarce sensible of it, but applies itself to the conception of the related idea with all the force and vivacity it acquired from the present impression.

If, in considering the nature of relation, and that facility of transition which is essential to it, we can satisfy ourselves concerning the reality of this phenomenon, it is well : but I must confess I place my chief confidence in experience to prove so material a principle. We may therefore observe, as the first experiment to our present purpose, that upon the appearance of the picture of an absent friend, our idea of him is evidently enlivened by the *resemblance*, and that every passion, which that idea occasions, whether of joy or sorrow, acquires new force and vigour. In producing this effect there concur both a relation and a present impression. Where the picture bears him no resemblance, or at least was not intended for him, it never so much as conveys our thought to him : and where it is absent as well as the person; though the mind may pass from the thought of the one to that of the other;

it feels its idea to be rather weakened than enlivened by that transition. We take a pleasure in viewing the picture of a friend, when it is set before us; but when it is removed, rather choose to consider him directly, than by reflection in an image, which is equally distant and obscure.

The ceremonies of the Roman Catholic religion may be considered as experiments of the same nature.† The devotees of that strange superstition usually plead in excuse of the mummeries with which they are upbraided, that they feel the good effect of those external motions, and postures, and actions, in enlivening their devotion, and quickening their fervour, which otherwise would decay away, if directed entirely to distant and immaterial objects. We shadow out the objects of our faith, they say, in sensible types and images, and render them more present to us by the immediate presence of these types, than it is possible for us to do, merely by an intellectual view and contemplation. Sensible objects have always a greater influence on the fancy than any other; and this influence they readily convey to those ideas to which they are related, and which they resemble. I shall only infer from these practices, and this reasoning, that the effect of resemblance in enlivening the idea is very common; and as in every case a resemblance and a present impression must concur, we are abundantly supplied with experiments to prove the reality of the foregoing principle.

We may add force to these experiments by others of a different kind, in considering the effects of *contiguity*, as well as of *resemblance*. It is certain that distance diminishes the force of every idea; and that, upon our approach to any object, though it does not discover itself to our senses, it operates upon the mind with an influence that imitates an immediate impression. The thinking on any object readily transports the mind to what is contiguous; but it is only the actual presence of an object, that transports it with a superior vivacity. When I am a few miles from home, whatever relates to it touches me more nearly than when I am two hundred leagues distant; though even at that distance the reflecting on anything in the neighbourhood of my friends and family naturally produces an idea of them. But as in this latter case, both the objects of the mind are ideas; notwithstanding there is an easy transition betwixt them; that transition alone is not able to give a superior vivacity to any of the ideas, for want of some immediate impression.[14]

No one can doubt but causation has the same influence as the other two relations of resemblance and contiguity. Superstitious people are fond of the relics of saints and holy men, for the same reason that they seek after types and images, in order to enliven their devotion, and give them a more intimate and strong conception of those exemplary lives, which they desire to imitate. Now, it is evident one of the best relics a devotee could procure would be the handywork of a saint; and if his clothes and furniture are ever to be considered in this light, it is because they were once at his disposal, and were moved and affected by him; in which respect they are to be considered as imperfect effects, and as connected with him by a shorter chain of consequences than any of those, from which we learn the reality of his existence. This phenomenon clearly proves, that a present impression with a relation of causation may enliven any idea, and consequently produce belief or assent, according to the precedent definition of it.

[14] Naturane nobis, inquit, datum dicam, an errore quodam, ut, cum ea loca videamus, in quibus memoria dignos viros acceperimus multum esse versatos, magis moveamur, quam siquando eorum ipsorum aut facta audiamus, aut scriptum aliquod legamus? velue ego nunc moveor. Venit enim mihi Platonis in mentem: quem accipimus primum his disputare solitum: cujus etiam illi hortuli propinqui non memoriam solum mihi afferunt, sed ipsum videntur in conspectu meo hic ponere. Hic Speusippus, hic Xenocrates, hic ejus auditor Polemo; cujus ipsa illa sessio fuit, quam videamus. Equidem etiam curiam nostram, hostiliam dico, non hanc novam, quae mihi minor esse videtur postquam est major, solebam intuens Scipionem, Catonem, Lælium, nostrum vero in primis avum cogitare. Tanta vis admonitionis inest in locis; ut non sine causa ex his memoriæ ducta sit disciplina.—*Cicero, de Finibus, lib.* 5.

But why need we seek for other arguments to prove, that a present impression with a relation or transition of the fancy may enliven any idea, when this very instance of our reasonings from cause and effect will alone suffice to that purpose? It is certain we must have an idea of every matter of fact which we believe. It is certain that this idea arises only from a relation to a present impression. It is certain that the belief superadds nothing to the idea, but only changes our manner of conceiving it, and renders it more strong and lively. The present conclusion concerning the influence of relation is the immediate consequence of all these steps; and every step appears to be sure and infallible. There enters nothing into this operation of the mind but a present impression, a lively idea, and a relation of association in the fancy betwixt the impression and the idea; so that there can be no suspicion of mistake.

In order to put this whole affair in a fuller light, let us consider it as a question in natural philosophy, which we must determine by experience and observation. I suppose there is an object presented, from which I draw a certain conclusion, and form to myself ideas, which I am said to believe or assent to. Here it is evident, that however that object, which is present to my senses, and that other, whose existence I infer by reasoning, may be thought to influence each other by their particular powers or qualities; yet as the phenomenon of belief, which we at present examine, is merely internal, these powers and qualities, being entirely unknown, can have no hand in producing it. It is the present impression which is to be considered as the true and real cause of the idea, and of the belief which attends it. We must therefore endeavour to discover, by experiments, the particular qualities by which it is enabled to produce so extraordinary an effect.

First then I observe, that the present impression has not this effect by its own proper power and efficacy, and, when considered alone as a single perception, limited to the present moment. I find that an impression, from which, on its first appearance, I can draw no conclusion, may afterwards become the foundation of belief, when I have had experience of its usual consequences. We must in every case have observed the same impression in past instances, and have found it to be constantly conjoined with some other impression. This is confirmed by such a multitude of experiments, that it admits not of the smallest doubt.

From a second observation I conclude, that the belief which attends the present impression, and is produced by a number of past impressions and conjunctions; that this belief, I say, arises immediately, without any new operation of the reason or imagination. Of this I can be certain, because I never am conscious of any such operation, and find nothing in the subject on which it can be founded. Now, as we call everything *custom* which proceeds from a past repetition, without any new reasoning or conclusion, we may establish it as a certain truth, that all the belief, which follows upon any present impression, is derived solely from that origin. When we are accustomed to see two impressions conjoined together, the appearance or idea of the one immediately carries us to the idea of the other.

Being fully satisfied on this head, I make a third set of experiments, in order to know whether anything be requisite, beside the customary transition, towards the production of this phenomenon of belief. I therefore change the first impression into an idea; and observe, that though the customary transition to the correlative idea still remains, yet there is in reality no belief nor persuasion. A present impression, then, is absolutely requisite to this whole operation; and when after this I compare an impression with an idea, and find that their only difference consists in their different degrees of force and vivacity, I conclude upon the whole, that belief is a more vivid and intense conception of an idea, proceeding from its relation to a present impression.

Thus, all probable reasoning is nothing but a species of sensation.† It is not solely in poetry and music we must follow our taste and sentiment, but likewise in philosophy.

When I am convinced of any principle, it is only an idea which strikes more strongly upon me. When I give the preference to one set of arguments above another, I do nothing but decide from my feeling concerning the superiority of their influence. Objects have no discoverable connection together; nor is it from any other principle but custom operating upon the imagination, that we can draw any inference from the appearance of one to the existence of another.

It will here be worth our observation, that the past experience, on which all our judgments concerning cause and effect depend, may operate on our mind in such an insensible manner as never to be taken notice of, and may even in some measure be unknown to us. A person, who stops short in his journey upon meeting a river in his way, foresees the consequences of his proceeding forward; and his knowledge of these consequences is conveyed to him by past experience, which informs him of such certain conjunctions of causes and effects. But can we think, that on this occasion he reflects on any past experience, and calls to remembrance instances that he has seen or heard of, in order to discover the effects of water on animal bodies? No, surely; this is not the method, in which he proceeds in his reasoning. The idea of sinking is so closely connected with that of water, and the idea of suffocating with that of sinking, that the mind makes the transition without the assistance of the memory. The custom operates before we have time for reflection. The objects seem so inseparable, that we interpose not a moment's delay in passing from the one or the other. But as this transition proceeds from experience, and not from any primary connection betwixt the ideas, we must necessarily acknowledge, that experience may produce a belief and a judgment of causes and effects by a separate operation, and without being once thought of. This removes all pretext, if there yet remains any, for asserting that the mind is convinced by reasoning of that principle, *that instances of which we have no experience, must necessarily resemble those of which we have*. For we here find, that the understanding or imagination can draw inference from past experience, without reflecting on it;† much more without forming any principle concerning it, or reasoning upon that principle.

In general we may observe, that in all the most established and uniform conjunctions of causes and effects, such as those of gravity, impulse, solidity, etc., the mind never carries its view expressly to consider any past experience : though in other associations of objects, which are more rare and unusual, it may assist the custom and transition of ideas by this reflection. Nay, we find in some cases, that the reflection produces the belief without the custom; or, more properly speaking, that the reflection produces the custom in an *oblique* and *artificial* manner. I explain myself. It is certain, that not only in philosophy, but even in common life, we may attain the knowledge of a particular cause merely by one experiment, provided it be made with judgment, and after a careful removal of all foreign and superfluous circumstances. Now, as after one experiment of this kind, the mind, upon the appearance either of the cause or the effect, can draw an inference concerning the existence of its correlative, and as a habit can never be acquired merely by one instance, it may be thought that belief cannot in this case be esteemed the effect of custom. But this difficulty will vanish, if we consider, that, though we are here supposed to have had only one experiment of a particular effect, yet we have many millions to convince us of this principle, *that like objects, placed in like circumstances, will always produce like effects;* and as this principle has established itself by a sufficient custom, it bestows an evidence and firmness on any opinion to which it can be applied. The connection of the ideas is not habitual after one experiment; but this connection is comprehended under another principle that is habitual; which brings us back to our hypothesis. In all cases we transfer our experience to instances of which we have no experience, either *expressly* or *tacitly,* either *directly* or *indirectly.*

I must not conclude this subject without observing, that it is very difficult to talk of the operations of the mind with perfect propriety and exactness; because common language has seldom made any very nice distinctions among them, but has generally called by the same term all such as nearly resemble each other. And as this is a source almost inevitable of obscurity and confusion in the author, so it may frequently give rise to doubts and objections in the reader, which otherwise he would never have dreamed of. Thus, my general position, that an opinion or belief is *nothing but a strong and lively idea derived from a present impression related to it,* may be liable to the following objection, by reason of a little ambiguity in those words *strong* and *lively.* It may be said, that not only an impression may give rise to reasoning, but that an idea may also have the same influence; especially upon my principle, *that all our ideas are derived from correspondent impressions.* For, suppose I form at present an idea, of which I have forgot the correspondent impression, I am able to conclude, from this idea, that such an impression did once exist; and as this conclusion is attended with belief, it may be asked, from whence are the qualities of force and vivacity derived which constitute this belief? And to this I answer very readily, *from the present idea.* For as this idea is not here considered as the representation of any absent object, but as a real perception in the mind, of which we are intimately conscious, it must be able to bestow, on whatever is related to it, the same quality, call it *firmness,* or *solidity,* or *force,* or *vivacity,* with which the mind reflects upon it, and is assured of its present existence. The idea here supplies the place of an impression, and is entirely the same, so far as regards our present purpose.

Upon the same principles we need not be surprised to hear of the remembrance of an idea; that is, of the idea of an idea, and of its force and vivacity superior to the loose conceptions of the imagination. In thinking of our past thoughts we not only delineate out the objects of which we were thinking, but also conceive the action of the mind in the meditation, that certain *je-ne-scai-quoi,* of which it is impossible to give any definition or description, but which every one sufficiently understands. When the memory offers an idea of this, and represents it as past, it is easily conceived how that idea may have more vigour and firmness than when we think of a past thought of which we have no remembrance.

After this, any one will understand how we may form the idea of an impression and of an idea, and how we may believe the existence of an impression and of an idea.†

SECTION IX

OF THE EFFECTS OF OTHER
RELATIONS AND OTHER HABITS

However convincing the foregoing arguments may appear, we must not rest contented with them, but must turn the subject on every side, in order to find some new points of view, from which we may illustrate and confirm such extraordinary and such fundamental principles. A scrupulous hesitation to receive any new hypothesis is so laudable a disposition in philosophers, and so necessary to the examination of truth, that it deserves to be complied with, and requires that every argument be produced which may tend to their satisfaction, and every objection removed which may stop them in their reasoning.

I have often observed, that, beside cause and effect, the two relations of resemblance and contiguity are to be considered as associating principles of thought, and as capable of conveying the imagination from one idea to another. I have also observed, that when of two objects, connected together by any of these relations, one is immediately present to the memory or senses, not only the mind is conveyed to its co-relative by means of the associating principle, but likewise conceives it with an additional force and vigour, by the united operation of that principle, and of the present impression. All this I have observed, in order to confirm, by analogy, my explication of our judgments concerning cause and effect. But this very argument may perhaps be turned against me, and instead of a confirmation of my hypothesis, may become an objection to it. For it may be said, that, if all the parts of that hypothesis be true, viz. *that* these three species of relation are derived from the same principles; *that* their effects, in enforcing and enlivening our ideas, are the same; and *that* belief is nothing but a more forcible and vivid conception of an idea; it should follow, that that action of the mind may not only be derived from the relation of cause and effect, but also from those of contiguity and resemblance. But as we find by experience that belief arises only from causation, and that we can draw no inference from one object to another, except they be connected by this relation, we may conclude, that there is some error in that reasoning which leads us into such difficulties.

This is the objection; let us now consider its solution. It is evident, that whatever is present to the memory, striking upon the mind with a vivacity which resembles an immediate impression, must become of considerable moment in all the operations of the mind, and must easily distinguish itself above the mere fictions of the imagination. Of these impressions or ideas of the memory we form a kind of system, comprehending whatever we remember to have been present, either to our internal perception or senses; and every particular of that system, joined to the present impressions, we are pleased to call a *reality*. But the mind stops not here. For finding, that with this system of perceptions there is another connected by custom, or, if you will, by the relation of cause or effect, it proceeds to the consideration of their ideas; and as it feels that it is in a manner necessarily determined to view these particular ideas, and that the custom or relation, by which it is determined, admits not of the least change, it forms them into a new system, which it likewise dignifies with the title of *realities*. The first of these systems is the object of the memory and senses; the second of the judgment.

It is this latter principle which peoples the world, and brings us acquainted with such existences as, by their removal in time and place, lie beyond the reach of the senses and memory. By means of it I paint the universe in my imagination, and fix my attention on any part of it I please. I form an idea of Rome, which I neither see nor remember, but which is connected with such impressions as I remember to have received from the conversation and books of travellers and historians. This idea of Rome I place in a certain situation on the idea of an object which I call the globe. I join to it the conception of a particular government, and religion, and manners. I look backward and consider its first foundation, its several revolutions, successes, and misfortunes. All this, and everything else which I believe, are nothing but ideas, though, by their force and settled order, arising from custom and the relation of cause and effect, they distinguish themselves from the other ideas, which are merely the offspring of the imagination.

As to the influence of contiguity and resemblance, we may observe, that if the contiguous and resembling object be comprehended in this system of realities, there is no doubt but these two relations will assist that of cause and effect, and infix the related idea with more force in the imagination. This I shall enlarge upon presently. Meanwhile I shall carry my observation a step further, and assert, that even where the related object is but feigned, the relation will serve to enliven the idea, and increase its influence. A poet, no doubt, will be the better able to form a strong description of the Elysian fields, that he prompts his imagination by the view of a beautiful meadow or garden; as at another time he may, by his fancy, place himself in the midst of these fabulous regions, that by the feigned contiguity he may enliven his imagination.

But though I cannot altogether exclude the relations of resemblance and contiguity from operating on the fancy in this manner, it is observable that, when single, their influence is very feeble and uncertain. As the relation of cause and effect is requisite to persuade us of any real existence, so is this persuasion requisite to give force to these other relations. For where upon the appearance of an impression we not only feign another object, but likewise arbitrarily, and of our mere good-will and pleasure give it a particular relation to the impression, this can have but a small effect upon the mind; nor is there any reason, why, upon the return of the same impression, we should be determined to place the same object in the same relation to it. There is no manner of necessity for the mind to feign any resembling and contiguous objects; and if it feigns such, there is as little necessity for it always to confine itself to the same, without any difference or variation. And indeed such a fiction is founded on so little reason, that nothing but pure *caprice* can determine the mind to form it; and that principle being fluctuating and uncertain, it is impossible it can ever operate with any considerable degree of force and constancy. The mind foresees and anticipates the change; and even from the very first instant feels the looseness of its actions, and the weak hold it has of its objects. And as this imperfection is very sensible in every single instance, it still increases by experience and observation, when we compare the several instances we may remember, and form a *general rule* against the reposing any assurance in those momentary glimpses of light, which arise in the imagination from a feigned resemblance and contiguity.

The relation of cause and effect has all the opposite advantages. The objects it presents are fixed and unalterable. The impressions of the memory never change in any considerable degree; and each impression draws along with it a precise idea, which takes its place in the imagination, as something solid and real, certain and invariable. The thought is always determined to pass from the impression to the idea, and from that particular impression to that particular idea, without any choice or hesitation.

But not content with removing this objection, I shall endeavour to extract from it a proof of the present doctrine. Contiguity and resemblance have an effect much inferior to causation; but still have some effect, and *augment the conviction of any opinion,* and the vivacity of any conception. If this can be proved in several new instances, beside what we have already observed, it will be allowed no inconsiderable argument, that belief is nothing but a lively idea related to a present impression.

To begin with contiguity; it has been remarked among the Mohametans as well as Christians, that those *pilgrims,* who have seen Mecca or the Holy Land, are ever after more faithful and zealous believers, than those who have not had that advantage. A man, whose memory presents him with a lively image of the Red Sea, and the Desert, and Jerusalem, and Galilee, can never doubt of any miraculous events, which are related either by Moses or the Evangelists. The lively idea of the places passes by an easy transition to the facts, which are supposed to have been related to them by contiguity, and increases the belief by increasing the vivacity of the conception. The remembrance of these fields and rivers has the same influence on the vulgar as a new argument, and from the same causes.

We may form a like observation concerning *resemblance.* We have remarked, that the conclusion which we draw from a present object to its absent cause or effect, is never founded on any qualities which we observe in that object, considered in itself; or, in other words, that it is impossible to determine otherwise than by experience, what will result from any phenomenon, or what has preceded it. But though this be so evident in itself, that it seemed not to require any proof, yet some philosophers have imagined that there is an apparent cause for the communication of motion, and that a reasonable man might immediately infer the motion of one body from the impulse of another, without having recourse to any past observation. That this opinion is false will admit of an easy proof. For if such an inference may be drawn merely from the ideas of body, of motion, and of impulse, it must amount to a demonstration, and must imply the absolute impossibility of any contrary supposition. Every effect, then, beside the communication of motion, implies a formal contradiction; and it is impossible not only that it can exist, but also that it can be conceived. But we may soon satisfy ourselves of the contrary, by forming a clear and consistent idea of one body's moving upon another, and of its rest immediately upon the contact; or of its returning back in the same line in which it came; or of its annihilation, or circular or elliptical motion; and in short, of an infinite number of other changes, which we may suppose it to undergo. These suppositions are all consistent and natural; and the reason why we imagine the communication of motion to be more consistent and natural, not only than those suppositions, but also than any other natural effect, is founded on the relation of *resemblance* betwixt the cause and effect, which is here united to experience, and binds the objects in the closest and most intimate manner to each other, so as to make us imagine them to be absolutely inseparable. Resemblance, then, has the same or a parallel influence with experience; and as the only immediate effect of experience is to associate our ideas together, it follows that all belief arises from the association of ideas, according to my hypothesis.

It is universally allowed by the writers on optics, that the eye at all times sees an equal number of physical points, and that a man on the top of a mountain has no larger an image presented to his senses, than when he is cooped up in the narrowest court or chamber. It is only by experience that he infers the greatness of the object from some peculiar qualities of the image; and this inference of the judgment he confounds with sensation, as is common on other occasions. Now it is evident, that the inference of the judgment is here much more lively than what is usual in our common reasonings, and that a man has a more vivid conception of the vast extent of the ocean from the image

3

he receives by the eye, when he stands on the top of the high promontory, than merely from hearing the roaring of the waters. He feels a more sensible pleasure from its magnificence, which is a proof of a more lively idea; and he confounds his judgment with sensation, which is another proof of it. But as the inference is equally certain and immediate in both cases, this superior vivacity of our conception in one case can proceed from nothing but this, that in drawing an inference from the sight, beside the customary conjunction, there is also a resemblance betwixt the image and the object we infer, which strengthens the relation, and conveys the vivacity of the impression to the related idea with an easier and more natural movement.

No weakness of human nature is more universal and conspicuous than what we commonly call *credulity,* or a too easy faith in the testimony of others; and this weakness is also very naturally accounted for from the influence of resemblance. When we receive any matter of fact upon human testimony, our faith arises from the very same origin as our inferences from causes to effects, and from effects to causes; nor is there anything but our *experience* of the governing principles of human nature, which can give us any assurance of the veracity of men. But though experience be the true standard of this, as well as of all other judgments, we seldom regulate ourselves entirely by it, but have a remarkable propensity to believe whatever is reported, even concerning apparitions, enchantments, and prodigies, however contrary to daily experience and observation. The words or discourses of others have an intimate connection with certain ideas in their mind; and these ideas have also a connection with the facts or objects which they represent. This latter connection is generally much overrated, and commands our assent beyond what experience will justify, which can proceed from nothing beside the resemblance betwixt the ideas and the facts. Other effects only point out their causes in an oblique manner; but the testimony of men does it directly, and is to be considered as an image as well as an effect. No wonder, therefore, we are so rash in drawing our inferences from it, and are less guided by experience in our judgments concerning it, than in those upon any other subject.

As resemblance, when conjoined with causation, fortifies our reasonings, so the want of it in any very great degree is able almost entirely to destroy them. Of this there is a remarkable instance in the universal carelessness and stupidity of men with regard to a future state, where they show as obstinate an incredulity, as they do a blind credulity on other occasions. There is not indeed a more ample matter of wonder to the studious, and of regret to the pious man, than to observe the negligence of the bulk of mankind concerning their approaching condition; and it is with reason, that many eminent theologians have not scrupled to affirm, that though the vulgar have no formal principles of infidelity, yet they are really infidels in their hearts, and have nothing like what we can call a belief of the eternal duration of their souls. For let us consider on the one hand what divines have displayed with such eloquence concerning the importance of eternity; and at the same time reflect, that though in matters of rhetoric we ought to lay our account with some exaggeration, we must in this case allow, that the strongest figures are infinitely inferior to the subject : and after this, let us view on the other hand the prodigious security of men in this particular : I ask, if these people really believe what is inculcated on them, and what they pretend to affirm; and the answer is obviously in the negative. As belief is an act of the mind arising from custom, it is not strange the want of resemblance should overthrow what custom has established, and diminish the force of the idea, as much as that latter principle increases it. A future state is so far removed from our comprehension, and we have so obscure an idea of the manner in which we shall exist after the dissolution of the body, that all the reasons we can invent, however strong in themselves, and however much assisted by education, are never able with slow imaginations to surmount this difficulty, or bestow a sufficient authority and force on the idea. I rather choose to ascribe this incredulity to the faint idea we form of our future condition, derived from its want of resemblance to the present life, than to that derived from its remoteness. For I observe, that men are everywhere concerned about what may happen after their death, provided it regard this world; and that there are few to whom their name, their family, their friends, and their country are in any period of time entirely indifferent.

And indeed the want of resemblance in this case so entirely destroys belief, that except those few who, upon cool reflection on the importance of the subject, have taken care by repeated meditation to imprint in their minds the arguments for a future state, there scarce are any who believe the immortality of the soul with a true and established judgment; such as is derived from the testimony of travellers and historians. This appears very conspicuously wherever men have occasion to compare the pleasures and pains, the rewards and punishments of this life with those of a future; even though the case does not concern themselves, and there is no violent passion to disturb their judgment. The Roman Catholics are certainly the most zealous of any sect in the Christian world; and yet you will find few among the more sensible part of that communion who do not blame the Gunpowder Treason, and the massacre of St. Bartholomew, as cruel and barbarous, though projected or executed against those very people, whom without any scruple they condemn to eternal and infinite punishments. All we can say in excuse for this inconsistency is, that they really do not believe what they affirm concerning a future state; nor is there any better proof of it than the very inconsistency.

We may add to this a remark, that in matters of religion men take a pleasure in being terrified, and that no preachers are so popular as those who excite the most dismal and gloomy passions. In the common affairs of life, where we feel and are penetrated with the solidity of the subject, nothing can be more disagreeable than fear and terror; and it is only in dramatic performances and in religious discourses that they ever give pleasure. In these latter cases the imagination reposes itself indolently on the idea; and the passion being softened by the want of belief in the subject, has no more than the agreeable effect of enlivening the mind and fixing the attention.

The present hypothesis will receive additional confirmation, if we examine the effects of other kinds of custom, as well as of other relations. To understand this, we must consider that custom, to which I attribute all belief and reasoning, may operate upon the mind in invigorating an idea after two several ways. For supposing that, in all past experience, we have found two objects to have been always conjoined together, it is evident, that upon the appearance of one of these objects in an impression, we must, from custom, make an easy transition to the idea of that object, which usually attends it; and by means of the present impression and easy transition must conceive that idea in a stronger and more lively manner than we do any loose floating image of the fancy. But let us next suppose, that a mere idea alone, without any of this curious and almost artificial preparation, should frequently make its appearance in the mind, this idea must, by degrees, acquire a facility and force; and both by its firm hold and easy introduction distinguish itself from any new and unusual idea. This is the only particular in which these two kinds of custom agree; and if it appear that their effects on the judgment are similar and proportionable, we may certainly conclude, that the foregoing explication of that faculty is satisfactory. But can we doubt of this agreement in their influence on the judgment, when we consider the nature and effects of *education*?

All those opinions and notions of things, to which we have been accustomed from our infancy, take such deep root, that it is impossible for us, by all the powers of reason and experience, to eradicate them; and this habit not only approaches in its influence, but even on many occasions prevails over that which arises from the constant and inseparable union of causes and effects. Here we must not be contented with saying, that the vividness of the idea produces the belief : we must maintain that they are individually the same. The frequent repetition of any idea infixes it in the imagination; but could never possibly of itself produce belief, if that act of the mind was, by the original constitution of our natures, annexed only to a reasoning and comparison of ideas. Custom may lead us into some false comparison of ideas : This is the utmost effect we can conceive of it; but it is certain it could never supply the place of that comparison, nor produce any act of the mind which naturally belonged to that principle.

A person that has lost a leg or an arm by amputation endeavours for a long time afterwards to serve himself with them. After the death of any one, it is a common remark of the whole family, but especially the servants, that they can scarce believe him to be dead, but still imagine him to be in his chamber or in any other place, where they were accustomed to find him. I have often heard in conversation, after talking of a person that is in any way celebrated, that one, who has no acquaintance with him, will say, *I have never seen such a one, but almost fancy I have, so often have I heard talk of him.* All these are parallel instances.

If we consider this argument from *education* in a proper light, it will appear very convincing; and the more so, that it is founded on one of the most common phenomena that is anywhere to be met with. I am persuaded that, upon examination, we shall find more than one half of those opinions that prevail among mankind to be owing to education, and that the principles which are thus implicitly embraced, over-balance those, which are owing either to abstract reasoning or experience. As liars, by the frequent repetition of their lies, come at last to remember them; so the judgment, or rather the imagination, by the like means, may have ideas so strongly imprinted on it, and conceive them in so full a light, that they may operate upon the mind in the same manner with those which the senses, memory, or reason present to us. But as education is an artificial and not a natural cause, and as its maxims are frequently contrary to reason, and even to themselves in different times and places, it is never upon that account recognised by philosophers; though in reality it be built almost on the same foundation of custom and repetition as our reasonings from causes and effects.[15]

SECTION X

OF THE INFLUENCE OF BELIEF

But though education be disclaimed by philosophy, as a fallacious ground of assent to any opinion, it prevails nevertheless in the world, and is the cause why all systems are apt to be rejected at first as new and unusual. This, perhaps, will be the fate of what I have here advanced concerning *belief;* and though the proofs I have produced appear to me perfectly conclusive, I expect not to make many proselytes to my opinion. Men will scarce ever be persuaded, that effects of such consequence can flow from principles which are seemingly so inconsiderable, and that the far greatest part of our reasonings, with all our actions and passions, can be derived from nothing but custom and habit. To obviate this objection, I shall here anticipate a little what would more properly fall under our considera-

---

[15] In general we may observe, that as our assent to all probable reasonings is founded on the vivacity of ideas, it resembles many of those whimsies and prejudices which are rejected under the opprobrious character of being the offspring of the imagination. By this expression it appears, that the word imagination, is commonly used in two different senses; and though nothing be more contrary to true philosophy than this inaccuracy, yet, in the following reasonings, I have often been obliged to fall into it. When I oppose the imagination to the memory, I mean the faculty by which we form our fainter ideas. When I oppose it to reason, I mean the same faculty, excluding only our demonstrative and probable reasonings. When I oppose it to neither, i⁺ is indifferent whether it be taken in the larger or more limited sense, or at least the context will sufficiently explain the meaning.

tion afterwards, when we come to treat of the Passions and the Sense of Beauty.[16]

There is implanted in the human mind a perception of pain and pleasure as the chief spring and moving principle of all its actions. But pain and pleasure have two ways of making their appearance in the mind; of which the one has effects very different from the other. They may either appear in impression to the actual feeling, or only in idea, as at present when I mention them. It is evident the influence of these upon our actions is far from being equal. Impressions always actuate the soul, and that in the highest degree; but it is not every idea which has the same effect. Nature has proceeded with caution in this case, and seems to have carefully avoided the inconveniences of two extremes. Did impressions alone influence the will, we should every moment of our lives be subject to the greatest calamities; because, though we foresaw their approach, we should not be provided by nature with any principle of action, which might impel us to avoid them. On the other hand, did every idea influence our actions, our condition would not be much mended. For such is the unsteadiness and activity of thought, that the images of everything, especially of goods and evils, are always wandering in the mind; and were it moved by every idle conception of this kind, it would never enjoy a moment's peace and tranquillity.

Nature has therefore chosen a medium, and has neither bestowed on every idea of good and evil[17] the power of actuating the will, nor yet has entirely excluded them from this influence. Though an idle fiction has no efficacy, yet we find by experience, that the ideas of those objects which we believe either are or will be existent, produce in a lesser degree the same effect with those impressions, which are immediately present to the senses and perception. The effect then of belief, is to raise up a simple idea to an equality with our impressions, and bestow on it a like influence on the passions. This effect it can only have by making an

---

[16] *Treatise, Book* II.　　　　[17] *i.e. pleasure and pain.*

idea approach an impression in force and vivacity. For as the different degrees of force make all the original difference betwixt an impression and an idea, they must of consequence be the source of all the differences in the effects of these perceptions, and their removal, in whole or in part, the cause of every new resemblance they acquire. Wherever we can make an idea approach the impressions in force and vivacity, it will likewise imitate them in its influence on the mind; and *vice versa,* where it imitates them in that influence, as in the present case, this must proceed from its approaching them in force and vivacity. Belief, therefore, since it causes an idea to imitate the effects of the impressions, must make it resemble them in these qualities, and is nothing but *a more vivid and intense conception of any idea.* This then may both serve as an additional argument for the present system, and may give us a notion after what manner our reasonings from causation are able to operate on the will and passions.

As belief is almost absolutely requisite to the exciting our passions, so the passions, in their turn, are very favourable to belief; and not only such facts as convey agreeable emotions, but very often such as give pain, do upon that account become more readily the objects of faith and opinion. A coward, whose fears are easily awakened, readily assents to every account of danger he meets with; as a person of a sorrowful and melancholy disposition is very credulous of everything that nourishes his prevailing passion. When any affecting object is presented, it gives the alarm, and excites immediately a degree of its proper passion; especially in persons who are naturally inclined to that passion. This emotion passes by an easy transition to the imagination; and diffusing itself over the idea of the affecting object, makes us form that idea with greater force and vivacity, and consequently assent to it, according to the precedent system. Admiration and surprise have the same effect as the other passions; and accordingly we may observe, that among the vulgar, quacks and projectors meet with a more easy faith upon account of their magnificent pretensions, than if they kept themselves within the bounds of moderation. The first astonishment, which naturally attends their miraculous relations, spreads itself over the whole soul, and so vivifies and enlivens the idea, that it resembles the inferences we draw from experience. This is a mystery, with which we may be already a little acquainted, and which we shall have further occasion to be let into in the progress of this Treatise.[18]

After this account of the influence of belief on the passions, we shall find less difficulty in explaining its effects on the imagination, however extraordinary they may appear. It is certain we cannot take pleasure in any discourse, where our judgment gives no assent to those images which are presented to our fancy. The conversation of those, who have acquired a habit of lying, though in affairs of no moment, never gives any satisfaction; and that because those ideas they present to us, not being attended with belief, make no impression upon the mind. Poets themselves, though liars by profession, always endeavour to give an air of truth to their fictions; and where that is totally neglected, their performances, however ingenious, will never be able to afford much pleasure. In short, we may observe, that even when ideas have no manner of influence on the will and passions, truth and reality are still requisite, in order to make them entertaining to the imagination.

But if we compare together all the phenomena that occur on this head, we shall find, that truth, however necessary it may seem in all works of genius, has no other effect than to procure an easy reception for the ideas, and to make the mind acquiesce in them with satisfaction, or at least without reluctance. But as this is an effect, which may easily be supposed to flow from that solidity and force, which, according to my system, attend those ideas that are established by reasonings from causation; it follows, that all the influence of belief upon the fancy may

[18] *This may be an allusion to a section on Miracles, which Hume cut out before publication.*

be explained from that system. Accordingly we may observe, that wherever that influence arises from any other principles beside truth or reality, they supply its place, and give an equal entertainment to the imagination. Poets have formed what they call a poetical system of things, which though it be believed neither by themselves nor readers, is commonly esteemed a sufficient foundation for any fiction. We have been so much accustomed to the names of Mars, Jupiter, Venus, that in the same manner as education infixes any opinion, the constant repetition of these ideas makes them enter into the mind with facility, and prevail upon the fancy, without influencing the judgment. In like manner tragedians always borrow their fable, or at least the names of their principal actors, from some known passage in history; and that not in order to deceive the spectators; for they will frankly confess, that truth is not in any circumstance inviolably observed, but in order to procure a more easy reception into the imagination for those extraordinary events, which they represent. But this is a precaution which is not required of comic poets, whose personages and incidents, being of a more familiar kind, enter easily into the conception, and are received without any such formality, even though at sight they be known to be fictitious, and the pure offspring of the fancy.

This mixture of truth and falsehood in the fables of tragic poets not only serves our present purpose, by showing that the imagination can be satisfied without any absolute belief or assurance; but may in another view be regarded as a very strong confirmation of this system. It is evident, that poets make use of this artifice of borrowing the names of their persons, and the chief events of their poems, from history, in order to procure a more easy reception for the whole, and cause it to make a deeper impression on the fancy and affections. The several incidents of the piece acquire a kind of relation by being united into one poem or representation; and if any of these incidents be an object of belief, it bestows a force and vivacity on the others, which are related to it. The vividness of the first conception diffuses itself along the relations, and is conveyed, as by so many pipes or canals, to every idea that has any communication with the primary one. This indeed can never amount to a perfect assurance; and that because the union among the ideas is in a manner accidental: but still it approaches so near in its influence, as may convince us that they are derived from the same origin. Belief must please the imagination by means of the force and vivacity which attends it; since every idea which has force and vivacity, is found to be agreeable to that faculty.

To confirm this we may observe, that the assistance is mutual betwixt the judgment and fancy, as well as betwixt the judgment and passion; and that belief not only gives vigour to the imagination, but that a vigorous and strong imagination is of all talents the most proper to procure belief and authority. It is difficult for us to withhold our assent from what is painted out to us in all the colours of eloquence; and the vivacity produced by the fancy is in many cases greater than that which arises from custom and experience. We are hurried away by the lively imagination of our author or companion; and even he himself is often a victim to his own fire and genius.

Nor will it be amiss to remark, that as a lively imagination very often degenerates into madness or folly, and bears it a great resemblance in its operations; so they influence the judgment after the same manner, and produce belief from the very same principles. When the imagination, from any extraordinary ferment of the blood and spirits, acquires such a vivacity as disorders all its powers and faculties, there is no means of distinguishing betwixt truth and falsehood: but every loose fiction or idea, having the same influence as the impressions of the memory, or the conclusions of the judgment, is received on the same footing, and operates with equal force on the passions. A present impression and a customary transition are now no longer necessary to enliven our ideas. Every chimera of the brain is as vivid and intense as any of those inferences, which we formerly dignified with the name of conclusions concerning matters of fact, and sometimes as the present impressions of the senses.

[We may observe the same effect of poetry in a lesser degree; and this is common both to poetry and madness, that the vivacity they bestow on the ideas is not derived from the particular situations or connections of the objects of these ideas, but from the present temper and disposition of the person. But how great soever the pitch may be to which this vivacity rise, it is evident, that in poetry it never has the same *feeling* with that which arises in the mind, when we reason, though even upon the lowest species of probability. The mind can easily distinguish betwixt the one and the other; and whatever emotion the poetical enthusiasm may give to the spirits, it is still the mere phantom of belief or persuasion. The case is the same with the idea as with the passion it occasions. There is no passion of the human mind but what may arise from poetry; though, at the same time, the *feelings* of the passions are very different when excited by poetical fictions, from what they are when they arise from belief and reality. A passion which is disagreeable in real life, may afford the highest entertainment in a tragedy or epic poem. In the latter case it lies not with that weight upon us : it feels less firm and solid, and has no other than the agreeable effect of exciting the spirits, and rousing the attention. The difference in the passions is a clear proof of a like difference in those ideas from which the passions are derived. Where the vivacity arises from a customary conjunction with a present impression, though the imagination may not, in appearance, be so much moved, yet there is always something more forcible and real in its actions than in the fervours of poetry and eloquence. The force of our mental actions in this case, no more than in any other, is not to be measured by the apparent agitation of the mind. A poetical description may have a more sensible effect on the fancy than an historical narration. It may collect more of those circumstances that form a complete image or picture. It may seem to set the object before us in more lively colours. But still the ideas it presents are different to the *feeling* from those which arise from the memory and the judgment.[19] There is something weak and imperfect amidst all that seeming vehemence of thought and sentiment which attends the fictions of poetry.

We shall afterwards have occasion to remark both the resemblances and differences betwixt a poetical enthusiasm and a serious conviction.[20] In the meantime, I cannot forbear observing, that the great difference in their feeling proceeds, in some measure, from reflection and *general rules*. We observe, that the vigour of conception which fictions receive from poetry and eloquence, is a circumstance merely accidental, of which every idea is equally susceptible; and that such fictions are connected with nothing that is real. This observation makes us only lend ourselves, so to speak, to the fiction, but causes the idea to feel very different from the eternal established persuasions founded on memory and custom. They are somewhat of the same kind; but the one is much inferior to the other, both in its causes and effects.

A like reflection on *general rules* keeps us from augmenting our belief upon every increase of the force and vivacity of our ideas. Where an opinion admits of no doubt, or opposite probability, we attribute to it a full conviction; though the want of resemblance, or contiguity, may render its force inferior to that of other opinions. It is thus the understanding corrects the appearances of the senses, and makes us imagine, that an object at twenty foot distance seems even to the eye as large as one of the same dimensions at ten.]

We may observe the same effect of poetry in a lesser degree; only with this difference, that the least reflection dissipates the illusions of poetry, and places the objects in

---

[19] *Note how the different feeling of a believed idea is here stressed more than its vivacity.*

[20] *I cannot find any later passages on this topic in the Treatise.*

their proper light. It is however certain, that in the warmth of a poetical enthusiasm, a poet has a counterfeit belief, and even a kind of vision of his objects; and if there be any shadow of argument to support this belief, nothing contributes more to his full conviction than a blaze of poetical figures and images, which have their effect upon the poet himself, as well as upon his readers.

SECTION XI

OF THE PROBABILITY OF CHANCES

But in order to bestow on this system its full force and evidence, we must carry our eye from it a moment to consider its consequences, and explain from the same principles some other species of reasoning which are derived from the same origin.

Those philosophers who have divided human reason into *knowledge and probability*, and have defined the first to be *that evidence which arises from the comparison of ideas*, are obliged to comprehend all our arguments from causes or effects under the general term of probability. But though every one be free to use his terms in what sense he pleases; and accordingly in the precedent part of this discourse I have followed this method of expression; it is however certain, that in common discourse we readily affirm, that many arguments from causation exceed probability, and may be received as a superior kind of evidence. One would appear ridiculous who would say, that it is only probable the sun will rise to-morrow, or that all men must die; though it is plain we have no further assurance of these facts than what experience affords us. For this reason it would perhaps be more convenient, in order at once to preserve the common signification of words, and mark the several degrees of evidence, to distinguish human reason into three kinds, viz. *that from knowledge, from proofs, and from probabilities*. By knowledge, I mean the assurance arising from the comparison of ideas. By proofs, those arguments which are derived from the relation of cause and effect, and which are entirely free from doubt and uncertainty. By probability, that evidence which is still attended with uncertainty. It is this last species of reasoning I proceed to examine.

Probability or reasoning from conjecture may be divided into two kinds, viz. that which is founded on *chance,* and that which arises from *causes*. We shall consider each of these in order.

The idea of cause and effect is derived from experience, which presenting us with certain objects constantly conjoined with each other, produces such a habit of surveying them in that relation, that we cannot without a sensible violence survey them in any other. On the other hand, as chance is nothing real in itself, and, properly speaking, is merely the negation of a cause, its influence on the mind is contrary to that of causation; and it is essential to it to leave the imagination perfectly indifferent, either to consider the existence or non-existence of that object which is regarded as contingent. A cause traces the way to our thought, and in a manner forces us to survey such certain objects in such certain relations. Chance can only destroy this determination of the thought, and leave the mind in its native situation of indifference; in which, upon the absence of a cause, it is instantly reinstated.

Since therefore an entire indifference is essential to chance, no one chance can possibly be superior to another, otherwise than as it is composed of a superior number of equal chances. For if we affirm that one chance can, after any other manner, be superior to another, we must at the same time affirm, that there is something which gives it the superiority, and determines the event rather to that side than the other : that is, in other words, we must allow of a cause, and destroy the supposition of chance, which we had before established. A perfect and total indifference is essential to chance, and one total indifference can never in itself be either superior or inferior to another. This truth is not peculiar to my system, but is acknowledged by every one that forms calculations concerning chances.

And here it is remarkable, that though chance and causation be directly contrary, yet it is impossible for us to conceive this combination of chances, which is requisite to render one hazard superior to another, without supposing a mixture of causes among the chances, and a conjunction of necessity in some particulars, with a total indifference in others. Where nothing limits the chances, every notion that the most extravagant fancy can form is upon a footing of equality; nor can there be any circumstance to give one the advantage above another. Thus, unless we allow that there are some causes to make the dice fall, and preserve their form in their fall, and lie upon some one of their sides, we can form no calculation concerning the laws of hazard. But supposing these causes to operate, and supposing likewise all the rest to be indifferent and to be determined by chance, it is easy to arrive at a notion of a superior combination of chances. A die that has four sides marked with a certain number of spots, and only two with another, affords us an obvious and easy instance of this superiority. The mind is here limited by the causes to such a precise number and quality of the events; and at the same time is undetermined in its choice of any particular event.

Proceeding then in that reasoning, wherein we have advanced three steps; *that* chance is merely the negation of a cause, and produces a total indifference in the mind; *that* one negation of a cause and one total indifference can never be superior or inferior to another; *that* there must always be a mixture of causes among the chances, in order to be the foundation of any reasoning; we are next to consider what effect a superior combination of chances can have upon the mind, and after what manner it influences our judgment and opinion. Here we may repeat all the same arguments we employed in examining that belief which arises from causes; and may prove, after the same manner, that a superior number of chances produces our assent neither by *demonstration* nor *probability*. It is indeed evident, that we can never, by the comparison of mere ideas, make any discovery which can be of consequence in this affair, and that it is impossible to prove with certainty that any event must fall on that side where there is a superior number of chances. To suppose in this case any certainty, were to overthrow what we have established concerning the opposition of chances, and their perfect equality and indifference.

Should it be said, that though in an opposition of chances, it is impossible to determine with *certainty* on which side the event will fall, yet we can pronounce with certainty, that it is more likely and probable it will be on that side where there is a superior number of chances, than where there is an inferior : should this be said, I would ask, what is here meant by *likelihood and probability*? The likelihood and probability of chances is a superior number of equal chances; and consequently, when we say it is likely the event will fall on the side which is superior, rather than on the inferior, we do no more than affirm, that where there is a superior number of chances there is actually a superior, and where there is an inferior there is an inferior, which are identical propositions, and of no consequence. The question is, by what means a superior number of equal chances operates upon the mind, and produces belief or assent, since it appears that it is neither by arguments derived from demonstration, nor from probability.[21]

In order to clear up this difficulty, we shall suppose a person to take a die, formed after such a manner as that four of its sides are marked with one figure, or one number of spots, and two with another; and to put this die into the box with an intention of throwing it : it is plain, he must conclude the one figure to be more probable than the

[21] *Up to this point, the section is a masterly non-technical introduction to the calculus of chances.*

other, and give the preference to that which is inscribed on the greatest number of sides. He in a manner believes that this will lie uppermost; though still with hesitation and doubt in proportion to the number of chances which are contrary : and according as these contrary chances diminish, and the superiority increases on the other side, his belief acquires new degrees of stability and assurance. This belief arises from an operation of the mind upon the simple and limited object before us; and therefore its nature will be the more easily discovered and explained. We have nothing but one single die to contemplate, in order to comprehend one of the most curious operations of the understanding.

This die formed as above, contains three circumstances worthy of our attention. *First,* certain causes, such as gravity, solidity, a cubical figure, etc., which determine it to fall, to preserve its form in its fall, and to turn up one of its sides. *Secondly,* a certain number of sides, which are supposed indifferent. *Thirdly,* a certain figure inscribed on each side. These three particulars form the whole nature of the die, so far as relates to our present purpose; and consequently are the only circumstances regarded by the mind in its forming a judgment concerning the result of such a throw. Let us therefore consider gradually and carefully what must be the influence of these circumstances on the thought and imagination.

First, we have already observed, that the mind is determined by custom to pass from any cause to its effect, and that upon the appearance of the one, it is almost impossible for it not to form an idea of the other. Their constant conjunction in past instances has produced such a habit in the mind, that it always conjoins them in its thought, and infers the existence of the one from that of its usual attendant. When it considers the die as no longer supported by the box, it cannot without violence regard it as suspended in the air; but naturally places it on the table, and views it as turning up one of its sides. This is the effect of the intermingled causes, which are requisite to our forming any calculation concerning chances.

Secondly, it is supposed, that though the die be necessarily determined to fall, and turn up one of its sides, yet there is nothing to fix the particular side, but that this is determined entirely by chance. The very nature and essence of chance is a negation of causes, and the leaving the mind in a perfect indifference among those events which are supposed contingent. When therefore the thought is determined by the causes to consider the die as falling and turning up one of its sides, the chances present all these sides as equal, and make us consider every one of them, one after another, as alike probable and possible. The imagination passes from the cause, viz. the throwing of the die, to the effect, viz. the turning up one of the six sides; and feels a kind of impossibility both of stopping short in the way, and of forming any other idea. But as all these six sides are incompatible, and the die cannot turn up above one at once, this principle directs us not to consider all of them at once as lying uppermost, which we look upon as impossible : neither does it direct us with its entire force to any particular side; for in that case this side would be considered as certain and inevitable; but it directs us to the whole six sides after such a manner as to divide its force equally among them. We conclude in general, that some one of them must result from the throw : we run all of them over in our minds : the determination of the thought is common to all; but no more of its force falls to the share of any one, than what is suitable to its proportion with the rest. It is after this manner the original impulse, and consequently the vivacity of thought arising from the causes, is divided and split in pieces by the intermingled chances.

We have already seen the influence of the two first qualities of the die, viz. the *causes,* and the *number,* and *indifference* of the sides, and have learned how they give an impulse to the thought, and divide that impulse into as many parts as there are units in the number of sides. We must now consider the effects of the third particular, viz. the *figures* inscribed on each side. It is evident that where several sides have the same figure inscribed on them, they must concur in their influence on the mind, and must unite upon one image or idea of a figure, all those divided impulses that were dispersed over the several sides upon which that figure is inscribed. Were the question only what side will be turned up, these are all perfectly equal, and no one could ever have any advantage above another. But as the question is concerning the figure, and as the same figure is presented by more than one side, it is evident that the impulses belonging to all these sides must reunite in that one figure, and become stronger and more forcible by the union.† Four sides are supposed in the present case to have the same figure inscribed on them, and two to have another figure. The impulses of the former are therefore superior to those of the latter. But as the events are contrary, and it is impossible both these figures can be turned up; the impulses, likewise, become contrary, and the inferior destroys the superior, as far as its strength goes. The vivacity of the idea is always proportionable to the degrees of the impulse or tendency to the transition; and belief is the same with the vivacity of the idea, according to the precedent doctrine.

SECTION XII

OF THE PROBABILITY OF CAUSES

What I have said concerning the probability of chances, can serve to no other purpose than to assist us in explaining the probability of causes; since it is commonly allowed by philosophers, that what the vulgar call chance is nothing but a secret and concealed cause. That species of probability, therefore, is what we must chiefly examine.

The probabilities of causes are of several kinds; but are

all derived from the same origin, viz. *the association of ideas to a present impression*. As the habit which produces the association arises from the frequent conjunction of objects, it must arrive at its perfection by degrees, and must acquire new force from each instance that falls under our observation. The first instance has little or no force : the second makes some addition to it : the third becomes still more sensible : and it is by these slow steps that our judgment arrives at a full assurance. But before it attains this pitch of perfection, it passes through several inferior degrees, and in all of them is only to be esteemed a presumption or probability. The gradation, therefore, from probabilities to proofs, is in many cases insensible; and the difference betwixt these kinds of evidence is more easily perceived in the remote degrees, than in the near and contiguous.

It is worthy of remark on this occasion, that though the species of probability here explained be the first in order, and naturally takes place before any entire proof can exist, yet no one, who is arrived at the age of maturity, can any longer be acquainted with it. It is true, nothing is more common than for people of the most advanced knowledge to have attained only an imperfect experience of many particular events; which naturally produces only an imperfect habit and transition : but then we must consider that the mind, having formed another observation concerning the connection of causes and effects, gives new force to its reasoning from that observation; and by means of it can build an argument on one single experiment, when duly prepared and examined. What we have found once to follow from any object, we conclude will for ever follow from it; and if this maxim be not always built upon as certain, it is not for want of a sufficient number of experiments, but because we frequently meet with instances to the contrary; which leads us to the second species of probability, where there is a *contrariety* in our experience and observation.

It would be very happy for men in the conduct of their

lives and actions, were the same objects always conjoined together, and we had nothing to fear but the mistakes of our own judgment, without having any reason to apprehend the uncertainty of nature. But as it is frequently found that one observation is contrary to another, and that causes and effects follow not in the same order, of which we have had experience, we are obliged to vary our reasoning on account of this uncertainty, and take into consideration the contrariety of events. The first question that occurs on this head is concerning the nature and causes of the contrariety.

The vulgar, who take things according to their first appearance, attribute the uncertainty of events to such an uncertainty in the causes, as makes them often fail of their usual influence, though they meet with no obstacle nor impediment in their operation. But philosophers observing that almost in every part of nature there is contained a vast variety of springs and principles, which are hid, by reason of their minuteness or remoteness, find that it is at least possible the contrariety of events may not proceed from any contingency in the cause, but from the secret operation of contrary causes. This possibility is converted into certainty by further observation, when they remark, that upon an exact scrutiny, a contrariety of effects always betrays a contrariety of causes, and proceeds from their mutual hinderance and opposition. A peasant can give no better reason for the stopping of any clock or watch than to say, that commonly it does not go right : but an artisan easily perceives that the same force in the spring or pendulum has always the same influence on the wheels; but fails of its usual effect, perhaps by reason of a grain of dust, which puts a stop to the whole movement. From the observation of several parallel instances, philosophers form a maxim, that the connection betwixt all causes and effects is equally necessary, and that its seeming uncertainty in some instances proceeds from the secret opposition of contrary causes.†

But however philosophers and the vulgar may differ in their explication of the contrariety of events, their inferences from it are always of the same kind, and founded on the same principles. A contrariety of events in the past may give us a kind of hesitating belief for the future, after two several ways. First, by producing an imperfect habit and transition from the present impression to the related idea. When the conjunction of any two objects is frequent, without being entirely constant, the mind is determined to pass from one object to the other; but not with so entire a habit as when the union is uninterrupted, and all the instances we have ever met with are uniform and of a piece. We find from common experience, in our actions as well as reasonings, that a constant perseverance in any course of life produces a strong inclination and tendency to continue for the future; though there are habits of inferior degrees of force, proportioned to the inferior degrees of steadiness and uniformity in our conduct.

There is no doubt but this principle sometimes takes place, and produces those inferences we draw from contrary phenomena; though I am persuaded that upon examination we shall not find it to be the principle that most commonly influences the mind in this species of reasoning. When we follow only the habitual determination of the mind, we make the transition without any reflection, and interpose not a moment's delay betwixt the view of one object, and the belief of that which is often found to attend it. As the custom depends not upon any deliberation, it operates immediately, without allowing any time for reflection. But this method of proceeding we have but few instances of in our probable reasonings; and even fewer than in those, which are derived from the uninterrupted conjunction of objects.[22] In the former species of reasoning we commonly take knowingly into consideration the contrariety of past events; we compare the different sides of the contrariety, and carefully weigh the experi-

[22] *Compare Part* III, *Sect.* VIII, *p.* 152.

ments, which we have on each side : whence we may conclude, that our reasonings of this kind arise not *directly*
from the habit, but in an *oblique* manner; which we must
now endeavour to explain.

It is evident that when an object is attended with contrary effects, we judge of them only by our past experience, and always consider those as possible, which we have
observed to follow from it. And as past experience regu-
lates our judgment concerning the possibility of these effects, so it does that concerning their probability; and that
effect, which has been the most common, we always esteem
the most likely. Here then are two things to be considered,
viz. the *reasons* which determine us to make the past a
standard for the future, and the *manner* how we extract a
single judgment from a contrariety of past events.

First we may observe, that the supposition, *that the
future resembles the past,* is not founded on arguments of
any kind, but is derived entirely from habit, by which we
are determined to expect for the future the same train of
objects to which we have been accustomed.[28] This habit or
determination to transfer the past to the future is full and
perfect; and consequently the first impulse of the imagination in this species of reasoning is endowed with the same
qualities.

But, *secondly,* when in considering past experiments we
find them of a contrary nature, this determination, though
full and perfect in itself, presents us with no steady object,
but offers us a number of disagreeing images in a certain
order and proportion. The first impulse therefore is here
broke into pieces, and diffuses itself over all those images,
of which each partakes an equal share of that force and
vivacity that is derived from the impulse. Any of these
past events may again happen; and we judge that when
they do happen, they will be mixed in the same proportion as in the past.

If our intention, therefore, be to consider the propor-

[28] *Compare Part* III, *Sect.* VI, *p.* 135.

tions of contrary events in a great number of instances, the images presented by our past experience must remain in their *first form*, and preserve their first proportions. Suppose, for instance, I have found by long observation that of twenty ships which go to sea, only nineteen return. Suppose I see at present twenty ships that leave the port : I transfer my past experience to the future, and represent to myself nineteen of these ships as returning in safety, and one as perishing. Concerning this there can be no difficulty. But as we frequently run over those several ideas of past events, in order to form a judgment concerning one single event, which appears uncertain; this consideration must change the *first form* of our ideas, and draw together the divided images presented by experience; since it is to *it* we refer the determination of that particular event, upon which we reason. Many of these images are supposed to concur, and a superior number to concur on one side. These agreeing images unite together, and render the idea more strong and lively, not only than a mere fiction of the imagination, but also than any idea, which is supported by a lesser number of experiments. Each new experiment is as a new stroke of the pencil, which bestows an additional vivacity on the colours, without either multiplying or enlarging the figure. This operation of the mind has been so fully explained in treating of the probability of chance, that I need not here endeavour to render it more intelligible. Every past experiment may be considered as a kind of chance; it being uncertain to us, whether the object will exist conformable to one experiment or another : and for this reason everything that has been said on the one subject is applicable to both.†

Thus, upon the whole, contrary experiments produce an imperfect belief, either by weakening the habit, or by dividing and afterwards joining in different parts, that *perfect* habit, which makes us conclude in general, that instances, of which we have no experience, must necessarily resemble those of which we have.

To justify still further this account of the second species of probability, where we reason with knowledge and reflection from a contrariety of past experiments, I shall propose the following considerations, without fearing to give offence by that air of subtilty which attends them. Just reasoning ought still, perhaps, to retain its force, however subtile; in the same manner as matter preserves its solidity in the air, and fire, and animal spirits, as well as in the grosser and more sensible forms.

First, we may observe, that there is no probability so great as not to allow of a contrary possibility; because otherwise it would cease to be a probability, and would become a certainty. That probability of causes, which is most extensive, and which we at present examine, depends on a contrariety of experiments; and it is evident an experiment in the past proves at least a possibility for the future.

Secondly, the component parts of this possibility and probability are of the same nature, and differ in number only, but not in kind. It has been observed, that all single chances are entirely equal, and that the only circumstance, which can give any event that is contingent a superiority over another, is a superior number of chances. In like manner, as the uncertainty of causes is discovered by experience, which presents us with a view of contrary events, it is plain that, when we transfer the past to the future, the known to the unknown, every past experiment has the same weight, and that it is only a superior number of them, which can throw the balance on any side. The possibility, therefore, which enters into every reasoning of this kind, is composed of parts, which are of the same nature both among themselves, and with those that compose the opposite probability.

Thirdly, we may establish it as a certain maxim, that in all moral as well as natural phenomena, wherever any cause consists of a number of parts, and the effect increases or diminishes, according to the variation of that number, the effect, properly speaking, is a compounded one, and arises from the union of the several effects, that proceed from each part of the cause. Thus, because the gravity of a body increases or diminishes by the increase or diminution of its parts, we conclude that each part contains this quality, and contributes to the gravity of the whole. The absence or presence of a part of the cause is attended with that of a proportionable part of the effect. This connection or constant conjunction sufficiently proves the one part to be the cause of the other. As the belief, which we have of any event, increases or diminishes according to the number of chances or past experiments, it is to be considered as a compounded effect, of which each part arises from a proportionable number of chances or experiments.

Let us now join these three observations, and see what conclusion we can draw from them. To every probability there is an opposite possibility. This possibility is composed of parts that are entirely of the same nature with those of the probability; and consequently have the same influence on the mind and understanding. The belief which attends the probability is a compounded effect, and is formed by the concurrence of the several effects, which proceed from each part of the probability. Since, therefore, each part of the probability contributes to the production of the belief, each part of the possibility must have the same influence on the opposite side; the nature of these parts being entirely the same. The contrary belief attending the possibility implies a view of a certain object, as well as the probability does an opposite view. In this particular both these degrees of belief are alike. The only manner then, in which the superior number of similar component parts in the one can exert its influence, and prevail above the inferior in the other, is by producing a stronger and more lively view of its object. Each part presents a particular view; and all these views uniting together produce one general view, which is fuller and more distinct by the greater number of causes or principles from which it is derived.

The component parts of the probability and possibility

being alike in their nature, must produce like effects; and the likeness of their effects consists in this, that each of them presents a view of a particular object. But though these parts be alike in their nature, they are very different in their quantity and number; and this difference must appear in the effect as well as the similarity. Now as the view they present is in both cases full and entire, and comprehends the object in all its parts, it is impossible that in this particular there can be any difference; nor is there anything but a superior vivacity in the probability, arising from the concurrence of a superior number of views, which can distinguish these effects.

Here is almost the same argument in a different light. All our reasonings concerning the probability of causes are founded on the transferring of past to future. The transferring of any past experiment to the future is sufficient to give us a view of the object; whether that experiment be single or combined with others of the same kind; whether it be entire, or opposed by others of a contrary kind. Suppose then it acquires both these qualities of combination and opposition, it loses not, upon that account, its former power of presenting a view of the object, but only concurs with and opposes other experiments that have a like influence. A question, therefore, may arise concerning the manner both of the concurrence and opposition. As to the *concurrence* there is only the choice left betwixt these two hypotheses. *First*, that the view of the object, occasioned by the transference of each past experiment, preserves itself entire, and only multiplies the number of views. Or, *secondly*, that it runs into the other similar and correspondent views, and gives them a superior degree of force and vivacity. But that the first hypothesis is erroneous is evident from experience, which informs us that the belief attending any reasoning consists in one conclusion, not in a multitude of similar ones, which would only distract the mind, and in many cases would be too numerous to be comprehended distinctly by any finite capacity. It remains, therefore, as the only reasonable opinion, that these similar views run into each other and unite their forces; so as to produce a stronger and clearer view than what arises from any one alone. This is the manner in which past experiments concur when they are transferred to any future event. As to the manner of their *opposition*, it is evident, that as the contrary views are incompatible with each other, and it is impossible the object can at once exist conformable to both of them, their influence becomes mutually destructive, and the mind is determined to the superior only with that force which remains after subtracting the inferior.

I am sensible how abstruse all this reasoning must appear to the generality of readers, who, not being accustomed to such profound reflections on the intellectual faculties of the mind, will be apt to reject as chimerical whatever strikes not in with the common received notions, and with the easiest and most obvious principles of philosophy. And no doubt there are some pains required to enter into these arguments; though perhaps very little are necessary to perceive the imperfection of every vulgar hypothesis on this subject, and the little light, which philosophy can yet afford us in such sublime and such curious speculations. Let men be once fully persuaded of these two principles, *that there is nothing in any object, considered in itself, which can afford us a reason for drawing a conclusion beyond it;* and, *that even after the observation of the frequent or constant conjunction of objects, we have no reason to draw any inference concerning any object beyond those of which we have had experience;* I say, let men be once fully convinced of these two principles, and this will throw them so loose from all common systems, that they will make no difficulty of receiving any, which may appear the most extraordinary. These principles we have found to be sufficiently convincing, even with regard to our most certain reasonings from causation : but I shall venture to affirm, that with regard to these conjectural or probable reasonings they still acquire a new degree of evidence.

First, it is obvious that in reasonings of this kind it is not the object presented to us, which, considered in itself, affords us any reason to draw a conclusion concerning any other object or event. For as this latter object is supposed uncertain, and as the uncertainty is derived from a concealed contrariety of causes in the former, were any of the causes placed in the known qualities of that object, they would no longer be concealed, nor would our conclusion be uncertain.

But, *secondly,* it is equally obvious in this species of reasoning, that if the transference of the past to the future were founded merely on a conclusion of the understanding, it could never occasion any belief or assurance. When we transfer contrary experiments to the future, we can only repeat these contrary experiments with their particular proportions; which could not produce assurance in any single event upon which we reason, unless the fancy melted together all those images that concur, and extracted from them one single idea or image, which is intense and lively in proportion to the number of experiments from which it is derived, and their superiority above their antagonists. Our past experience presents no determinate object; and as our belief, however faint, fixes itself on a determinate object, it is evident that the belief arises not merely from the transference of past to future, but from some operation of the *fancy* conjoined with it. This may lead us to conceive the manner in which that faculty enters into all our reasonings.

I shall conclude this subject with two reflections which may deserve our attention. The *first* may be explained after this manner. When the mind forms a reasoning concerning any matter of fact, which is only probable, it casts its eye backward upon past experience, and transferring it to the future, is presented with so many contrary views of its object, of which those that are of the same kind uniting together and running into one act of the mind, serve to fortify and enliven it. But suppose that this multitude of views or glimpses of an object proceeds not from experience, but from a voluntary act of the imagination; this effect does not follow, or at least follows not in the same degree. For though custom and education produce belief by such a repetition as is not derived from experience, yet this requires a long tract of time, along with a very frequent and *undesigned* repetition. In general we may pronounce that a person, who would *voluntarily* repeat any idea in his mind, though supported by one past experience, would be no more inclined to believe the existence of its object, than if he had contented himself with one survey of it. Beside the effect of design, each act of the mind, being separate and independent, has a separate influence, and joins not its force with that of its fellows. Not being united by any common object producing them, they have no relation to each other; and consequently make no transition or union of forces. This phenomenon we shall understand better afterwards.

My *second* reflection is founded on those large probabilities which the mind can judge of, and the minute differences it can observe betwixt them. When the chances or experiments on one side amount to ten thousand, and on the other to ten thousand and one, the judgment gives the preference to the latter on account of that superiority; though it is plainly impossible for the mind to run over every particular view, and distinguish the superior vivacity of the image arising from the superior number, where the difference is so inconsiderable. We have a parallel instance in the affections. It is evident, according to the principles above mentioned, that when an object produces any passion in us, which varies according to the different quantity of the object; I say, it is evident, that the passion, properly speaking, is not a simple emotion, but a compounded one, of a great number of weaker passions, derived from a view of each part of the object; for otherwise it were impossible the passion should increase by the increase of these parts. Thus a man, who desires a thousand pounds, has in reality a thousand or more desires, which uniting together, seem to make only one passion;

though the composition evidently betrays itself upon every alteration of the object, by the preference he gives to the larger number, if superior only by an unit. Yet nothing can be more certain than that so small a difference would not be discernible in the passions, nor could render them distinguishable from each other. The difference, therefore, of our conduct in preferring the greater number depends not upon our passions, but upon custom and *general rules*. We have found in a multitude of instances that the augmenting the numbers of any sum augments the passion, where the numbers are precise and the difference sensible. The mind can perceive, from its immediate feeling, that three guineas produce a greater passion than two; and *this* it transfers to larger numbers, because of the resemblance; and by a general rule assigns to a thousand guineas a stronger passion than to nine hundred and ninety-nine. These general rules we shall explain presently.

But besides these two species of probability, which are derived from an *imperfect* experience and from *contrary* causes, there is a third arising from *analogy,* which differs from them in some material circumstances. According to the hypothesis above explained, all kinds of reasoning from causes or effects are founded on two particulars, viz. the constant conjunction of any two objects in all past experience, and the resemblance of a present object to any one of them. The effect of these two particulars is, that the present object invigorates and enlivens the imagination; and the resemblance, along with the constant union, conveys this force and vivacity to the related idea; which we are therefore said to believe or assent to. If you weaken either the union or resemblance, you weaken the principle of transition, and of consequence that belief which arises from it. The vivacity of the first impression cannot be fully conveyed to the related idea, either where the conjunction of their objects is not constant, or where the present impression does not perfectly resemble any of those whose union we are accustomed to observe. In those probabilities of chance and causes above explained, it is the constancy of the union which is diminished; and in the probability derived from analogy, it is the resemblance only which is affected. Without some degree of resemblance, as well as union, it is impossible there can be any reasoning. But as this resemblance admits of many different degrees, the reasoning becomes proportionably more or less firm and certain. An experiment loses of its force when transferred to instances which are not exactly resembling; though it is evident it may still retain as much as may be the foundation of probability, as long as there is any resemblance remaining.

SECTION XIII

OF UNPHILOSOPHICAL PROBABILITY

All these kinds of probability are received by philosophers, and allowed to be reasonable foundations of belief and opinion. But there are others that are derived from the same principles, though they have not had the good fortune to obtain the same sanction. The *first* probability of this kind may be accounted for thus. The diminution of the union and of the resemblance, as above explained, diminishes the facility of the transition, and by that means weakens the evidence; and we may further observe, that the same diminution of the evidence will follow from a diminution of the impression, and from the shading of those colours under which it appears to the memory or senses. The argument which we found on any matter of fact we remember is more or less convincing, according as the fact is recent or remote; and though the difference in these degrees of evidence be not received by philosophy as solid and legitimate; because in that case an argument must have a different force to-day from what it shall have a month hence; yet, notwithstanding the opposition of philosophy, it is certain this circumstance has a considerable influence on the understanding, and secretly changes the authority of the same argument, according to the different times in which it is proposed to us. A greater force and vivacity in the impression naturally conveys a greater to the related idea; and it is on the degrees of force and vivacity that the belief depends, according to the foregoing system.

There is a *second* difference which we may frequently observe in our degrees of belief and assurance, and which never fails to take place, though disclaimed by philosophers. An experiment that is recent and fresh in the memory affects us more than one that is in some measure obliterated; and has a superior influence on the judgment as well as on the passions. A lively impression produces more assurance than a faint one, because it has more original force to communicate to the related idea, which thereby acquires a greater force and vivacity. A recent observation has a like effect; because the custom and transition is there more entire, and preserves better the original force in the communication. Thus a drunkard, who has seen his companion die of a debauch, is struck with that instance for some time, and dreads a like accident for himself; but as the memory of it decays away by degrees, his former security returns, and the danger seems less certain and real.

I add, as a *third* instance of this kind, that though our reasonings from proofs and from probabilities be considerably different from each other, yet the former species of reasoning often degenerates insensibly into the latter, by nothing but the multitude of connected arguments. It is certain that when an inference is drawn immediately from an object, without any intermediate cause or effect, the conviction is much stronger and the persuasion more lively, than when the imagination is carried through a long chain of connected arguments, however infallible the connection of each link may be esteemed. It is from the original impression that the vivacity of all the ideas is derived, by means of the customary transition of the imagination; and it is evident this vivacity must gradually decay in proportion to the distance, and must lose somewhat in each transition. Sometimes this distance has a greater influence than even contrary experiments would have; and a man may receive a more lively conviction from a probable reasoning which is close and immediate, than from a long chain of consequences, though just and conclusive in each part. Nay, it is seldom such reasonings produce any conviction; and one must have a very strong and firm imagination to preserve the evidence to the end, where it passes through so many stages.

But here it may not be amiss to remark a very curious phenomenon which the present subject suggests to us. It is evident there is no point of ancient history, of which we can have any assurance, but by passing through many millions of causes and effects, and through a chain of arguments of almost an immeasurable length. Before the knowledge of the fact could come to the first historian, it must be conveyed through many mouths; and after it is committed to writing, each new copy is a new object, of which the connection with the foregoing is known only by experience and observation. Perhaps therefore it may be concluded, from the precedent reasoning, that the evidence of all ancient history must now be lost, or at least will be lost in time, as the chain of causes increases, and runs on to a greater length. But as it seems contrary to common sense to think, that if the republic of letters and the art of printing continue on the same footing as at present, our posterity, even after a thousand ages, can ever doubt if there has been such a man as Julius Cæsar; this may be considered as an objection to the present system. If belief consisted only in a certain vivacity, conveyed from an original impression, it would decay by the length of the transition, and must at last be utterly extinguished. And, *vice versa,* if belief, on some occasions, be not capable of such an extinction, it must be something different from that vivacity.

Before I answer this objection I shall observe, that from this topic there has been borrowed a very celebrated argument against the *Christian Religion;* but with this difference, that the connection betwixt each link of the chain in human testimony has been there supposed not to go beyond probability, and to be liable to a degree of doubt and uncertainty. And indeed it must be confessed, that in this manner of considering the subject (which however is not a true one), there is no history or tradition but what must in the end lose all its force and evidence. Every new probability diminishes the original conviction; and however great that conviction may be supposed, it is impossible it can subsist under such reiterated diminutions. This is true in general, though we shall find afterwards,[24] that there is one very memorable exception, which is of vast consequence in the present subject of the understanding.

Meanwhile, to give a solution of the preceding objection upon the supposition that historical evidence amounts at first to an entire proof, let us consider that, though the links are innumerable that connect any original fact with the present impression, which is the foundation of belief, yet they are all of the same kind, and depend on the fidelity of printers and copyists. One edition passes into another, and that into a third, and so on, till we come to that volume we peruse at present. There is no variation in the steps. After we know one, we know all of them; and after we have made one, we can have no scruple as to the rest. This circumstance alone preserves the evidence of history, and will perpetuate the memory of the present age to the latest posterity. If all the long chain of causes and effects, which connect any past event with any volume of history, were composed of parts different from each other, and which it were necessary for the mind distinctly to conceive, it is impossible we should preserve to the end any

[24] Part IV, Sect. I.

belief or evidence. But as most of these proofs are perfectly resembling, the mind runs easily along them, jumps from one part to another with facility, and forms but a confused and general notion of each link. By this means a long chain of argument has as little effect in diminishing the original vivacity, as a much shorter would have if composed of parts which were different from each other, and of which each required a distinct consideration.

A fourth unphilosophical species of probability is that derived from *general rules,* which we rashly form to ourselves, and which are the source of what we properly call *prejudice.* An Irishman cannot have wit, and a Frenchman cannot have solidity; for which reason, though the conversation of the former in any instance be visibly very agreeable, and of the latter very judicious, we have entertained such a prejudice against them, that they must be dunces or fops in spite of sense and reason. Human nature is very subject to errors of this kind, and perhaps this nation as much as any other.

Should it be demanded why men form general rules, and allow them to influence their judgment, even contrary to present observation and experience, I should reply, that in my opinion it proceeds from those very principles on which all judgments concerning causes and effects depend. Our judgments concerning cause and effect are derived from habit and experience; and when we have been accustomed to see one object united to another, our imagination passes from the first to the second by a natural transition, which precedes reflection, and which cannot be prevented by it. Now, it is the nature of custom not only to operate with its full force, when objects are presented that are exactly the same with those to which we have been accustomed, but also to operate in an inferior degree when we discover such as are similar; and though the habit loses somewhat of its force by every difference, yet it is seldom entirely destroyed where any considerable circumstances remain the same. A man who has contracted a custom of eating fruit by the use of pears or peaches, will satisfy himself with melons where he cannot find his favourite fruit; as one, who has become a drunkard by the use of red wines, will be carried almost with the same violence to white, if presented to him. From this principle I have accounted for that species of probability, derived from analogy, where we transfer our experience in past instances to objects which are resembling, but are not exactly the same with those concerning which we have had experience. In proportion as the resemblance decays, the probability diminishes, but still has some force as long as there remain any traces of the resemblance.

This observation we may carry further, and may remark, that though custom be the foundation of all our judgments, yet sometimes it has an effect on the imagination in opposition to the judgment, and produces a contrariety in our sentiments concerning the same object. I explain myself. In almost all kinds of causes there is a complication of circumstances, of which some are essential, and others superfluous; some are absolutely requisite to the production of the effect, and others are only conjoined by accident. Now we may observe, that when these superfluous circumstances are numerous and remarkable, and frequently conjoined with the essential, they have such an influence on the imagination, that even in the absence of the latter they carry us on to the conception of the usual effect, and give to that conception a force and vivacity which make it superior to the mere fictions of the fancy. We may correct this propensity by a reflection on the nature of those circumstances; but it is still certain that custom takes the start, and gives a bias to the imagination.

To illustrate this by a familiar instance, let us consider the case of a man, who being hung out from a high tower in a cage of iron cannot forbear trembling when he surveys the precipice below him, though he knows himself to be perfectly secure from falling, by his experience of the solidity of the iron which supports him, and though the ideas of fall and descent, and harm and death, be derived solely from custom and experience. The same custom goes beyond the instances from which it is derived, and to which it perfectly corresponds; and influences his ideas of such objects as are in some respect resembling, but fall not precisely under the same rule. The circumstances of depth and descent strike so strongly upon him, that their influence cannot be destroyed by the contrary circumstances of support and solidity, which ought to give him a perfect security. His imagination runs away with its object, and excites a passion proportioned to it. That passion returns back upon the imagination, and enlivens the idea; which lively idea has a new influence on the passion, and in its turn augments its force and violence; and both his fancy and affections, thus mutually supporting each other, cause the whole to have a very great influence upon him.

But why need we seek for other instances, while the present subject of philosophical[25] probabilities offers us so obvious a one, in the opposition betwixt the judgment and imagination, arising from these effects of custom? According to my system, all reasonings are nothing but the effects of custom, and custom has no influence, but by enlivening the imagination, and giving us a strong conception of any object. It may therefore be concluded,[26] that our judgment and imagination can never be contrary, and that custom cannot operate on the latter faculty after such a manner, as to render it opposite to the former. This difficulty we can remove after no other manner than by supposing the influence of general rules. We shall afterwards[27] take notice of some general rules, by which we ought to regulate our judgment concerning causes and effects; and these rules are formed on the nature of our understanding, and on our experience of its operations in the judgments we form concerning objects. By them we learn to distinguish the accidental circumstances from the

[25] *This may be a misprint in the original edition for " unphilosophical."*
[26] *Sc. by an invalid argument or unphilosophical probability.*
[27] Sect. 15.

efficacious causes; and when we find that an effect can be produced without the concurrence of any particular circumstance, we conclude that that circumstance makes not a part of the efficacious cause, however frequently conjoined with it. But as this frequent conjunction necessarily makes it have some effect on the imagination, in spite of the opposite conclusion from general rules, the opposition of these two principles produces a contrariety in our thoughts, and causes us to ascribe the one inference to our judgment, and the other to our imagination. The general rule is attributed to our judgment, as being more extensive and constant; the exception to the imagination, as being more capricious and uncertain.

Thus our general rules are in a manner set in opposition to each other. When an object appears, that resembles any cause in very considerable circumstances, the imagination naturally carries us to a lively conception of the usual effect, though the object be different in the most material and most efficacious circumstances from that cause. Here is the first influence of general rules. But when we take a review of this act of the mind, and compare it with the more general and authentic operations of the understanding, we find it to be of an irregular nature, and destructive of all the most established principles of reasonings, which is the cause of our rejecting it.† This is a second influence of general rules, and implies the condemnation of the former. Sometimes the one, sometimes the other prevails, according to the disposition and character of the person. The vulgar are commonly guided by the first, and wise men by the second. Meanwhile the sceptics may here have the pleasure of observing a new and signal contradiction in our reason, and of seeing all philosophy ready to be subverted by a principle of human nature, and again saved by a new direction of the very same principle. The following of general rules is a very unphilosophical species of probability; and yet it is only by following them that we can correct this, and all other unphilosophical probabilities.

Since we have instances where general rules operate on

the imagination, even contrary to the judgment, we need not be surprised to see their effects increase, when conjoined with that latter faculty, and to observe that they bestow on the ideas they present to us a force superior to what attends any other. Every one knows there is an indirect manner of insinuating praise or blame, which is much less shocking than the open flattery or censure of any person. However he may communicate his sentiments by such secret insinuations, and make them known with equal certainty as by the open discovery of them, it is certain that their influence is not equally strong and powerful. One who lashes me with concealed strokes of satire, moves not my indignation to such a degree, as if he flatly told me I was a fool and a coxcomb; though I equally understand his meaning as if he did. This difference is to be attributed to the influence of general rules.

Whether a person openly abuses me, or slily intimates his contempt, in neither case do I immediately perceive his sentiment or opinion; and it is only by signs, that is, by its effects, I become sensible of it. The only difference then, betwixt these two cases consists in this, that in the open discovery of his sentiments he makes use of signs, which are general and universal; and in the secret intimation employs such as are more singular and uncommon. The effect of this circumstance is, that the imagination, in running from the present impression to the absent idea, makes the transition with greater facility, and consequently conceives the object with greater force, where the connection is common and universal, than where it is more rare and particular. Accordingly, we may observe, that the open declaration of our sentiments is called the taking off the mask, as the secret intimation of our opinions is said to be the veiling of them. The difference betwixt an idea produced by a general connection, and that arising from a particular one, is here compared to the difference betwixt an impression and an idea. This difference in the imagination has a suitable effect on the passions, and this effect is augmented by another circumstance. A secret intimation of anger or contempt shows that we still have some consideration for the person, and avoid the directly abusing him. This makes a concealed satire less disagreeable, but still this depends on the same principle. For if an idea were not more feeble, when only intimated, it would never be esteemed a mark of greater respect to proceed in this method than in the other.

Sometimes scurrility is less displeasing than delicate satire, because it revenges us in a manner for the injury at the very time it is committed, by affording us a just reason to blame and contemn the person who injures us. But this phenomenon likewise depends upon the same principle. For why do we blame all gross and injurious language, unless it be because we esteem it contrary to good breeding and humanity? And why is it contrary, unless it be more shocking than any delicate satire? The rules of good breeding condemn whatever is openly disobliging, and gives a sensible pain and confusion to those with whom we converse. After this is once established, abusive language is universally blamed, and gives less pain upon account of its coarseness and incivility, which render the person despicable that employs it. It becomes less disagreeable, merely because originally it is more so; and it is more disagreeable, because it affords an inference by general and common rules that are palpable and undeniable.

To this explication of the different influence of open and concealed flattery or satire, I shall add the consideration of another phenomenon, which is analogous to it. There are many particulars in the point of honour, both of men and women, whose violations, when open and avowed, the world never excuses, but which it is more apt to overlook, when the appearances are saved, and the transgression is secret and concealed. Even those who know with equal certainty that the fault is committed, pardon it more easily, when the proofs seem in some measure oblique and equivocal, than when they are direct and undeniable. The same idea is presented in both cases, and, properly speaking, is equally assented to by the judgment; and yet its influence is different, because of the different manner in which it is presented.

Now, if we compare these two cases, of the *open* and *concealed* violations of the laws of honour, we shall find that the difference betwixt them consists in this, that in the first case the sign, from which we infer the blamable action, is single, and suffices alone to be the foundation of our reasoning and judgment; whereas in the latter the signs are numerous, and decide little or nothing when alone and unaccompanied with many minute circumstances, which are almost imperceptible. But it is certainly true, that any reasoning is always the more convincing the more single and united it is to the eye, and the less exercise it gives to the imagination to collect all its parts, and run from them to the correlative idea, which forms the conclusion. The labour of the thoughts disturbs the regular progress of the sentiments, as we shall observe presently.[28] The idea strikes not on us with such vivacity, and consequently has no such influence on the passion and imagination.

From the same principles we may account for those observations of the Cardinal de Retz, *that there are many things in which the world wishes to be deceived,* and *that it more easily excuses a person in acting than in talking contrary to the decorum of his profession and character.* A fault in words is commonly more open and distinct than one in actions, which admit of many palliating excuses, and decide not so clearly concerning the attention and views of the actor.

Thus it appears, upon the whole, that every kind of opinion or judgment which amounts not to knowledge, is derived entirely from the force and vivacity of the perception, and that these qualities constitute in the mind what we call the *belief* of the existence of any object. This force and this vivacity are most conspicuous in the memory; and therefore our confidence in the veracity of that faculty is

[28] Part iv, Sect. i.

the greatest imaginable, and equals in many respects the assurance of a demonstration. The next degree of these qualities is that derived from the relation of cause and effect; and this too is very great, especially when the conjunction is found by experience to be perfectly constant, and when the object, which is present to us, exactly resembles those of which we have had experience. But below this degree of evidence there are many others which have an influence on the passions and imagination, proportioned to that degree of force and vivacity which they communicate to the ideas. It is by habit we make the transition from cause to effect; and it is from some present impression we borrow that vivacity which we diffuse over the correlative idea. But when we have not observed a sufficient number of instances to produce a strong habit; or when these instances are contrary to each other; or when the resemblance is not exact; or the present impression is faint and obscure; or the experience in some measure obliterated from the memory; or the connection dependent on a long chain of objects; or the inference derived from general rules, and yet not conformable to them: in all these cases the evidence diminishes by the diminution of the force and intenseness of the idea. This therefore is the nature of the judgment and probability.

What principally gives authority to this system is, beside the undoubted arguments, upon which each part is founded, the agreement of these parts, and the necessity of one to explain another. The belief which attends our memory is of the same nature with that which is derived from our judgments: nor is there any difference betwixt that judgment which is derived from a constant and uniform connection of causes and effects, and that which depends upon an interrupted and uncertain. It is indeed evident, that in all determinations where the mind decides from contrary experiments, it is first divided within itself, and has an inclination to either side in proportion to the number of experiments we have seen and remember. This contest is at last determined to the advantage of that side where we observe a superior number of these experiments; but still with a diminution of force in the evidence correspondent to the number of the opposite experiments. Each possibility, of which the probability is composed, operates separately upon the imagination; and it is the larger collection of possibilities which at last prevails, and that with a force proportionable to its superiority. All these phenomena lead directly to the precedent system; nor will it ever be possible upon any other principles to give a satisfactory and consistent explication of them. Without considering these judgments as the effects of custom on the imagination, we shall lose ourselves in perpetual contradiction and absurdity.

SECTION XIV

OF THE IDEA OF NECESSARY CONNECTION

Having thus explained the manner *in which we reason beyond our immediate impressions, and conclude that such particular causes must have such particular effects;* we must now return upon our footsteps to examine that question[29] which first occurred to us, and which we dropped in our way, viz. *What is our idea of necessity, when we say that two objects are necessarily connected together?* Upon this head I repeat, what I have often had occasion to observe, that as we have no idea that is not derived from an impression, we must find some impression that gives rise to this idea of necessity, if we assert we have really such an idea. In order to do this, I consider in what objects necessity is commonly supposed to lie; and finding that it is always ascribed to causes and effects, I turn my eye to two objects supposed to be placed in that relation, and examine them in all the situations of which they are susceptible. I immediately perceive that they are *contiguous* in time and

[29] Sect. 2.

place, and that the object we call cause *precedes* the other we call effect. In no one instance can I go any further, nor is it possible for me to discover any third relation betwixt these objects. I therefore enlarge my view to comprehend several instances, where I find like objects always existing in like relations of contiguity and succession. At first sight this seems to serve but little to my purpose. The reflection on several instances only repeats the same objects; and therefore can never give rise to a new idea. But upon further inquiry I find that the repetition is not in every particular the same, but produces a new impression, and by that means the idea which I at present examine. For after a frequent repetition, I find that upon the appearance of one of the objects the mind is *determined* by custom to consider its usual attendant, and to consider it in a stronger light upon account of its relation to the first object. It is this impression, then, or *determination,* which affords me the idea of necessity.

I doubt not but these consequences will at first sight be received without difficulty, as being evident deductions from principles which we have already established, and which we have often employed in our reasonings. This evidence, both in the first principles and in the deductions, may seduce us unwarily into the conclusion, and make us imagine it contains nothing extraordinary, nor worthy of our curiosity. But though such an inadvertence may facilitate the reception of this reasoning, it will make it be the more easily forgot; for which reason I think it proper to give warning, that I have just now examined one of the most sublime questions in philosophy, viz. *that concerning the power and efficacy of causes* where all the sciences seem so much interested. Such a warning will naturally rouse up the attention of the reader, and make him desire a more full account of my doctrine, as well as of the arguments on which it is founded. This request is so reasonable that I cannot refuse complying with it; especially as I am hopeful that these principles, the more they are examined, will acquire the more force and evidence.

There is no question which, on account of its importance, as well as difficulty, has caused more disputes both among ancient and modern philosophers, than this concerning the efficacy of causes, or that quality which makes them be followed by their effects. But before they entered upon these disputes, methinks it would not have been improper to have examined what idea we have of that efficacy, which is the subject of the controversy. This is what I find principally wanting in their reasonings, and what I shall here endeavour to supply.

I begin with observing that the terms of *efficacy, agency, power, force, energy, necessity, connection,* and *productive quality,* are all nearly synonymous; and therefore it is an absurdity to employ any of them in defining the rest. By this observation we reject at once all the vulgar definitions which philosophers have given of power and efficacy; and instead of searching for the ideas in these definitions, must look for it in the impressions from which it is originally derived. If it be a compound idea, it must arise from compound impressions. If simple, from simple impressions.

I believe the most general and most popular explication of this matter, is to say,[30] that finding from experience that there are several new productions in matter, such as the motions and variations of body, and concluding that there must somewhere be a power capable of producing them, we arrive at last by this reasoning at the idea of power and efficacy. But to be convinced that this explication is more popular than philosophical, we need but reflect on two very obvious principles. *First,* that reason alone can never give rise to any original idea; and, *secondly,* that reason, as distinguished from experience, can never make us conclude that a cause or productive quality is absolutely requisite to every beginning of existence. Both these considerations have been sufficiently explained; and therefore shall not at present be any further insisted on.

I shall only infer from them, that since reason can never

[30] See Mr. Locke: chapter of Power. (*Essay Concerning the Human Understanding. Ed.*)

give rise to the idea of efficacy, that idea must be derived from experience, and from some particular instances of this efficacy, which make their passage into the mind by the common channels of sensation or reflection. Ideas always represent their objects or impressions; and *vice versa,* there are some objects necessary to give rise to every idea. If we pretend, therefore, to have any just idea of this efficacy, we must produce some instance wherein the efficacy is plainly discoverable to the mind, and its operations obvious to our consciousness or sensation. By the refusal of this, we acknowledge that the idea is impossible and imaginary; since the principle of innate ideas, which alone can save us from this dilemma, has been already refuted, and is now almost universally rejected in the learned world. Our present business, then, must be to find some natural production, where the operation and efficacy of a cause can be clearly conceived and comprehended by the mind, without any danger of obscurity or mistake.

In this research we meet with very little encouragement from that prodigious diversity which is found in the opinions of those philosophers who have pretended to explain the secret force and energy of causes.[31] There are some who maintain that bodies operate by their substantial form; others, by their accidents or qualities; several, by their matter and form; some, by their form and accidents; others, by certain virtues and faculties distinct from all this. All these sentiments, again, are mixed and varied in a thousand different ways, and form a strong presumption that none of them have any solidity or evidence, and that the supposition of an efficacy in any of the known qualities of matter is entirely without foundation. This presumption must increase upon us when we consider that these principles of substantial forms, and accidents, and faculties, are not in reality any of the known properties of bodies, but are perfectly unintelligible and inexplicable. For it is

[31] See Father Malebranche, Book VI, *Part* II, Chap. 3, and the illustrations upon it. (*Recherche de la Verité.*)

evident philosophers would never have had recourse to such obscure and uncertain principles, had they met with any satisfaction in such as are clear and intelligible; especially in such an affair as this, which must be an object of the simplest understanding, if not of the senses. Upon the whole, we may conclude that it is impossible, in any one instance, to show the principle in which the force and agency of a cause is placed; and that the most refined and most vulgar understandings are equally at a loss in this particular. If any one think proper to refute this assertion, he need not put himself to the trouble of inventing any long reasonings, but may at once show us an instance of a cause where we discover the power or operating principle. This defiance we are obliged frequently to make use of, as being almost the only means of proving a negative in philosophy.

The small success which has been met with in all the attempts to fix this power, has at last obliged philosophers to conclude that the ultimate force and efficacy of nature is perfectly unknown to us, and that it is in vain we search for it in all the known qualities of matter. In this opinion they are almost unanimous; and it is only in the inference they draw from it that they discover any difference in their sentiments. For some of them, as the Cartesians in particular, having established it as a principle that we are perfectly acquainted with the essence of matter, have very naturally inferred that it is endowed with no efficacy, and that it is impossible for it of itself to communicate motion, or produce any of those effects which we ascribe to it. As the essence of matter consists in extension, and as extension implies not actual motion, but only mobility; they conclude that the energy which produces the motion cannot lie in the extension.

This conclusion leads them into another, which they regard as perfectly unavoidable. Matter, say they, is in itself entirely unactive and deprived of any power by which it may produce, or continue, or communicate motion : but since these effects are evident to our senses, and since the power that produces them must be placed somewhere, it must lie in the Deity, or that Divine Being who contains in his nature all excellency and perfection. It is the Deity, therefore, who is the prime mover of the universe, and who not only first created matter, and gave it its original impulse, but likewise, by a continued exertion of omnipotence, supports its existence, and successively bestows on it all those motions, and configurations, and qualities, with which it is endowed.

This opinion is certainly very curious, and well worth our attention; but it will appear superfluous to examine it in this place, if we reflect a moment on our present purpose in taking notice of it. We have established it as a principle, that as all ideas are derived from impressions, or some precedent *perceptions*, it is impossible we can have any idea of power and efficacy, unless some instances can be produced, wherein this power *is perceived* to exert itself. Now as these instances can never be discovered in body, the Cartesians, proceeding upon their principle of innate ideas, have had recourse to a Supreme Spirit or Deity, whom they consider as the only active being in the universe, and as the immediate cause of every alteration in matter. But the principle of innate ideas being allowed to be false, it follows, that the supposition of a Deity can serve us in no stead, in accounting for that idea of agency, which we search for in vain in all the objects which are presented to our senses, or which we are internally conscious of in our own minds. For if every idea be derived from an impression, the idea of a Deity proceeds from the same origin; and if no impression, either of sensation or reflection, implies any force or efficacy, it is equally impossible to discover or even imagine any such active principle in the Deity. Since these philosophers, therefore, have concluded that matter cannot be endowed with any efficacious principle, because it is impossible to discover in it such a principle, the same course of reasoning should determine them to exclude it from the Supreme Being. Or if they esteem that opinion absurd and impious, as it really is, I shall tell them how they may avoid it; and that is, by concluding from the very first, that they have no adequate idea of power or efficacy in any object; since neither in body nor spirit, neither in superior nor inferior natures are they able to discover one single instance of it.

The same conclusion is unavoidable upon the hypothesis of those who maintain the efficacy of second causes, and attribute a derivative, but a real power and energy to matter. For as they confess that this energy lies not in any of the known qualities of matter, the difficulty still remains concerning the origin of its idea. If we have really an idea of power, we may attribute power to an unknown quality: but as it is impossible that that idea can be derived from such a quality, and as there is nothing in known qualities which can produce it, it follows that we deceive ourselves when we imagine we are possessed of any idea of this kind, after the manner we commonly understand it. All ideas are derived from and represent impressions. We never have any impression that contains any power or efficacy. We never therefore have any idea of power.

[Some have asserted that we feel an energy or power in our own mind; and that having in this manner acquired the idea of power, we transfer that quality to matter, where we are not able immediately to discover it. The motions of our body, and the thoughts and sentiments of our mind (say they) obey the will; nor do we seek any further to acquire a just notion of force or power. But to convince us how fallacious this reasoning is, we need only consider, that the will being here considered as a cause has no more a discoverable connection with its effects than any material cause has with its proper effect. So far from perceiving the connection betwixt an act of volition and a motion of the body, it is allowed that no effect is more inexplicable from the powers and essence of thought and matter.

Nor is the empire of the will over our mind more intelligible. The effect is there distinguishable and separable from the cause, and could not be foreseen without the experience of their constant conjunction. We have command over our mind to a certain degree, but beyond *that* lose all empire over it : and it is evidently impossible to fix any precise bounds to our authority, where we consult not experience. In short, the actions of the mind are, in this respect, the same with those of matter. We perceive only their constant conjunction; nor can we ever reason beyond it. No internal impression has an apparent energy, more than external objects have. Since, therefore, matter is confessed by philosophers to operate by an unknown force, we should in vain hope to attain an idea of force by consulting our own minds.[32]]†

It has been established as a certain principle, that general or abstract ideas are nothing but individual ones taken in a certain light, and that, in reflecting on any object, it is as impossible to exclude from our thought all particular degrees of quantity and quality as from the real nature of things. If we be possessed, therefore, of any idea of power in general, we must also be able to conceive some particular species of it; and as power cannot subsist alone, but is always regarded as an attribute of some being or existence, we must be able to place this power in some particular being, and conceive that being as endowed with a real force and energy, by which such a particular effect necessarily results from its operation. We must distinctly and particularly conceive the connection betwixt the cause and effect, and be able to pronounce, from a simple view of the one, that it must be followed or preceded by the other. This is the true manner of conceiving a partic-

---

[32] The same imperfection attends our ideas of the Deity; but this can have no effect either on religion or morals. The order of the universe proves an omnipotent mind; that is, a mind whose will is *constantly attended* with the obedience of every creature and being. Nothing more is requisite to give a foundation to all the articles of religion; nor is it necessary we should form a distinct idea of the force and energy of the Supreme Being.

ular power in a particular body : and a general idea being impossible without an individual; where the latter is impossible, it is certain the former can never exist. Now nothing is more evident than that the human mind cannot form such an idea of two objects, as to conceive any connection betwixt them, or comprehend distinctly that power or efficacy by which they are united. Such a connection would amount to a demonstration, and would imply the absolute impossibility for the one object not to follow, or to be conceived not to follow upon the other : which kind of connection has already been rejected in all cases. If any one is of a contrary opinion, and thinks he has attained a notion of power in any particular object, I desire he may point out to me that object. But till I meet with such a one, which I despair of, I cannot forbear concluding, that since we can never distinctly conceive how any particular power can possibly reside in any particular object, we deceive ourselves in imagining we can form any such general idea.

Thus, upon the whole, we may infer, that when we talk of any being, whether of a superior or inferior nature, as endowed with a power or force, proportioned to any effect; when we speak of a necessary connection betwixt objects, and suppose that this connection depends upon an efficacy or energy, with which any of these objects are endowed; in all the expressions, *so applied,* we have really no distinct meaning, and make use only of common words, without any clear and determinate ideas. But as it is more probable that these expressions do here lose their true meaning by being *wrong applied,* than that they never have any meaning; it will be proper to bestow another consideration on this subject, to see if possibly we can discover the nature and origin of those ideas we annex to them.†

Suppose two objects to be presented to us, of which the one is the cause and the other the effect; it is plain that, from the simple consideration of one or both these objects, we never shall perceive the tie by which they are united, or be able certainly to pronounce, that there is a connection betwixt them. It is not, therefore, from any one instance, that we arrive at the idea of cause and effect, of a necessary connection of power, of force, of energy, and of efficacy. Did we never see any but particular conjunctions of objects, entirely different from each other, we should never be able to form any such ideas.

But, again, suppose we observe several instances in which the same objects are always conjoined together, we immediately conceive a connection betwixt them, and begin to draw an inference from one to another. This multiplicity of resembling instances, therefore, constitutes the very essence of power or connection, and is the source from which the idea of it arises. In order, then, to understand the idea of power, we must consider that multiplicity; nor do I ask more to give a solution of that difficulty which has so long perplexed us. For thus I reason. The repetition of perfectly similar instances can never *alone* give rise to an original idea, different from what is to be found in any particular instance, as has been observed, and as evidently follows from our fundamental principle, *that all ideas are copied from impressions*. Since therefore the idea of power is a new original idea, not to be found in any one instance, and which yet arises from the repetition of several instances, it follows that the repetition *alone* has not that effect, but must either *discover* or *produce* something new, which is the source of that idea. Did the repetition neither discover nor produce anything new, our ideas might be multiplied by it, but would not be enlarged above what they are upon the observation of one single instance. Every enlargement, therefore (such as the idea of power or connection), which arises from the multiplicity of similar instances, is copied from some effects of the multiplicity, and will be perfectly understood by understanding these effects. Wherever we find anything new to be discovered or produced by the repetition, there we must place the power, and must never look for it in any other object.

But it is evident, in the first place, that the repetition of like objects in like relations of succession and contiguity, *discovers* nothing new in any one of them; since we can draw no inference from it, nor make it a subject either of our demonstrative or probable reasonings; as has been already proved.[33]   Nay, suppose we could draw an inference, it would be of no consequence in the present case; since no kind of reasoning can give rise to a new idea, such as this of power is; but wherever we reason, we must antecedently be possessed of clear ideas, which may be the objects of our reasoning. The conception always precedes the understanding; and where the one is obscure, the other is uncertain; where the one fails, the other must fail also.

Secondly, it is certain that this repetition of similar objects in similar situations, *produces* nothing new either in these objects, or in any external body. For it will readily be allowed, that the several instances we have of the conjunction of resembling causes and effects, are in themselves entirely independent, and that the communication of motion, which I see result at present from the shock of two billiard-balls, is totally distinct from that which I saw result from such an impulse a twelvemonth ago. These impulses have no influence on each other. They are entirely divided by time and place; and the one might have existed and communicated motion, though the other never had been in being.

There is, then, nothing new either discovered or produced in any objects by their constant conjunction, and by the uninterrupted resemblance of their relations of succession and contiguity. But it is from this resemblance that the ideas of necessity, of power, and of efficacy, are derived. These ideas, therefore, represent not anything that does or can belong to the objects which are constantly conjoined. This is an argument which, in every view we can examine it, will be found perfectly unanswerable. Similar instances are still the first source of our idea of power or necessity; at the same time that they have no

[33] Sect. 6.

influence by their similarity either on each other, or on any external object. We must, therefore, turn ourselves to some other quarter to seek the origin of that idea.

Though the several resembling instances, which give rise to the idea of power, have no influence on each other, and can never produce any new quality *in the object,* which can be the model of that idea, yet the *observation* of this resemblance produces a new impression *in the mind,* which is its real model. For after we have observed the resemblance in a sufficient number of instances, we immediately feel a determination of the mind to pass from one object to its usual attendant, and to conceive it in a stronger light upon account of that relation. This determination is the only effect of the resemblance; and therefore must be the same with power or efficacy, whose idea is derived from the resemblance. The several instances of resembling conjunctions lead us into the notion of power and necessity. These instances are in themselves totally distinct from each other, and have no union but in the mind, which observes them, and collects their ideas. Necessity then is the effect of this observation, and is nothing but an internal impression of the mind, or a determination to carry our thoughts from one object to another. Without considering it in this view, we can never arrive at the most distant notion of it, or be able to attribute it either to external or internal objects, to spirit or body, to causes or effects.

The necessary connection betwixt causes and effects is the foundation of our inference from one to the other. The foundation of our inference is the transition arising from the accustomed union. These are, therefore, the same.

The idea of necessity arises from some impression. There is no impression conveyed by our senses which can give rise to that idea. It must, therefore, be derived from some internal impression, or impression of reflection. There is no internal impression which has any relation to the present business, but that propensity, which custom produces, to pass from an object to the idea of its usual attendant. This, therefore, is the essence of necessity. Upon the whole, necessity is something that exists in the mind, not in objects; nor is it possible for us ever to form the most distant idea of it, considered as a quality in bodies. Either we have no idea of necessity, or necessity is nothing but that determination of the thought to pass from causes to effects, and from effects to causes, according to their experienced union.

Thus, as the necessity, which makes two times two equal to four, or three angles of a triangle equal to two right ones, lies only in the act of the understanding, by which we consider and compare these ideas; in like manner the necessity of power, which unites causes and effects, lies in the determination of the mind to pass from the one to the other.† The efficacy or energy of causes is neither placed in the causes themselves, nor in the Deity, nor in the concurrence of these two principles; but belongs entirely to the soul, which considers the union of two or more objects in all past instances. It is here that the real power of causes is placed, along with their connection and necessity.

I am sensible that of all the paradoxes which I have had, or shall hereafter have occasion to advance in the course of this Treatise, the present one is the most violent, and that it is merely by dint of solid proof and reasoning I can ever hope it will have admission, and overcome the inveterate prejudices of mankind. Before we are reconciled to this doctrine, how often must we repeat to ourselves, *that* the simple view of any two objects or actions, however related, can never give us any idea of power, or of a connection betwixt them : *that* this idea arises from the repetition of their union : *that* the repetition neither discovers nor causes anything in the objects, but has an influence only on the mind, by that customary transition it produces : *that* this customary transition is therefore the same with the power and necessity; which are consequently qualities of perceptions, not of objects, and are internally felt by the soul, and not perceived externally in bodies? There is commonly an astonishment attending everything extraordinary; and this astonishment changes immediately into the highest degree of esteem or contempt, according as we approve or disapprove of the subject. I am much afraid, that though the foregoing reasoning appears to me the shortest and most decisive imaginable, yet, with the generality of readers, the bias of the mind will prevail, and give them a prejudice against the present doctrine.

This contrary bias is easily accounted for. It is a common observation, that the mind has a great propensity to spread itself on external objects, and to conjoin with them any internal impressions which they occasion, and which always make their appearance at the same time that these objects discover themselves to the senses. Thus, as certain sounds and smells are always found to attend certain visible objects, we naturally imagine a conjunction, even in place, betwixt the objects and qualities, though the qualities be of such a nature as to admit of no such conjunction, and really exist nowhere. But of this more fully hereafter.[34] Meanwhile, it is sufficient to observe, that the same propensity is the reason why we suppose necessity and power to lie in the objects we consider, not in our mind, that considers them; notwithstanding it is not possible for us to form the most distant idea of that quality, when it is not taken for the determination of the mind, to pass from the idea of an object to that of its usual attendant.

But though this be the only reasonable account we can give of necessity, the contrary notion is so riveted in the mind from the principles above mentioned, that I doubt not but my sentiments will be treated by many as extravagant and ridiculous. What! the efficacy of causes lie in the determination of the mind! As if causes did not operate entirely independent of the mind, and would not continue their operation, even though there was no mind existent to contemplate them, or reason concerning them. Thought may well depend on causes for its operation, but not causes on thought. This is to reverse the order of nature, and make that secondary, which is really primary.

[34] Part **IV**, Sect. 5.

To every operation there is a power proportioned; and this power must be placed on the body that operates. If we remove the power from one cause, we must ascribe it to another; but to remove it from all causes, and bestow it on a being that is noways related to the cause or effect, but by perceiving them, is a gross absurdity, and contrary to the most certain principles of human reason.

I can only reply to all these arguments, that the case is here much the same, as if a blind man should pretend to find a great many absurdities in the supposition, that the colour of scarlet is not the same with the sound of a trumpet, nor light the same with solidity. If we have really no idea of a power or efficacy in any object, or of any real connection betwixt causes and effects, it will be to little purpose to prove that an efficacy is necessary in all operations. We do not understand our own meaning in talking so, but ignorantly confound ideas which are entirely distinct from each other. I am, indeed, ready to allow, that there may be several qualities, both in material and immaterial objects, with which we are utterly unacquainted; and if we please to call these *power* or *efficacy,* it will be of little consequence to the world. But when, instead of meaning these unknown qualities, we make the terms of power and efficacy signify something, of which we have a clear idea, and which is incompatible with those objects to which we apply it, obscurity and error begin then to take place, and we are led astray by a false philosophy. This is the case when we transfer the determination of the thought to external objects, and suppose any real intelligible connection betwixt them; that being a quality which can only belong to the mind that considers them.

As to what may be said, that the operations of nature are independent of our thought and reasoning, I allow it; and accordingly have observed, that objects bear to each other the relations of contiguity and succession; that like objects may be observed, in several instances, to have like relations; and that all this is independent of, and antecedent to, the operations of the understanding. But if we go any further, and ascribe a power or necessary connection to these objects, this is what we can never observe in them, but must draw the idea of it from what we feel internally in contemplating them. And this I carry so far, that I am ready to convert my present reasoning into an instance of it, by a subtilty which it will not be difficult to comprehend.

When any object is presented to us, it immediately conveys to the mind a lively idea of that object which is usually found to attend it; and this determination of the mind forms the necessary connection of these objects. But when we change the point of view from the objects to the perceptions, in that case the impression is to be considered as the cause, and the lively idea as the effect; and their necessary connection is that new determination, which we feel to pass from the idea of the one to that of the other. The uniting principle among our internal perceptions is as unintelligible as that among external objects, and is not known to us any other way than by experience. Now, the nature and effects of experience have been already sufficiently examined and explained. It never gives us any insight into the internal structure or operating principle of objects, but only accustoms the mind to pass from one to another.†

It is now time to collect all the different parts of this reasoning, and, by joining them together, form an exact definition of the relation of cause and effect, which makes the subject of the present inquiry. This order would not have been excusable, of first examining our inference from the relation before we had explained the relation itself, had it been possible to proceed in a different method. But as the nature of the relation depends so much on that of the inference, we have been obliged to advance in this seemingly preposterous manner, and make use of terms before we were able exactly to define them, or fix their meaning. We shall now correct this fault by giving a precise definition of cause and effect.

There may two definitions be given of this relation,

which are only different by their presenting a different view of the same object, and making us consider it either as a *philosophical* or as a *natural* relation; either as a comparison of two ideas, or as an association betwixt them. We may define a *cause* to be "An object precedent and contiguous to another, and where all the objects resembling the former are placed in like relations of precedency and contiguity to those objects that resemble the latter." If this definition be esteemed defective, because drawn from objects foreign to the cause, we may substitute this other definition in its place, viz. "A *cause* is an object precedent and contiguous to another, and so united with it that the idea of the one determines the mind to form the idea of the other, and the impression of the one to form a more lively idea of the other." Should this definition also be rejected for the same reason, I know no other remedy, than that the persons, who express this delicacy, should substitute a juster definition in its place. But, for my part, I must own my incapacity for such an undertaking. When I examine with the utmost accuracy those objects which are commonly denominated causes and effects, I find, in considering a single instance, that the one object is precedent and contiguous to the other; and in enlarging my view to consider several instances, I find only that like objects are constantly placed in like relations of succession and contiguity. Again, when I consider the influence of this constant conjunction, I perceive that such a relation can never be an object of reasoning, and can never operate upon the mind but by means of custom, which determines the imagination to make a transition from the idea of one object to that of its usual attendant, and from the impression of one to a more lively idea of the other. However extraordinary these sentiments may appear, I think it fruitless to trouble myself with any further inquiry or reasoning upon the subject, but shall repose myself on them as on established maxims.

It will only be proper, before we leave this subject, to draw some corollaries from it, by which we may remove several prejudices and popular errors that have very much prevailed in philosophy. First, we may learn from the foregoing doctrine, that all causes are of the same kind, and that in particular there is no foundation for that distinction which we sometimes make betwixt efficient causes, and causes *sine qua non*;† or betwixt efficient causes, and formal, and material, and exemplary, and final causes. For as our idea of efficiency is derived from the constant conjunction of two objects, wherever this is observed, the cause is efficient; and where it is not, there can never be a cause of any kind. For the same reason we must reject the distinction betwixt *cause* and *occasion,* when supposed to signify anything essentially different from each other. If constant conjunction be implied in what we call occasion, it is a real cause; if not, it is no relation at all, and cannot give rise to any argument or reasoning.

Secondly, the same course of reasoning will make us conclude, that there is but one kind of *necessity,* as there is but one kind of cause, and that the common distinction betwixt *moral* and *physical* necessity is without any foundation in nature.† This clearly appears from the precedent explication of necessity. It is the constant conjunction of objects along with the determination of the mind, which constitutes a physical necessity : and the removal of these is the same thing with *chance.* As objects must either be conjoined or not, and as the mind must either be determined or not to pass from one object to another, it is impossible to admit of any medium betwixt chance and an absolute necessity. In weakening this conjunction and determination you do not change the nature of the necessity; since even in the operation of bodies these have different degrees of constancy and force, without producing a different species of that relation.

The distinction, which we often make betwixt *power* and the *exercise* of it, is equally without foundation.†

Thirdly, we may now be able fully to overcome all that repugnance, which it is so natural for us to entertain against the foregoing reasoning, by which we endeavoured to prove, that the necessity of a cause to every beginning of existence is not founded on any arguments either demonstrative or intuitive. Such an opinion will not appear strange after the foregoing definitions. If we define a cause to be *an object precedent and contiguous to another, and where all the objects resembling the former are placed in a like relation of priority and contiguity to those objects that resemble the latter;* we may easily conceive that there is no absolute nor metaphysical necessity, that every beginning of existence should be attended with such an object. If we define a cause to be, *an object precedent and contiguous to another, and so united with it in the imagination, that the idea of the one determines the mind to form the idea of the other, and the impression of the one to form a more lively idea of the other;* we shall make still less difficulty of assenting to this opinion. Such an influence on the mind is in itself perfectly extraordinary and incomprehensible; nor can we be certain of its reality, but from experience and observation.

I shall add as a fourth corollary, that we can never have reason to believe that any object exists, of which we cannot form an idea. For as all our reasonings concerning existence are derived from causation, and as all our reasonings concerning causation are derived from the experienced conjunction of objects, not from any reasoning or reflection, the same experience must give us a notion of these objects, and must remove all mystery from our conclusions. This is so evident that it would scarce have merited our attention, were it not to obviate certain objections of this kind which might arise against the following reasonings concerning *matter* and *substance*.[35] I need not observe, that a full knowledge of the object is not requisite, but only of those qualities of it which we believe to exist.

[35] *Part* iv, *Sects.* ii, iii, v.

RULES BY WHICH TO JUDGE OF CAUSES AND EFFECTS

According to the precedent doctrine, there are no objects which, by the mere survey, without consulting experience, we can determine to be the causes of any other; and no objects which we can certainly determine in the same manner not to be the causes. Anything may produce anything. Creation, annihilation, motion, reason, volition; all these may arise from one another, or from any other object we can imagine. Nor will this appear strange if we compare two principles explained about, *that the constant conjunction of objects determines their causation,* and *that, properly speaking, no objects are contrary to each other but existence and non-existence.*[36] Where objects are not contrary, nothing hinders them from having that constant conjunction on which the relation of cause and effect totally depends.

Since, therefore, it is possible for all objects to become causes or effects to each other, it may be proper to fix some general rules[37] by which we may know when they really are so.

1. The cause and effect must be contiguous in space and time.

2. The cause must be prior to the effect.

3. There must be a constant union betwixt the cause and effect. It is chiefly this quality that constitutes the relation.

4. The same cause always produces the same effect, and the same effect never arises but from the same cause. This principle we derive from experience, and is the source of most of our philosophical reasonings. For when by any

[36] Part I, Sect. 5.   [37] *Compare Sect.* XIII.

3

clear experiment we have discovered the causes or effects of any phenomenon, we immediately extend our observation to every phenomenon of the same kind, without waiting for that constant repetition, from which the first idea of this relation is derived.

5. There is another principle which hangs upon this, viz. that where several different objects produce the same effect, it must be by means of some quality which we discover to be common amongst them. For as like effects imply like causes, we must always ascribe the causation to the circumstance wherein we discover the resemblance.

6. The following principle is founded on the same reason. The difference in the effects of two resembling objects must proceed from that particular in which they differ. For as like causes always produce like effects, when in any instance we find our expectation to be disappointed, we must conclude that this irregularity proceeds from some difference in the causes.

7. When any object increases or diminishes with the increase or diminution of its cause, it is to be regarded as a compounded effect, derived from the union of the several different effects which arise from the several different parts of the cause. The absence or presence of one part of the cause is here supposed to be always attended with the absence or presence of a proportionable part of the effect. This constant conjunction sufficiently proves that the one part is the cause of the other. We must, however, beware not to draw such a conclusion from a few experiments. A certain degree of heat gives pleasure; if you diminish that heat, the pleasure diminishes; but it does not follow, that if you augment it beyond a certain degree, the pleasure will likewise augment; for we find that it degenerates into pain.

8. The eighth and last rule I shall take notice of is, that an object, which exists for any time in its full perfection without any effect, is not the sole cause of that effect, but requires to be assisted by some other principle, which may

forward its influence and operation. For as like effects necessarily follow from like causes, and in a contiguous time and place, their separation for a moment shows that these causes are not complete ones.

Here is all the *logic* I think proper to employ in my reasoning; and perhaps even this was not very necessary, but might have been supplied by the natural principles of our understanding. Our scholastic headpieces and logicians show no such superiority above the mere vulgar in their reason and ability, as to give us any inclination to imitate them in delivering a long system of rules and precepts to direct our judgment in philosophy. All the rules of this nature are very easy in their invention, but extremely difficult in their application; and even experimental philosophy, which seems the most natural and simple of any, requires the utmost stretch of human judgment. There is no phenomenon in nature but what is compounded and modified by so many different circumstances, that, in order to arrive at the decisive point, we must carefully separate whatever is superfluous, and inquire, by new experiments, if every particular circumstance of the first experiment was essential to it. These new experiments are liable to a discussion of the same kind; so that the utmost constancy is required to make us persevere in our inquiry, and the utmost sagacity to choose the right way among so many that present themselves. If this be the case even in natural philosophy, how much more in moral, where there is a much greater complication of circumstances, and where those views and sentiments, which are essential to any action of the mind, are so implicit and obscure, that they often escape our strictest attention, and are not only unaccountable in their causes, but even unknown in their existence? I am much afraid, lest the small success I meet with in my inquiries, will make this observation bear the air of an apology rather than of boasting.

If anything can give me security in this particular, it will be the enlarging the sphere of my experiments as much as possible; for which reason, it may be proper, in this place, to examine the reasoning faculty of brutes, as well as that of human creatures.

SECTION XVI

OF THE REASON OF ANIMALS

Next to the ridicule of denying an evident truth, is that of taking much pains to defend it; and no truth appears to me more evident, than that the beasts are endowed with thought and reason as well as men. The arguments are in this case so obvious, that they never escape the most stupid and ignorant.

We are conscious that we ourselves, in adapting means to ends, are guided by reason and design, and that it is not ignorantly nor casually we perform those actions which tend to self-preservation, to the obtaining pleasure, and avoiding pain. When, therefore, we see other creatures, in millions of instances, perform like actions, and direct them to like ends, all our principles of reason and probability carry us with an invincible force to believe the existence of a like cause. It is needless, in my opinion, to illustrate this argument by the enumeration of particulars. The smallest attention will supply us with more than are requisite. The resemblance betwixt the actions of animals and those of men is so entire, in this respect, that the very first action of the first animal we shall please to pitch on, will afford us an incontestable argument for the present doctrine.

This doctrine is as useful as it is obvious, and furnishes us with a kind of touchstone, by which we may try every system in this species of philosophy. It is from the resemblance of the external actions of animals to those we ourselves perform, that we judge their internal likewise to resemble ours; and the same principle of reasoning, carried one step further, will make us conclude, that since our internal actions resemble each other, the causes, from which they are derived, must also be resembling. When any hypothesis, therefore, is advanced to explain a mental operation, which is common to men and beasts, we must apply the same hypothesis to both; and as every true hypothesis will abide this trial, so I may venture to affirm, that no false one will ever be able to endure it. The common defect of those systems, which philosophers have employed to account for the actions of the mind, is, that they suppose such a subtilty and refinement of thought, as not only exceeds the capacity of mere animals, but even of children and the common people in our own species; who are, notwithstanding, susceptible of the same emotions and affections as persons of the most accomplished genius and understanding. Such a subtilty is a clear proof of the falsehood, as the contrary simplicity of the truth, of any system.†

Let us, therefore, put our present system, concerning the nature of the understanding, to this decisive trial, and see whether it will equally account for the reasonings of beasts as for those of the human species.

Here we must make a distinction betwixt those actions of animals, which are of a vulgar nature, and seem to be on a level with their common capacities, and those more extraordinary instances of sagacity, which they sometimes discover for their own preservation, and the propagation of their species. A dog that avoids fire and precipices, that shuns strangers, and caresses his master, affords us an instance of the first kind. A bird, that chooses with such care and nicety the place and materials of her nest, and sits upon her eggs for a due time, and in a suitable season, with all the precaution that a chemist is capable of in the most delicate projection, furnishes us with a lively instance of the second.

As to the former actions, I assert they proceed from a reasoning, that is not in itself different, nor founded on different principles, from that which appears in human nature. It is necessary in the first place, that there be some impression immediately present to their memory or senses, in order to be the foundation of their judgment. From the tone of voice the dog infers his master's anger, and foresees his own punishment. From a certain sensation affecting his smell, he judges his game not to be far distant from him.

Secondly, the inference he draws from the present impression is built on experience, and on his observation of the conjunction of objects in past instances. As you vary this experience, he varies his reasoning. Make a beating follow upon one sign or motion for some time, and afterwards upon another; and he will successively draw different conclusions, according to his most recent experience.

Now let any philosopher make a trial, and endeavour to explain that act of the mind which we call *belief,* and give an account of the principles, from which it is derived, independent of the influence of custom on the imagination, and let his hypothesis be equally applicable to beasts as to the human species; and after he has done this, I promise to embrace his opinion. But at the same time I demand as an equitable condition, that if my system be the only one, which can answer to all these terms, it may be received as entirely satisfactory and convincing. And that it is the only one is evident almost without any reasoning. Beasts certainly never perceive any real connection among objects. It is therefore by experience they infer one from another. They can never by any arguments form a general conclusion, that those objects of which they have had no experience, resemble those of which they have. It is therefore by means of custom alone that experience operates upon them. All this was sufficiently evident with respect to man. But with respect to beasts there cannot be the least suspicion of mistake; which must be owned to be a strong confirmation, or rather an invincible proof of my system.

Nothing shows more the force of habit in reconciling us to any phenomenon, than this, that men are not astonished at the operations of their own reason, at the same time that they admire the *instinct* of animals, and find a difficulty in explaining it, merely because it cannot be reduced to the very same principles. To consider the matter aright, reason is nothing but a wonderful and unintelligible instinct in our souls, which carries us along a certain train of ideas, and endows them with particular qualities, according to their particular situations and relations. This instinct, it is true, arises from past observation and experience; but can any one give the ultimate reason why past experience and observation produces such an effect, any more than why nature alone should produce it? Nature may certainly produce whatever can arise from habit : nay, habit is nothing but one of the principles of nature, and derives all its force from that origin.[36]

---

[36] *Hume ignores a distinction between habit (conditioned response) and intelligence. By the former an animal repeats a response that has succeeded in the past. By the latter it finds a new response the success of which is likely in relation to general features of its experience. (Consult Holloway " Language and Intelligence " and Kohler " The Mentality of Apes ".)*

PART IV

OF THE SCEPTICAL AND OTHER SYSTEMS OF PHILOSOPHY

SECTION I

OF SCEPTICISM WITH REGARD TO REASON

In all demonstrative sciences the rules are certain and infallible; but when we apply them, our fallible and uncertain faculties are very apt to depart from them, and fall into error. We must, therefore, in every reasoning form a new judgment, as a check or control on our first judgment or belief; and must enlarge our view to comprehend a kind of history of all the instances, wherein our understanding has deceived us, compared with those wherein its testimony was just and true. Our reason must be considered as a kind of cause, of which truth is the natural effect; but such a one as, by the irruption of other causes, and by the inconstancy of our mental powers, may frequently be prevented. By this means all knowledge degenerates into probability; and this probability is greater or less, according to our experience of the veracity or deceitfulness of our understanding, and according to the simplicity or intricacy of the question.

There is no algebraist nor mathematician so expert in his science, as to place entire confidence in any truth immediately upon his discovery of it, or regard it as anything but a mere probability. Every time he runs over his proofs, his confidence increases; but still more by the approbation of his friends; and is raised to its utmost perfection by the universal assent and applauses of the learned world. Now, it is evident that this gradual increase of assurance is nothing but the addition of new probabilities, and is derived from the constant union of causes and effects, according to past experience and observation.

In accounts of any length or importance, merchants seldom trust to the infallible certainty of numbers for their security; but by the artificial structure of the accounts, produce a probability beyond what is derived from the skill and experience of the accountant. For that is plainly of itself some degree of probability; though uncertain and variable, according to the degrees of his experience and length of the account. Now as none will maintain that our assurance in a long numeration exceeds probability, I may safely affirm, that there scarce is any proposition concerning numbers of which we can have a fuller security. For it is easily possible, by gradually diminishing the numbers, to reduce the longest series of addition to the most simple question which can be formed, to an addition of two single numbers; and upon this supposition we shall find it impracticable to show the precise limits of knowledge and of probability, or discover that particular number at which the one ends and the other begins. But knowledge and probability are of such contrary and disagreeing natures, that they cannot well run insensibly into each other, and that because they will not divide, but must be either entirely present, or entirely absent. Besides, if any single addition were certain, every one would be so, and consequently the whole or total sum; unless the whole can be different from all its parts. I had almost said that this was certain; but I reflect that it must reduce *itself,* as well as every other reasoning, and from knowledge degenerate into probability.

Since therefore all knowledge resolves itself into probability, and becomes at last of the same nature with that evidence which we employ in common life, we must now examine this latter species of reasoning, and see on what foundation it stands.

In every judgment, which we can form concerning probability, as well as concerning knowledge, we ought always to correct the first judgment, derived from the nature of the object, by another judgment, derived from the nature of the understanding. It is certain a man of solid sense and long experience ought to have, and usually has, a greater assurance in his opinions than one that is foolish and ignorant, and that our sentiments have different degrees of authority, even with ourselves, in proportion to the degrees of our reason and experience. In the man of the best sense and longest experience, this authority is never entire; since even such a one must be conscious of many errors in the past, and must still dread the like for the future. Here then arises a new species of probability to correct and regulate the first, and fix its just standard and proportion. As demonstration is subject to the control of probability, so is probability liable to a new correction by a reflex act of the mind, wherein the nature of our understanding, and our reasoning from the first probability, become our objects.

Having thus found in every probability, beside the original uncertainty inherent in the subject, a new uncertainty, derived from the weakness of that faculty which judges, and having adjusted these two together, we are obliged by our reason to add a new doubt, derived from the possibility of error in the estimation we make of the truth and fidelity of our faculties. This is a doubt which immediately occurs to us, and of which, if we would closely pursue our reason, we cannot avoid giving a decision. But this decision, though it should be favourable to our preceding judgment, being founded only on probability, must weaken still further our first evidence, and must itself be weakened by a fourth doubt of the same kind, and so on *in infinitum;* till at last there remain nothing of the original probability, however great we may suppose it to have been, and however small the diminution by every new uncertainty. No finite object can subsist under a decrease repeated *in infinitum;* and even the vastest quantity which can enter into human imagination, must in this manner be reduced to nothing. Let our first belief be never so strong, it must infallibly perish, by passing through so many new examinations, of which each diminishes somewhat of its force and vigour. When I reflect on the natural fallibility of my judgment, I have less confidence in my opinions than when I only consider the objects concerning which I reason; and when I proceed still further, to turn the scrutiny against every successive estimation I make of my faculties, all the rules of logic require a continual diminution, and at last a total extinction of belief and evidence.[1]

Should it here be asked me, whether I sincerely assent to this argument, which I seem to take such pains to inculcate, and whether I be really one of those sceptics who hold that all is uncertain, and that our judgment is not in *any* thing possessed of *any* measures of truth and falsehood; I should reply, that this question is entirely superfluous, and that neither I, nor any other person, was ever sincerely and constantly of that opinion. Nature, by an absolute and uncontrollable necessity, has determined us to judge as well as to breathe and feel; nor can we any more forbear viewing certain objects in a stronger and fuller light, upon account of their customary connection with a present impression, than we can hinder ourselves from thinking, as long as we are awake, or seeing the surrounding bodies, when we turn our eyes towards them in broad sunshine. Whoever has taken the pains to refute the cavils of this *total* scepticism, has really disputed without an antagonist, and endeavoured by arguments to establish a faculty, which nature has antecedently implanted in the mind, and rendered unavoidable.

My intention then in displaying so carefully the arguments of that fantastic sect, is only to make the reader sensible of the truth of my hypothesis, *that all our reasonings concerning causes and effects, are derived from nothing but custom; and that belief is more properly an act of the sensitive, than of the cogitative part of our natures.*

[1] *See editor's introduction, p. 24-5.*

I have here proved, that the very same principles, which make us form a decision upon any subject, and correct that decision by the consideration of our genius and capacity, and of the situation of our mind, when we examined that subject; I say, I have proved that these same principles, when carried further, and applied to every new reflex judgment, must, by continually diminishing the original evidence, at last reduce it to nothing, and utterly subvert all belief and opinion. If belief, therefore, were a simple act of the thought, without any peculiar manner of conception, or the addition of a force and vivacity, it must infallibly destroy itself, and in every case terminate in a total suspense of judgment. But as experience will sufficiently convince any one, who thinks it worth while to try, that though he can find no error in the foregoing arguments, yet he still continues to believe, and think, and reason, as usual, he may safely conclude that his reasoning and belief is some sensation or peculiar manner of conception, which it is impossible for mere ideas and reflections to destroy.

But here, perhaps, it may be demanded, how it happens, even upon my hypothesis, that these arguments above explained produce not a total suspense of judgment, and after what manner the mind ever retains a degree of assurance in any subject? For as these new probabilities, which by their repetition perpetually diminish the original evidence, are founded on the very same principles, whether of thought or sensation, as the primary judgment, it may seem unavoidable, that in either case they must equally subvert it, and by the opposition, either of contrary thoughts or sensations, reduce the mind to a total uncertainty. I suppose there is some question proposed to me, and that after revolving over the impressions of my memory and senses, and carrying my thoughts from them to such objects as are commonly conjoined with them, I feel a stronger and more forcible conception on the one side than on the other. This strong conception forms my first decision. I suppose, that afterwards I examine my judgment itself, and observing from experience, that it is sometimes just and sometimes erroneous, I consider it as regulated by contrary principles or causes, of which some lead to truth, and some to error; and in balancing these contrary causes, I diminish by a new probability the assurance of my first decision. This new probability is liable to the same diminution as the foregoing, and so on, *in infinitum.* It is therefore demanded, *how it happens, that, even after all, we retain a degree of belief, which is sufficient for our purpose, either in philosophy or common life?*

I answer, that after the first and second decision, as the action of the mind becomes forced and unnatural, and the ideas faint and obscure, though the principles of judgment, and the balancing of opposite causes be the same as at the very beginning, yet their influence on the imagination, and the vigour they add to, or diminish from the thought, is by no means equal. Where the mind reaches not its objects with easiness and facility, the same principles have not the same effect as in a more natural conception of the ideas; nor does the imagination feel a sensation, which holds any proportion with that which arises from its common judgments and opinions. The attention is on the stretch; the posture of the mind is uneasy; and the spirits being diverted from their natural course, are not governed in their movements by the same laws, at least not to the same degree, as when they flow in their usual channel.

If we desire similar instances, it will not be very difficult to find them. The present subject of metaphysics will supply us abundantly. The same argument, which would have been esteemed convincing in a reasoning concerning history or politics, has little or no influence in these abstruser subjects, even though it be perfectly comprehended; and that because there is required a study and an effort of thought, in order to its being comprehended: and this effort of thought disturbs the operation of our sentiments, on which the belief depends. The case is the same in other subjects. The straining of the imagination always hinders the regular flowing of the passions and sentiments. A tragic poet, that would represent his heroes as very ingenious and witty in their misfortunes, would never touch the passions. As the emotions of the soul prevent any subtile reasoning and reflection, so these latter actions of the mind are equally prejudicial to the former. The mind, as well as the body, seems to be endowed with a certain precise degree of force and activity, which it never employs in one action, but at the expense of all the rest. This is more evidently true, where the actions are of quite different natures; since in that case the force of the mind is not only diverted, but even the disposition changed, so as to render us incapable of a sudden transition from one action to the other, and still more of performing both at once. No wonder, then, the conviction, which arises from a subtile reasoning, diminishes in proportion to the efforts which the imagination makes to enter into the reasoning, and to conceive it in all its parts. Belief, being a lively conception, can never be entire, where it is not founded on something natural and easy.

This I take to be the true state of the question, and cannot approve of that expeditious way, which some take with the sceptics, to reject at once all their arguments without inquiry or examination. If the sceptical reasonings be strong, say they, it is a proof that reason may have some force and authority; if weak, they can never be sufficient to invalidate all the conclusions of our understanding. This argument is not just; because the sceptical reasonings, were it possible for them to exist, and were they not destroyed by their subtilty, would be successively both strong and weak, according to the successive dispositions of the mind. Reason first appears in possession of the throne, prescribing laws, and imposing maxims, with an absolute sway and authority. Her enemy, therefore, is obliged to take shelter under her protection, and by making use of rational arguments to prove the fallaciousness and imbecility of reason, produces, in a manner, a patent under her hand and seal. This patent has at first an authority, proportioned to the present and immediate authority of reason, from which it is derived. But as it is supposed to be contradictory to reason, it gradually diminishes the force of that governing power and its own at the same time; till at last they both vanish away into nothing, by a regular and just diminution. The sceptical and dogmatical reasons are of the same kind, though contrary in their operation and tendency; so that where the latter is strong, it has an enemy of equal force in the former to encounter; and as their forces were at first equal, they still continue so, as long as either of them subsists; nor does one of them lose any force in the contest, without taking as much from its antagonist. It is happy, therefore, that nature breaks the force of all sceptical arguments in time, and keeps them from having any considerable influence on the understanding. Were we to trust entirely to their self-destruction, that can never take place, until they have first subverted all conviction, and have totally destroyed human reason.

SECTION II

OF SCEPTICISM WITH REGARD TO THE SENSES

Thus the sceptic still continues to reason and believe, even though he asserts that he cannot defend his reason by reason; and by the same rule he must assent to the principle concerning the existence of body, though he cannot pretend, by any arguments of philosophy, to maintain its veracity. Nature has not left this to his choice, and has doubtless esteemed it an affair of too great importance, to be trusted to our uncertain reasonings and speculations. We may well ask, *What causes induce us to believe in the existence of body?* but it is in vain to ask, *Whether there be body or not?* That is a point which we must take for granted in all our reasonings.

The subject, then, of our present inquiry, is concerning the *causes* which induce us to believe in the existence of body: and my reasonings on this head I shall begin with a distinction, which at first sight may seem superfluous, but which will contribute very much to the perfect understanding of what follows. We ought to examine apart those two questions, which are commonly confounded together, viz. Why we attribute a *continued* existence to objects, even when they are not present to the senses; and why we suppose them to have an existence *distinct* from the mind and perception? Under this last head I comprehend their situation as well as relations, their *external* position as well as the *independence* of their existence and operation. These two questions concerning the continued and distinct existence of body are intimately connected together. For if the objects of our senses continue to exist, even when they are not perceived, their existence is of course independent of and distinct from the perception; and *vice versa*, if their existence be independent of the perception, and distinct from it, they must continue to exist, even though they be not perceived. But though the decision of the one question decides the other; yet that we may the more easily discover the principles of human nature, from whence the decision arises, we shall carry along with us this distinction, and shall consider, whether it be the *senses, reason,* or the *imagination,* that produces the opinion of a *continued* or of a *distinct* existence. These are the only questions that are intelligible on the present subject. For as to the notion of external existence, when taken for something specifically different from our perceptions, we have already shown its absurdity.[2]

To begin with the *senses,* it is evident these faculties are incapable of giving rise to the notion of the *continued* existence of their objects, after they no longer appear to the senses. For that is a contradiction in terms, and supposes that the senses continue to operate, even after they have ceased all manner of operation. These faculties,

[2] Part II, Sect. 6.

therefore, if they have any influence in the present case, must produce the opinion of a distinct, not of a continued existence; and in order to that, must present their impressions either as images and representations, or as these very distinct and external existences.†

That our senses offer not their impressions as the images of something *distinct,* or *independent,* and *external,* is evident; because they convey to us nothing but a single perception, and never give us the least intimation of anything beyond. A single perception can never produce the idea of a double existence, but by some inference either of the reason or imagination. When the mind looks further than what immediately appears to it, its conclusions can never be put to the account of the senses; and it certainly looks further, when from a single perception it infers a double existence, and supposes the relations of resemblance and causation betwixt them.

If our senses, therefore, suggest any idea of distinct existences, they must convey the impressions as those very existences, by a kind of fallacy and illusion. Upon this head we may observe that all sensations are felt by the mind, such as they really are, and that, when we doubt whether they present themselves as distinct objects, or as mere impressions, the difficulty is not concerning their nature, but concerning their relations and situation. Now, if the senses presented our impressions as external to, and independent of ourselves, both the objects and ourselves must be obvious to our senses, otherwise they could not be compared by these faculties. The difficulty then is, how far we are *ourselves* the objects of our senses.

It is certain there is no question in philosophy more abstruse than that concerning identity, and the nature of the uniting principle, which constitutes a person.[3] So far from being able by our senses merely to determine this question, we must have recourse to the most profound metaphysics to give a satisfactory answer to it; and in common life it is evident these ideas of self and person

[3] *See Section* VI.

are never very fixed nor determinate. It is absurd therefore to imagine the senses can ever distinguish betwixt
ourselves and external objects.

Add to this, that every impression, external and internal,
passions, affections, sensations, pains, and pleasures, are
originally on the same footing; and that whatever other
differences we may observe among them, they appear, all
of them, in their true colours, as impressions or perceptions.
And indeed, if we consider the matter aright, it is scarce
possible it should be otherwise; nor is it conceivable that
our senses should be more capable of deceiving us in the
situation and relations, than in the nature of our impressions. For since all actions and sensations of the mind
are known to us by consciousness, they must necessarily
appear in every particular what they are, and be what they
appear. Everything that enters the mind, being in *reality*
[a] perception,[4] it is impossible anything should to *feeling*
appear different. This were to suppose, that even where we
are most intimately conscious, we might be mistaken.

But not to lose time in examining, whether it is possible
for our senses to deceive us, and represent our perceptions
as distinct from ourselves, that is as *external* to and *independent* of us; let us consider whether they really do so,
and whether this error proceeds from an immediate sensation, or from some other causes.

To begin with the question concerning *external* existence, it may perhaps be said, that setting aside the metaphysical question of the identity of a thinking substance,
our own body evidently belongs to us; and as several
impressions appear exterior to the body, we suppose them
also exterior to ourselves. The paper on which I write at
present is beyond my hand. The table is beyond the paper.
The walls of the chamber beyond the table. And in casting
my eye towards the window, I perceive a great extent of
fields and buildings beyond my chamber. From all this it
may be inferred, that no other faculty is required, beside

[4] *The original edition reads " as the ". Corrected by Hume in
his Appendix.*

the senses, to convince us of the external existence of body. But to prevent this inference, we need only weigh the three following considerations. *First,* that, properly speaking, it is *not* our body we perceive, when we regard our limbs and members, but certain impressions, which enter by the senses; so that the ascribing a real and corporeal existence to these impressions, or to their objects, is an act of the mind as difficult to explain as that which we examine at present. *Secondly,* sounds, and tastes, and smells, though commonly regarded by the mind as continued independent qualities, appear not to have any existence in extension, and consequently cannot appear to the senses as situated externally to the body. The reason why we ascribe a place to them shall be considered afterwards.[5] *Thirdly,* even our sight informs us not of distances or outness (so to speak) immediately and without a certain reasoning and experience, as is acknowledged by the most rational philosophers.[6]

As to the *independency* of our perceptions on ourselves, this can never be an object of the senses; but any opinion we form concerning it must be derived from experience and observation : and we shall see afterwards, that our conclusions from experience are far from being favourable to the doctrine of the independency of our perceptions. Meanwhile we may observe, that when we talk of real distinct existences, we have commonly more in our eye their independency than external situation in place, and think an object has a sufficient reality, when its being is uninterrupted, and independent of the incessant revolutions, which we are conscious of in ourselves.

Thus to resume what I have said concerning the senses; they give us no notion of continued existence, because they cannot operate beyond the extent, in which they really operate. They as little produce the opinion of a distinct existence, because they neither can offer it to the mind as represented, nor as original. To offer it as represented, they must present both an object and an image. To make

[5] Sect. 5.   [6] *E.g. Locke and Berkeley.*

it appear as original, they must convey a falsehood; and this falsehood must lie in the relations and situation : in order to which, they must be able to compare the object with ourselves; and even in that case they do not, nor is it possible they should deceive us. We may therefore conclude with certainty, that the opinion of a continued and of a distinct existence never arises from the senses.

To confirm this, we may observe that there are three different kinds of impressions conveyed by the senses. The first are those of the figure, bulk, motion, and solidity of bodies. The second, those of colours, tastes, smells, sounds, heat, and cold. The third are the pains and pleasures that arise from the application of objects to our bodies, as by the cutting of our flesh with steel, and such like. Both philosophers and the vulgar suppose the first of these to have a distinct continued existence. The vulgar only regard the second as on the same footing.[7] Both philosophers and the vulgar, again, esteem the third to be merely perceptions; and consequently interrupted and dependent beings.

Now, it is evident, that whatever may be our philosophical opinion, colour, sounds, heat, and cold, as far as appears to the senses, exist after the same manner with motion and solidity; and that the difference we make betwixt them, in this respect, arises not from the mere perception. So strong is the prejudice for the distinct continued existence of the former qualities, that when the contrary opinion is advanced by modern philosophers, people imagine they can almost refute it from their feeling and experience, and that their very senses contradict this philosophy. It is also evident, that colours, sounds, etc., are originally on the same footing with the pain that arises from steel, and pleasure that proceeds from a fire; and that the difference betwixt them is founded neither on perception nor reason, but on the imagination. For as they are confessed to be, both of them, nothing but per-

[7] *Compare Locke, Essay conc. Human Understanding, Book* II, *ch.* 8.

ceptions arising from the particular configurations and motions of the parts of body, wherein possibly can their difference consist? Upon the whole, then, we may conclude that, as far as the senses are judges, all perceptions are the same in the manner of their existence.

We may also observe, in this instance of sounds and colours, that we can attribute a distinct continued existence to objects without ever consulting *reason*, or weighing our opinions by any philosophical principles. And, indeed, whatever convincing arguments philosophers may fancy they can produce to establish the belief of objects independent of the mind, it is obvious these arguments are known but to very few; and that it is not by them that children, peasants, and the greatest part of mankind, are induced to attribute objects to some impressions, and deny them to others. Accordingly, we find that all the conclusions which the vulgar form on this head, are directly contrary to those which are confirmed by philosophy. For philosophy informs us that everything which appears to the mind is nothing but a perception, and is interrupted and dependent on the mind; whereas the vulgar confound perceptions and objects, and attribute a distinct continued existence to the very things they feel or see. This sentiment, then, as it is entirely unreasonable, must proceed from some other faculty than the understanding. To which we may add, that as long as we take our perceptions and objects to be the same, we can never infer the existence of the one from that of the other, nor form any argument from the relation of cause and effect; which is the only one that can assure us of matter of fact. Even after we distinguish our perceptions from our objects, it will appear presently that we are still incapable of reasoning from the existence of one to that of the other : so that, upon the whole, our reason neither does, nor is it possible it ever should, upon any supposition, give us an assurance of the continued and distinct existence of body. That opinion must be entirely owing to the *imagination:* which must now be the subject of our inquiry.

Since all impressions are internal and perishing existences, and appear as such, the notion of their distinct and continued existence must arise from a concurrence of some of their qualities with the qualities of the imagination; and since this notion does not extend to all of them, it must arise from certain qualities peculiar to some impressions. It will, therefore, be easy for us to discover these qualities by a comparison of the impressions, to which we attribute a distinct and continued existence, with those which we regard as internal and perishing.

We may observe, then, that it is neither upon account of the involuntariness of certain impressions, as is commonly supposed, nor of their superior force and violence, that we attribute to them a reality and continued existence, which we refuse to others, that are voluntary or feeble. For it is evident our pains and pleasures, our passions and affections, which we never suppose to have any existence beyond our perception, operate with greater violence, and are equally involuntary, as the impressions of figure and extension, colour and sound, which we suppose to be permanent beings. The heat of a fire, when moderate, is supposed to exist in the fire; but the pain which it causes upon a near approach is not taken to have any being except in the perception.

These vulgar opinions, then, being rejected, we must search for some other hypothesis, by which we may discover those peculiar qualities in our impressions, which makes us attribute to them a distinct and continued existence.

After a little examination, we shall find that all those objects, to which we attribute a continued existence, have a peculiar *constancy*, which distinguishes them from the impressions whose existence depends upon our perception. Those mountains, and houses, and trees, which lie at present under my eye, have always appeared to me in the same order; and when I lose sight of them by shutting my eyes or turning my head, I soon after find them return upon me without the least alteration. My bed and table, my books and papers, present themselves in the same uniform manner, and change not upon account of any interruption in my seeing or perceiving them. This is the case with all the impressions whose objects are supposed to have an external existence; and is the case with no other impressions, whether gentle or violent, voluntary or involuntary.

This constancy, however, is not so perfect as not to admit of very considerable exceptions. Bodies often change their position and qualities, and, after a little absence or interruption, may become hardly knowable. But here it is observable, that even in these changes they preserve a *coherence*, and have a regular dependence on each other; which is the foundation of a kind of reasoning from causation, and produces the opinion of their continued existence. When I return to my chamber after an hour's absence, I find not my fire in the same situation in which I left it; but then I am accustomed, in other instances, to see a like alteration produced in a like time, whether I am present or absent, near or remote. This coherence, therefore, in their changes, is one of the characteristics of external objects, as well as their constancy.

Having found that the opinion of the continued existence of body depends on the *coherence* and *constancy* of certain impressions, I now proceed to examine after what manner these qualities give rise to so extraordinary an opinion. To begin with the coherence; we may observe, that though those internal impressions, which we regard as fleeting and perishing, have also a certain coherence or regularity in their appearances, yet it is of somewhat a different nature from that which we discover in our bodies. Our passions are found by experience to have a mutual connection with and dependence on each other; but on no occasion is it necessary to suppose that they have existed and operated, when they were not perceived, in order to preserve the same dependence and connection, of which we have had experience. The case is not the same with relation to external objects. Those require a continued existence, or otherwise lose, in a great measure, the regularity of their operation. I am here seated in my chamber, with my face to the fire; and all the objects that strike my senses are contained in a few yards around me. My memory, indeed, informs me of the existence of many objects; but, then, this information extends not beyond their past existence, nor do either my senses or memory give any testimony to the continuance of their being. When, therefore, I am thus seated, and revolve over these thoughts, I hear on a sudden a noise as of a door turning upon its hinges; and a little after see a porter who advances towards me. This gives occasion to many new reflections and reasonings. First, I never have observed that this noise could proceed from anything but the motion of a door; and therefore conclude that the present phenomenon is a contradiction to all past experience, unless the door, which I remember on the other side of the chamber, be still in being. Again, I have always found, that a human body was possessed of a quality which I call gravity, and which hinders it from mounting in the air, as this porter must have done to arrive at my chamber, unless the stairs I remember be not annihilated by my absence. But this is not all. I receive a letter, which, upon opening it, I perceive by the handwriting and subscription to have come from a friend, who says he is two hundred leagues distant. It is evident I can never account for this phenomenon, conformable to my experience in other instances, without spreading out in my mind the whole sea and continent between us, and supposing the effects and continued existence of posts and ferries, according to my memory and observation. To consider these phenomena of the porter and letter in a certain light, they are contradictions to common experience, and may be regarded as objections to those maxims which we form concerning the connections of causes and effects. I am accustomed to hear such a sound, and see such an object in motion at the same time. I have not received, in this particular instance, both these perceptions. These observations are contrary, unless I suppose that the door still remains, and that it was opened without my perceiving it : and this supposition, which was at first entirely arbitrary and hypothetical, acquires a force and evidence by its being the only one upon which I can reconcile these contradictions. There is scarce a moment of my life wherein there is not a similar instance presented to me, and I have not occasion to suppose the continued existence of objects, in order to connect their past and present appearances, and give them such a union with each other, as I have found, by experience, to be suitable to their particular natures and circumstances. Here, then, I am naturally led to regard the world as something real and durable, and as preserving its existence, even when it is no longer present to my perception.

But, though this conclusion, from the coherence of appearances, may seem to be of the same nature with our reasonings concerning causes and effects, as being derived from custom, and regulated by past experience, we shall find upon examination, that they are at the bottom considerably different from each other, and that this inference arises from the understanding, and from custom in an indirect and oblique manner. For it will readily be allowed, that since nothing is ever really present to the mind, besides its own perceptions, it is not only impossible that any habit should ever be acquired otherwise than by the regular succession of these perceptions, but also that any habit should ever exceed that degree of regularity. Any degree, therefore, of regularity in our perceptions, can never be a foundation for us to infer a greater degree of regularity in some objects which are not perceived, since this supposes a contradiction, viz. a habit acquired by what was never present to the mind. But it is evident that, whenever we infer the continued existence of the objects of sense from their coherence, and the frequency of their union, it is in order to bestow on the objects a greater regularity than what is observed in our mere perceptions. We remark a connection betwixt two kinds of objects in their past appearance to the senses, but are not able to observe this connection to be perfectly constant, since the turning about of our head, or the shutting of our eyes, is able to break it. What, then, do we suppose in this case, but that these objects still continue their usual connection, notwithstanding their apparent interruption, and that the irregular appearances are joined by something of which we are insensible? But as all reasoning concerning matters of fact arises only from custom, and custom can only be the effect of repeated perceptions, the extending of custom and reasoning beyond the perceptions can never be the direct and natural effect of the constant repetition and connection, but must arise from the co-operation of some other principles.

I have already observed,[8] in examining the foundation of mathematics, that the imagination, when set into any train of thinking, is apt to continue even when its object fails it, and, like a galley put in motion by the oars, carries on its course without any new impulse. This I have assigned for the reason, why, after considering several loose standards of equality, and correcting them by each other, we proceed to imagine so correct and exact a standard of that relation as is not liable to the least error or variation. The same principle makes us easily entertain this opinion of the continued existence of body. Objects have a certain coherence even as they appear to our senses; but this coherence is much greater and more uniform if we suppose the objects to have a continued existence; and as the mind is once in the train of observing a uniformity among objects, it naturally continues till it renders the uniformity as complete as possible. The simple supposition of their continued existence suffices for this purpose, and gives us a notion of a much greater regularity among objects, than what they have when we look no further than our senses.†

But whatever force we may ascribe to this principle, I am afraid it is too weak to support alone so vast an edifice as is that of the continued existence of all external bodies; and that we must join the *constancy* of their appearance

[8] Part II, Sect. 4.

to the *coherence,* in order to give a satisfactory account of that opinion. As the explication of this will lead me into a considerable compass of very profound reasoning, I think it proper, in order to avoid confusion, to give a short sketch or abridgment of my system, and afterwards draw out all its parts in their full compass. This inference from the constancy of our perceptions, like the precedent from their coherence, gives rise to the opinion of the *continued* existence of body, which is prior to that of its *distinct* existence, and produces that latter principle.†

When we have been accustomed to observe a constancy in certain impressions, and have found that the perception of the sun or ocean, for instance, returns upon us, after an absence or annihilation, with like parts and in a like order as at its first appearance, we are not apt to regard these interrupted perceptions as different (which they really are), but on the contrary consider them as individually the same, upon account of their resemblance. But as this interruption of their existence is contrary to their perfect identity, and makes us regard the first impression as annihilated, and the second as newly created, we find ourselves somewhat at a loss, and are involved in a kind of contradiction. In order to free ourselves from this difficulty, we disguise, as much as possible, the interruption, or rather remove it entirely, by supposing that these interrupted perceptions are connected by a real existence, of which we are insensible. This supposition, or idea of continued existence, acquires a force and vivacity from the memory of these broken impressions, and from that propensity which they give us to suppose them the same; and according to the precedent reasoning, the very essence of belief consists in the force and vivacity of the conceptions.

In order to justify this system, there are four things requisite. *First,* to explain the *principium individuationis,* or principle of identity. *Secondly,* give a reason why the resemblance of our broken and interrupted perceptions induces us to attribute an identity to them. *Thirdly,* account for that propensity, which this illusion gives, to unite these broken appearances by a continued existence. *Fourthly,* and lastly, explain that force and vivacity of conception which arises from the propensity.

First, as to the principle of individuation, we may observe, that the view of any one object is not sufficient to convey the idea of identity. For in that proposition, *an object is the same with itself,* if the idea expressed by the word *object* were noways distinguished from that meant by *itself;* we really should mean nothing, nor would the proposition contain a predicate and a subject, which, however, are implied in this affirmation. One single object conveys the idea of unity, not that of identity.

On the other hand, a multiplicity of objects can never convey this idea, however resembling they may be supposed. The mind always pronounces the one not to be the other, and considers them as forming two, three, or any determinate number of objects, whose existences are entirely distinct and independent.

Since then both number and unity are incompatible with the relation of identity, it must lie in something that is neither of them. But to tell the truth, at first sight this seems utterly impossible. Betwixt unity and number there can be no medium; no more than betwixt existence and non-existence. After one object is supposed to exist, we must either suppose another also to exist; in which case we have the idea of number : or we must suppose it not to exist; in which case the first object remains at unity.

To remove this difficulty, let us have recourse to the idea of time or duration. I have already observed,[9] that time, in a strict sense, implies succession, and that, when we apply its idea to any unchangeable object, it is only by a fiction of the imagination by which the unchangeable object is supposed to participate of the changes of the co-existing objects, and in particular of that of our perceptions. This fiction of the imagination almost universally takes place; and it is by means of it that a single object, placed before us, and surveyed for any time without our

[9] Part II, Sect. 5.

discovering in it any interruption or variation, is able to give us a notion of identity. For when we consider any two points of this time, we may place them in different lights: we may either survey them at the very same instant; in which case they give us the idea of number, both by themselves and by the object; which must be multiplied in order to be conceived at once, as existent in these two different points of time: or, on the other hand, we may trace the succession of time by a like succession of ideas, and conceiving first one moment, along with the object then existent, imagine afterwards a change in the time without any *variation* or *interruption* in the object; in which case it gives us the idea of unity. Here then is an idea, which is a medium, betwixt unity and number; or, more properly speaking, is either of them, according to the view in which we take it: and this idea we call that of identity. We cannot, in any propriety of speech, say that an object existent at one time is the same with itself existent at another, unless we mean that the object existent at one time is the same with itself existent at another. By this means we make a difference betwixt the idea meant by the word *object,* and that meant by *itself,* without going the length of number, and at the same time without restraining ourselves to a strict and absolute unity.†

Thus the principle of individuation is nothing but the *invariableness* and *uninterruptedness* of any object, through a supposed variation of time, by which the mind can trace it in the different periods of its existence, without any break of the view, and without being obliged to form the idea of multiplicity or number.

I now proceed to explain the *second* part of my system, and show why the constancy of our perceptions makes us ascribe to them a perfect numerical identity, though there be very long intervals betwixt their appearance, and they have only one of the essential qualities of identity, viz. *invariableness.* That I may avoid all ambiguity and confusion on this head, I shall observe, that I here account for the opinions and belief of the vulgar with regard to the existence of body; and therefore must entirely conform myself to their manner of thinking and of expressing themselves. Now we have already observed, that however philosophers may distinguish betwixt the objects and perceptions of the senses; which they suppose co-existent and resembling; yet this is a distinction which is not comprehended by the generality of mankind, who as they perceive only one being, can never assent to the opinion of a double existence and representation. Those very sensations which enter by the eye or ear are with them the true objects, nor can they readily conceive that this pen or paper, which is immediately perceived, represents another which is different from, but resembling it. In order, therefore, to accommodate myself to their notions, I shall at first suppose that there is only a single existence, which I shall call indifferently *object* or *perception*, according as it shall seem best to suit my purpose, understanding by both of them what any common man means by a hat, or shoe, or stone, or any other impression conveyed to him by his senses.† I shall be sure to give warning when I return to a more philosophical way of speaking and thinking.

To enter therefore upon the question concerning the source of the error and deception with regard to identity, when we attribute it to our resembling perceptions, notwithstanding their interruption, I must here recall an observation which I have already proved and explained.[10] Nothing is more apt to make us mistake one idea for another, than any relation betwixt them, which associates them together in the imagination, and makes it pass with facility from one to the other. Of all relations, that of resemblance is in this respect the most efficacious; and that because it not only causes an association of ideas, but also of dispositions, and makes us conceive the one idea by an act or operation of the mind, similar to that by which we conceive the other. This circumstance I have observed to be of great moment; and we may establish it for a general

[10] Part II, Sect. 5.

rule, that whatever ideas place the mind in the same disposition or in similar ones, are very apt to be confounded. The mind readily passes from one to the other, and perceives not the change without a strict attention, of which, generally speaking, it is wholly incapable.

In order to apply this general maxim, we must first examine the disposition of the mind in viewing any object which preserves a perfect identity, and then find some other object that is confounded with it, by causing a similar disposition. When we fix our thought on any object, and suppose it to continue the same for some time, it is evident we suppose the change to lie only in the time, and never exert ourselves to produce any new image or idea of the object. The faculties of the mind repose themselves in a manner, and take no more exercise than what is necessary to continue that idea of which we were formerly possessed, and which subsists without variation or interruption. The passage from one moment to another is scarce felt, and distinguishes not itself by a different perception or idea, which may require a different direction of the spirits, in order to its conception.

Now what other objects, besides identical ones, are capable of placing the mind in the same disposition, when it considers them, and of causing the same uninterrupted passage of the imagination from one idea to another? This question is of the last importance. For if we can find any such objects, we may certainly conclude, from the foregoing principle, that they are very naturally confounded with identical ones, and are taken for them in most of our reasonings. But though this question be very important, it is not very difficult nor doubtful. For I immediately reply, that a succession of related objects places the mind in this disposition, and is considered with the same smooth and uninterrupted progress of the imagination, as attends the view of the same invariable object. The very nature and essence of relation is to connect our ideas with each other, and upon the appearance of one, to facilitate the transition to its correlative. The passage betwixt related ideas is

therefore so smooth and easy, that it produces little alteration of the mind, and seems like the continuation of the
same action; and as the continuation of the same action is
an effect of the continued view of the same object, it is for
this reason we attribute sameness to every succession of
related objects. The thought slides along the succession
with equal facility, as if it considered only one object; and
therefore confounds the succession with the identity.

We shall afterwards see many instances of this tendency
of relation to make us ascribe an *identity* to *different*
objects; but shall here confine ourselves to the present
subject. We find by experience that there is such a *constancy* in almost all the impressions of the senses, that
their interruption produces no alteration on them, and
hinders them not from returning the same in appearance
and in situation as at their first existence. I survey the
furniture of my chamber; I shut my eyes, and afterwards
open them; and find the new perceptions to resemble perfectly those which formerly struck my senses. This resemblance is observed in a thousand instances, and naturally connects together our ideas of these interrupted perceptions by the strongest relation, and conveys the mind
with an easy transition from one to another. An easy transition or passage of the imagination, along the ideas of
these different and interrupted perceptions, is almost the
same disposition of mind with that in which we consider
one constant and uninterrupted perception. It is therefore
very natural for us to mistake the one for the other.[11]

[11] This reasoning, it must be confessed, is somewhat abstruse and
difficult to be comprehended; but it is remarkable, that this very
difficulty may be converted into a proof of the reasoning. We
may observe that there are two relations, and both of them
resemblances, which contribute to our mistaking the succession of
our interrupted perceptions for an identical object. The first is,
the resemblance of the perceptions: the second is, the resemblance
which the act of the mind, in surveying a succession of resembling
objects, bears to that in surveying an identical object. Now
these resemblances we are apt to confound with each other; and
it is natural we should, according to this very reasoning. But let
us keep them distinct, and we shall find no difficulty in conceiving
the precedent argument.

The persons who entertain this opinion concerning the identity of our resembling perceptions, are in general all the unthinking and unphilosophical part of mankind, (that is, all of us at one time or other,) and consequently such as suppose their perceptions to be their only objects, and never think of a double existence internal and external, representing and represented. The very image which is present to the senses is with us the real body; and it is to these interrupted images we ascribe a perfect identity. But as the interruption of the appearance seems contrary to the identity, and naturally leads us to regard these resembling perceptions as different from each other, we here find ourselves at a loss how to reconcile such opposite opinions. The smooth passage of the imagination along the ideas of the resembling perceptions makes us ascribe to them a perfect identity. The interrupted manner of their appearance makes us consider them as so many resembling, but still distinct beings, which appear after certain intervals. The perplexity arising from this contradiction produces a propension to unite these broken appearances by the fiction of a continued existence, which is the *third* part of that hypothesis I proposed to explain.

Nothing is more certain from experience than that any contradiction either to the sentiments or passions gives a sensible uneasiness, whether it proceeds from without or from within; from the opposition of external objects, or from the combat of internal principles. On the contrary, whatever strikes in with the natural propensities, and either externally forwards their satisfaction, or internally concurs with their movements, is sure to give a sensible pleasure. Now, there being here an opposition betwixt the notion of the identity of resembling perceptions, and the interruption of their appearance, the mind must be uneasy in that situation, and will naturally seek relief from the uneasiness. Since the uneasiness arises from the opposition of two contrary principles, it must look for relief by sacrificing the one to the other. But as the smooth passage of our thought along our resembling perceptions makes us ascribe to them an identity, we can never, without reluctance, yield up that opinion. We must therefore turn to the other side, and suppose that our perceptions are no longer interrupted, but preserve a continued as well as an invariable existence, and are by that means entirely the same. But here the interruption in the appearance of these perceptions are so long and frequent, that it is impossible to overlook them; and as the *appearance* of a perception in the mind and its *existence* seem at first sight entirely the same, it may be doubted whether we can ever assent to so palpable a contradiction, and suppose a perception to exist without being present to the mind. In order to clear up this matter, and learn how the interruption in the appearance of a perception implies not necessarily an interruption in its existence, it will be proper to touch upon some principles which we shall have occasion to explain more fully afterwards.[12]

We may begin with observing, that the difficulty in the present case is not concerning the matter of fact, or whether the mind forms such a conclusion concerning the continued existence of its perceptions, but only concerning the manner in which the conclusion is formed, and principles from which it is derived. It is certain that almost all mankind, and even philosophers themselves, for the greatest part of their lives, take their perceptions to be their only objects, and suppose that the very being which is intimately present to the mind, is the real body or material existence. It is also certain that this very perception or object is supposed to have a continued uninterrupted being, and neither to be annihilated by our absence, nor to be brought into existence by our presence. When we are absent from it, we say it still exists, but that we do not feel, we do not see it. When we are present, we say we feel or see it. Here then may arise two questions; *first,* how we can satisfy ourselves in supposing a perception to be absent from the mind without being annihilated. *Secondly,* after what manner we conceive an object to become pre-

[12] Sect. 6.

I

sent to the mind, without some new creation of a perception or image; and what we mean by this *seeing,* and *feeling,* and *perceiving.*

As to the first question, we may observe, that what we call a *mind,* is nothing but a heap or collection of different perceptions, united together by certain relations, and supposed, though falsely, to be endowed with a perfect simplicity and identity.[18] Now, as every perception is distinguishable from another, and may be considered as separately existent; it evidently follows, that there is no absurdity in separating any particular perception from the mind; that is, in breaking off all its relations with that connected mass of perceptions which constitute a thinking being.

The same reasoning affords us an answer to the second question. If the name of *perception* renders not this separation from a mind absurd and contradictory, the name of *object,* standing for the same thing, can never render their conjunction impossible. External objects are seen and felt, and become present to the mind; that is, they acquire such a relation to a connected heap of perceptions as to influence them very considerably in augmenting their number by present reflections and passions, and in storing the memory with ideas. The same continued and uninterrupted being may, therefore, be sometimes present to the mind and sometimes absent from it without any real or essential change in the being itself. An interrupted appearance to the senses implies not necessarily an interruption in the existence. The supposition of the continued existence of sensible objects or perceptions involves no contradiction. We may easily indulge our inclination to that supposition. When the exact resemblance of our perceptions makes us ascribe to them an identity, we may remove the seeming interruption by feigning a continued being, which may fill those intervals, and preserve a perfect and entire identity to our perceptions.†

But as we here not only *feign* but *believe* this continued existence, the question is, *from whence arises such a belief?*

18 *Compare Section* vi.

and this question leads us to the *fourth* member of this system. It has been proved already, that belief, in general, consists in nothing but the vivacity of an idea; and that an idea may acquire this vivacity by its relation to some present impression. Impressions are naturally the most vivid perceptions of the mind; and this quality is in part conveyed by the relation to every connected idea. The relation causes a smooth passage from the impression to the idea, and even gives a propensity to that passage. The mind falls so easily from the one perception to the other, that it scarce perceives the change, but retains in the second a considerable share of the vivacity of the first. It is excited by the lively impression, and this vivacity is conveyed to the related idea, without any great diminution in the passage, by reason of the smooth transition and the propensity of the imagination.

But suppose that this propensity arises from some other principle, besides that of relation; it is evident it must still have the same effect, and convey the vivacity from the impression to the idea. Now, this is exactly the present case. Our memory presents us with a vast number of instances of perceptions perfectly resembling each other, that return at different distances of time, after considerable interruptions. This resemblance gives us a propension to consider these interrupted perceptions as the same; and also a propension to connect them by a continued existence, in order to justify this identity, and avoid the contradiction in which the interrupted appearance of these perceptions seems necessarily to involve us. Here then we have a propensity to feign the continued existence of all sensible objects; and as this propensity arises from some lively impressions of the memory, it bestows a vivacity on that fiction; or, in other words, makes us believe the continued existence of body. If sometimes we ascribe a continued existence to objects, which are perfectly new to us, and of whose constancy and coherence we have no experience, it is because the manner, in which they present themselves to our senses, resembles that of constant and coherent objects; and this resemblance is a source of reasoning and analogy, and leads us to attribute the same qualities to the similar objects.

I believe an intelligent reader will find less difficulty to assent to this system, than to comprehend it fully and distinctly, and will allow, after a little reflection, that every part carries its own proof along with it. It is indeed evident, that as the vulgar *suppose* their perceptions to be their only objects, and at the same time *believe* the continued existence of matter, we must account for the origin of the belief upon that supposition. Now upon that supposition, it is a false opinion that any of our objects, or perceptions, are identically the same after an interruption; and consequently the opinion of their identity can never arise from reason, but must arise from the imagination. The imagination is seduced into such an opinion only by means of the resemblance of certain perceptions; since we find they are only our resembling perceptions, which we have a propension to suppose the same. This propension to bestow an identity on our resembling perceptions, produces the fiction of a continued existence; since that fiction, as well as the identity, is really false, as is acknowledged by all philosophers, and has no other effect than to remedy the interruption of our perceptions, which is the only circumstance that is contrary to their identity. In the last place, this propension causes belief by means of the present impressions of the memory; since, without the remembrance of former sensations, it is plain we never should have any belief of the continued existence of body. Thus, in examining all these parts, we find that each of them is supported by the strongest proofs; and that all of them together form a consistent system, which is perfectly convincing. A strong propensity or inclination alone, without any present impression, will sometimes cause a belief or opinion. How much more when aided by that circumstance!

But though we are led after this manner, by the natural propensity of the imagination, to ascribe a continued existence to those sensible objects or perceptions, which we find to resemble each other in their interrupted appearance; yet a very little reflection and philosophy is sufficient to make us perceive the fallacy of that opinion. I have already observed that there is an intimate connection betwixt those two principles, of a *continued* and of a *distinct* or *independent* existence, and that we no sooner establish the one than the other follows as a necessary consequence. It is the opinion of a continued existence, which first takes place, and without much study or reflection draws the other along with it, wherever the mind follows its first and most natural tendency. But when we compare experiments, and reason a little upon them, we quickly perceive that the doctrine of the independent existence of our sensible perceptions is contrary to the plainest experience. This leads us backward upon our footsteps to perceive our error in attributing a continued existence to our perceptions, and is the origin of many very curious opinions, which we shall here endeavour to account for.

It will first be proper to observe a few of those experiments, which convince us that our perceptions are not possessed of any independent existence. When we press one eye with a finger, we immediately perceive all the objects to become double, and one half of them to be removed from their common and natural position. But as we do not attribute a continued existence to both these perceptions, and as they are both of the same nature, we clearly perceive that all our perceptions are dependent on our organs and the disposition of our nerves and animal spirits. This opinion is confirmed by the seeming increase and diminution of objects according to their distance; by the apparent alterations in their figure; by the changes in their colour and other qualities, from our sickness and distempers, and by an infinite number of other experiments of the same kind; from all which we learn that our sensible perceptions are not possessed of any distinct or independent existence.

The natural consequence of this reasoning should be,

that our perceptions have no more a continued than an independent existence; and, indeed, philosophers have so far run into this opinion, that they change their system, and distinguish (as we shall do for the future) betwixt perceptions and objects, of which the former are supposed to be interrupted and perishing, and different at every different return; the latter to be uninterrupted, and to preserve a continued existence and identity. But however philosophical this new system may be esteemed, I assert that it is only a palliative remedy, and that it contains all the difficulties of the vulgar system, with some others that are peculiar to itself. There are no principles either of the understanding or fancy, which lead us directly to embrace this opinion of the double existence of perceptions and objects, nor can we arrive at it but by passing through the common hypothesis of the identity and continuance of our interrupted perceptions. Were we not first persuaded that our perceptions are our only objects, and continue to exist even when they no longer make their appearance to the senses, we should never be led to think that our perceptions and objects are different, and that our objects alone preserve a continued existence. " The latter hypothesis has no primary recommendation either to reason or the imagination, but acquires all its influence on the imagination from the former." This proposition contains two parts which we shall endeavour to prove as distinctly and clearly as such abstruse subjects will permit.

As to the first part of the proposition, *that this philosophical hypothesis has no primary recommendation, either to reason or the imagination,* we may soon satisfy ourselves with regard to *reason,* by the following reflections. The only existences, of which we are certain, are perceptions, which being immediately present to us by consciousness, command our strongest assent, and are the first foundation of all our conclusions. The only conclusion we can draw from the existence of one thing to that of another, is by means of the relation of cause and effect, which shows that there is a connection betwixt them, and that the existence of one is dependent on that of the other. The idea of this relation is derived from past experience, by which we find that two beings are constantly conjoined together, and are always present at once to the mind. But as no beings are ever present to the mind but perceptions, it follows that we may observe a conjunction or a relation of cause and effect between different perceptions, but can never observe it between perceptions and objects. It is impossible, therefore, that from the existence or any of the qualities of the former, we can ever form any conclusion concerning the existence of the latter, or ever satisfy our reason in this particular.

It is no less certain that this philosophical system has no primary recommendation to the *imagination,* and that that faculty would never, of itself, and by its original tendency, have fallen upon such a principle. I confess it will be somewhat difficult to prove this to the full satisfaction of the reader; because it implies a negative, which in many cases will not admit of any positive proof. If any one would take the pains to examine this question, and would invent a system to account for the direct origin of this opinion from the imagination, we should be able, by the examination of that system, to pronounce a certain judgment in the present subject. Let it be taken for granted, that our perceptions are broken and interrupted, and however like, are still different from each other; and let any one, upon this supposition, show why the fancy, directly and immediately, proceeds to the belief of another existence, resembling these perceptions in their nature, but yet continued, and uninterrupted, and identical; and after he has done this to my satisfaction, I promise to renounce my present opinion. Meanwhile I cannot forbear concluding, from the very abstractedness and difficulty of the first supposition, that it is an improper subject for the fancy to work upon. Whoever would explain the origin of the *common* opinion concerning the continued and distinct existence of body, must take the mind in its *common* situation, and must proceed upon the supposition, that our per-

ceptions are our only objects, and continue to exist even
when they are not perceived. Though this opinion be
false, it is the most natural of any, and has alone any
primary recommendation to the fancy.

As to the second part of the proposition, *that the philosophical system acquires all its influence on the imagination from the vulgar one;* we may observe that this is a
natural and unavoidable consequence of the foregoing
conclusion, *that it has no primary recommendation to
reason or the imagination.* For as the philosophical system
is found by experience to take hold of many minds, and,
in particular, of all those who reflect ever so little on this
subject, it must derive all its authority from the vulgar
system, since it has no original authority of its own. The
manner in which these two systems, though directly contrary, are connected together, may be explained as follows.

The imagination naturally runs on in this train of thinking. Our perceptions are our only objects : resembling perceptions are the same, however broken or uninterrupted in
their appearance : this appearing interruption is contrary
to the identity : the interruption consequently extends not
beyond the appearance, and the perception or object really
continues to exist, even when absent from us : our sensible perceptions have, therefore, a continued and uninterrupted existence. But as a little reflection destroys this
conclusion, that our perceptions have a continued existence, by showing that they have a dependent one, it would
naturally be expected that we must altogether reject the
opinion, that there is such a thing in nature as a continued
existence, which is preserved even when it no longer appears to the senses. The case, however, is otherwise.
Philosophers are so far from rejecting the opinion of a
continued existence upon rejecting that of the independence and continuance of our sensible perceptions, that
though all sects agree in the latter sentiment, the former,
which is in a manner its necessary consequence, has been
peculiar to a few extravagant sceptics; who, after all, main-

tained that opinion in words only, and were never able to bring themselves sincerely to believe it.[14]

There is a great difference betwixt such opinions as we form after a calm and profound reflection, and such as we embrace by a kind of instinct or natural impulse, on account of their suitableness and conformity to the mind. If these opinions become contrary, it is not difficult to foresee which of them will have the advantage. As long as our attention is bent upon the subject, the philosophical and studied principle may prevail; but the moment we relax our thoughts, nature will display herself, and draw us back to our former opinion. Nay she has sometimes such an influence, that she can stop our progress, even in the midst of our most profound reflections, and keep us from running on with all the consequences of any philosophical opinion. Thus though we clearly perceive the dependence and interruption of our perceptions, we stop short in our career, and never upon that account reject the notion of an independent and continued existence. That opinion has taken such deep root in the imagination, that it is impossible ever to eradicate it, nor will any strained metaphysical conviction of the dependence of our perceptions be sufficient for that purpose.

But though our natural and obvious principles here prevail above our studied reflections, it is certain there must be some struggle and opposition in this case; at least so long as these reflections retain any force or vivacity. In order to set ourselves at ease in this particular, we contrive a new hypothesis, which seems to comprehend both these principles of reason and imagination. This hypothesis is the philosophical one of the double existence of perceptions and objects; which pleases our reason, in allowing that our dependent perceptions are interrupted and different, and at the same time is agreeable to the imagination, in attributing a continued existence to something else, which we call *objects*. This philosophical system, therefore, is the monstrous offspring of two prin-

[14] *Compare Enquiry, Sect. XII, Part II . . . footnote on Berkeley.*

ciples, which are contrary to each other, which are both at once embraced by the mind, and which are unable mutually to destroy each other. The imagination tells us that our resembling perceptions have a continued and uninterrupted existence, and are not annihilated by their absence. Reflection tells us, that even our resembling perceptions are interrupted in their existence, and different from each other. The contradiction betwixt these opinions we elude by a new fiction, which is conformable to the hypothesis both of reflection and fancy, by ascribing these contrary qualities to different existences; the *interruption* to perceptions, and the *continuance* to objects. Nature is obstinate, and will not quit the field, however strongly attacked by reason; and at the same time reason is so clear in the point that there is no possibility of disguising her. Not being able to reconcile these two enemies, we endeavour to set ourselves at ease as much as possible, by successively granting to each whatever it demands, and by feigning a double existence, where each may find something that has all the conditions it desires. Were we fully convinced that our resembling perceptions are continued, and identical, and independent, we should never run into this opinion of a double existence; since we should find satisfaction in our first supposition, and would not look beyond. Again, were we fully convinced that our perceptions are dependent, and interrupted, and different, we should be as little inclined to embrace the opinion of a double existence; since in that case we should clearly perceive the error of our first supposition of a continued existence, and would never regard it any further. It is therefore from the intermediate situation of the mind that this opinion arises, and from such an adherence to these two contrary principles, as makes us seek some pretext to justify our receiving both; which happily at last is found in the system of a double existence.[15]

Another advantage of this philosophical system is its

[15] *For further developments and difficulties of the double existence theory, see Section* IV.

similarity to the vulgar one, by which means we can humour our reason for a moment, when it becomes troublesome and solicitous; and yet upon its least negligence or inattention, can easily return to our vulgar and natural notions. Accordingly we find that philosophers neglect not this advantage, but immediately upon leaving their closets, mingle with the rest of mankind in those exploded opinions, that our perceptions are our only objects, and continue identically and uninterruptedly the same in all their interrupted appearances.

There are other particulars of this system, wherein we may remark its dependence on the fancy, in a very conspicuous manner. Of these, I shall observe the two following. *First*, we suppose external objects to resemble internal perceptions. I have already shown that the relation of cause and effect can never afford us any just conclusion from the existence or qualities of our perceptions to the existence of external continued objects : and I shall further add, that even though they could afford such a conclusion, we should never have any reason to infer that our objects resemble our perceptions. That opinion, therefore, is derived from nothing but the quality of the fancy above explained, *that it borrows all its ideas from some precedent perception*. We never can conceive anything but perceptions, and therefore must make everything resemble them.

Secondly, as we suppose our objects in general to resemble our perceptions, so we take it for granted that every particular object resembles that perception which it causes. The relation of cause and effect determines us to join the other of resemblance; and the ideas of these existences being already united together in the fancy by the former relation, we naturally add the latter to complete the union. We have a strong propensity to complete every union by joining new relations to those which we have before observed betwixt any ideas, as we shall have occasion to observe presently.[16]

Having thus given an account of all the systems, both

[16] Sect. 5.

popular and philosophical, with regard to external existences, I cannot forbear giving vent to a certain sentiment
which arises upon reviewing those systems. I began this
subject with premising that we ought to have an implicit
faith in our senses, and that this would be the conclusion I
should draw from the whole of my reasoning. But to be
ingenuous, I feel myself *at present* of a quite contrary
sentiment, and am more inclined to repose no faith at all
in my senses, or rather imagination, than to place in it such
an implicit confidence. I cannot conceive how such trivial
qualities of the fancy, conducted by such false suppositions, can ever lead to any solid and rational system. They
are the coherence and constancy of our perceptions, which
produce the opinion of their continued existence; though
these qualities of perceptions have no perceivable connection with such an existence. The constancy of our perceptions has the most considerable effect, and yet is
attended with the greatest difficulties. It is a gross illusion
to suppose that our resembling perceptions are numerically
the same; and it is this illusion which leads us into the
opinion that these perceptions are uninterrupted, and are
still existent, even when they are not present to the senses.
This is the case with our popular system. And as to our
philosophical one, it is liable to the same difficulties; and
is over and above loaded with this absurdity, that it at
once denies and establishes the vulgar supposition. Philosophers deny our resembling perceptions to be identically
the same, and uninterrupted; and yet have so great a
propensity to believe them such, that they arbitrarily invent
a new set of perceptions, to which they attribute these
qualities. I say, a new set of perceptions : for we may well
suppose in general, but it is impossible for us distinctly to
conceive, objects to be in their nature anything but exactly
the same with perceptions.[17] What then can we look for
from this confusion of groundless and extraordinary
opinions but error and falsehood? And how can we justify
to ourselves any belief we repose in them?

[17] *Compare Part* ii, *Sect.* vi, *conclusion.*

This sceptical doubt, both with respect to reason and the senses, is a malady which can never be radically cured, but must return upon us every moment, however we may chase it away, and sometimes may seem entirely free from it. It is impossible, upon any system, to defend either our understanding or senses; and we but expose them further when we endeavour to justify them in that manner. As the sceptical doubt arises naturally from a profound and intense reflection on those subjects, it always increases the further we carry our reflections, whether in opposition or conformity to it. Carelessness and inattention alone can afford us any remedy. For this reason I rely entirely upon them; and take it for granted, whatever may be the reader's opinion at this present moment, that an hour hence he will be persuaded there is both an external and internal world; and, going upon that supposition, I intend to examine some general systems, both ancient and modern, which have been proposed of both, before I proceed to a more particular inquiry concerning our impressions. This will not, perhaps, in the end, be found foreign to our present purpose.

SECTION III

OF THE ANCIENT PHILOSOPHY

Several moralists have recommended it as an excellent method of becoming acquainted with our own hearts, and knowing our progress in virtue, to recollect our dreams in a morning, and examine them with the same rigour that we would our most serious and most deliberate actions. Our character is the same throughout, say they, and appears best where artifice, fear, and policy, have no place, and men can neither be hypocrites with themselves nor others. The generosity or baseness of our temper, our meekness or cruelty, our courage or pusillanimity, influence the fictions of the imagination with the most unbounded liberty, and discover themselves in the most glaring colours. In like manner, I am persuaded, there might be several useful discoveries made from a criticism of the fictions of the ancient philosophy concerning *substances, and substantial forms, and accidents, and occult qualities,* which, however unreasonable and capricious, have a very intimate connection with the principles of human nature.

It is confessed by the most judicious philosophers, that our ideas of bodies are nothing but collections formed by the mind of the ideas of the several distinct sensible qualities, of which objects are composed, and which we find to have a constant union with each other. But however these qualities may in themselves be entirely distinct, it is certain we commonly regard the compound, which they form, as *one* thing, and as continuing the *same* under very considerable alterations. The acknowledged composition is evidently contrary to this supposed *simplicity,* and the variation to the *identity.* It may therefore be worth while to consider the *causes,* which make us almost universally fall into such evident contradictions, as well as the *means* by which we endeavour to conceal them.

It is evident that as the ideas of the several distinct *successive* qualities of objects are united together by a very close relation, the mind, in looking along the succession, must be carried from one part of it to another by an easy transition, and will no more perceive the change than if it contemplated the same unchangeable object. This easy transition is the effect, or rather essence of relation; and as the imagination readily takes one idea for another, where their influence on the mind is similar; hence it proceeds, that any such succession of related qualities is readily considered as one continued object, existing without any variation. The smooth and uninterrupted progress of the thought, being alike in both cases, readily deceives the mind, and makes us ascribe an identity to the changeable succession of connected qualities.

But when we alter our method of considering the succession, and instead of tracing it gradually through the successive points of time, survey at once any two distinct periods of its duration, and compare the different conditions of the successive qualities; in that case the variations, which were insensible when they arose gradually, do now appear of consequence, and seem entirely to destroy the identity. By this means there arises a kind of contrariety in our method of thinking, from the different points of view, in which we survey the object, and from the nearness or remoteness of those instants of time, which we compare together. When we gradually follow an object in its successive changes, the smooth progress of the thought makes us ascribe an identity to the succession; because it is by a similar act of the mind we consider an unchangeable object. When we compare its situation after a considerable change the progress of the thought is broken; and consequently we are presented with the idea of diversity; in order to reconcile which contradictions, the imagination is apt to feign something unknown and invisible, which it supposes to continue the same under all these variations; and this unintelligible something it calls a *substance, or original and first matter*.

We entertain a like notion with regard to the *simplicity* of substances, and from like causes. Suppose an object perfectly simple and indivisible to be presented, along with another object, whose *co-existent* parts are connected together by a strong relation, it is evident the actions of the mind, in considering these two objects, are not very different. The imagination conceives the simple object at once, with facility, by a single effort of thought, without change or variation. The connection of parts in the compound object has almost the same effect, and so unites the object within itself, that the fancy feels not the transition in passing from one part to another. Hence the colour, taste, figure, solidity, and other qualities, combined in a peach or melon, are conceived to form *one thing;* and that on account of their close relation, which makes them affect the thought in the same manner, as if perfectly uncompounded. But the mind rests not here. Whenever it views the object in another light, it finds that all these qualities are different, and distinguishable, and separable from each other; which view of things being destructive of its primary and more natural notions, obliges the imagination to feign an unknown something, or *original* substance and matter, as a principle of union or cohesion among these qualities, and as what may give the compound object a title to be called one thing, notwithstanding its diversity and composition.

The Peripatetic philosophy asserts the *original* matter to be perfectly homogeneous in all bodies, and considers fire, water, earth, and air, as of the very same substance, on account of their gradual revolutions and changes into each other. At the same time it assigns to each of these species of objects a distinct *substantial form,* which it supposes to be the source of all those different qualities they possess, and to be a new foundation of simplicity and identity to each particular species. All depends on our manner of viewing the objects. When we look along the insensible changes of bodies, we suppose all of them to be of the same substance or essence. When we consider their sensible differences, we attribute to each of them a substantial and essential difference. And in order to indulge ourselves in both these ways of considering our objects, we suppose all bodies to have at once a substance and a substantial form.

The notion of *accidents* is an unavoidable consequence of this method of thinking with regard to substances and substantial forms; nor can we forbear looking upon colours, sounds, tastes, figures, and other properties of bodies, as existences, which cannot subsist apart, but require a subject of inhesion to sustain and support them. For having never discovered any of these sensible qualities, where, for the reasons above mentioned, we did not likewise fancy a substance to exist; the same habit, which makes us infer a connection betwixt cause and effect, makes us here infer a dependence of every quality on the unknown substance. The custom of imagining a dependence has the same effect as the custom of observing it would have. This conceit, however, is no more reasonable than any of the foregoing. Every quality being a distinct thing from another, may be conceived to exist apart, and may exist apart not only from every other quality, but from that unintelligible chimera of a substance.

But these philosophers carry their fictions still further in their sentiments concerning *occult qualities,* and both suppose a substance supporting, which they do not understand, and an accident supported, of which they have as imperfect an idea. The whole system, therefore, is entirely incomprehensible, and yet is derived from principles as natural as any of these above explained.

In considering this subject, we may observe a gradation of three opinions that rise above each other, according as the persons who form them acquire new degrees of reason and knowledge. These opinions are that of the vulgar, that of a false philosophy, and that of the true; where we shall find upon inquiry, that the true philosophy approaches nearer to the sentiments of the vulgar than to those of a mistaken knowledge. It is natural for men, in their common and careless way of thinking, to imagine they perceive a connection betwixt such objects as they have constantly found united together; and because custom has rendered it difficult to separate the ideas, they are apt to fancy such a separation to be in itself impossible and absurd. But philosophers, who abstract from the effects of custom, and compare the ideas of objects, immediately perceive the falsehood of these vulgar sentiments, and discover that there is no known connection among objects. Every different object appears to them entirely distinct and separate; and they perceive that it is not from a view of the nature and qualities of objects we infer one from another, but only when in several instances we observe them to have been constantly conjoined. But these philosophers, instead of drawing a just inference from this observation, and concluding that we have no idea of power or agency, separate from the mind and belonging to causes;

I say, instead of drawing this conclusion, they frequently search for the qualities in which this agency consists, and are displeased with every system which their reason suggests to them in order to explain it. They have sufficient force of genius to free them from the vulgar error, that there is a natural and perceivable connection betwixt the several sensible qualities and actions of matter, but not sufficient to keep them from ever seeking for this connection in matter or causes. Had they fallen upon the just conclusion, they would have returned back to the situation of the vulgar, and would have regarded all these disquisitions with indolence and indifference. At present they seem to be in a very lamentable condition, and such as the poets have given us but a faint notion of in their descriptions of the punishment of Sisyphus and Tantalus. For what can be imagined more tormenting than to seek with eagerness what for ever flies us, and seek for it in a place where it is impossible it can ever exist?

But as Nature seems to have observed a kind of justice and comprehension in everything, she has not neglected philosophers more than the rest of the creation, but has reserved them a consolation amid all their disappointments and afflictions. This consolation principally consists in their invention of the words *faculty* and *occult quality*. For it being usual, after the frequent use of terms, which are really significant and intelligible, to omit the idea which we would express by them, and preserve only the custom by which we recall the idea at pleasure; so it naturally happens, that after the frequent use of terms which are wholly insignificant and unintelligible, we fancy them to be on the same footing with the precedent, and to have a secret meaning which we might discover by reflection. The resemblance of their appearance deceives the mind, as is usual, and makes us imagine a thorough resemblance and conformity. By this means these philosophers set themselves at ease, and arrive at last, by an illusion, at the same indifference which the people attain by their stupidity, and true philosophers by their moderate scepticism. They need only say, that any phenomenon which puzzles them arises from a faculty or an occult quality, and there is an end of all dispute and inquiry upon the matter.

But among all the instances wherein the Peripatetics have shown they were guided by every trivial propensity of the imagination, no one is more remarkable than their *sympathies, antipathies, and horrors of a vacuum*. There is a very remarkable inclination in human nature to bestow on external objects the same emotions which it observes in itself, and to find everywhere those ideas which are most present to it. This inclination, it is true, is suppressed by a little reflection, and only takes place in children, poets, and the ancient philosophers. It appears in children, by their desire of beating the stones which hurt them; in poets by their readiness to personify everything; and in the ancient philosophers, by these fictions of sympathy and antipathy. We must pardon children, because of their age; poets, because they profess to follow implicitly the suggestions of their fancy; but what excuse shall we find to justify our philosophers in so signal a weakness?

SECTION IV

OF THE MODERN PHILOSOPHY

But here it may be objected, that the imagination, according to my own confession, being the ultimate judge of all systems of philosophy, I am unjust in blaming the ancient philosophers for making use of that faculty, and allowing themselves to be entirely guided by it in their reasonings. In order to justify myself, I must distinguish in the imagination betwixt the principles which are permanent, irresistible, and universal; such as the customary transition from causes to effects, and from effects to causes : and the principles, which are changeable, weak, and irregular; such as those I have just now taken notice of. The former are the foundation of all our thoughts and actions, so that upon their removal, human nature must immediately perish and go to ruin. The latter are neither unavoidable to mankind, nor necessary, or so much as useful in the conduct of life; but, on the contrary, are observed only to take place in weak minds, and being opposite to the other principles of custom and reasoning, may easily be subverted by a due contrast and opposition. For this reason, the former are received by philosophy, and the latter rejected. One who concludes somebody to be near him, when he hears an articulate voice in the dark, reasons justly and naturally; though that conclusion be derived from nothing but custom, which infixes and enlivens the idea of a human creature, on account of his usual conjunction with the present impression. But one who is tormented he knows not why, with the apprehension of spectres in the dark, may perhaps be said to reason, and to reason naturally too : but then it must be in the same sense that a malady is said to be natural; as arising from natural causes, though it be contrary to health, the most agreeable and most natural situation of man.

The opinions of the ancient philosophers, their fictions of substance and accident, and their reasonings concerning substantial forms and occult qualities, are like the spectres in the dark, and are derived from principles, which, however common, are neither universal nor unavoidable in human nature. The *modern philosophy* pretends to be entirely free from this defect, and to arise only from the solid, permanent, and consistent principles of the imagination. Upon what grounds this pretension is founded must now be the subject of our inquiry.

The fundamental principle of that philosophy is the opinion concerning colours, sounds, tastes, smells, heat, and cold; which it asserts to be nothing but impressions in the mind, derived from the operation of external objects, and without any resemblance to the qualities of the objects.[18] Upon examination, I find only one of the reasons

[18] *Compare Locke, Essay conc. Human Understanding, Book* II, *ch.* 8.

commonly produced for this opinion to be satisfactory; viz. that derived from the variation of those impressions, even while the external object, to all appearance, continues the same. These variations depend upon several circumstances. Upon the different situations of our health : a man in a malady feels a disagreeable taste in meats, which before pleased him the most. Upon the different complexions and constitutions of men : that seems bitter to one, which is sweet to another. Upon the difference of their external situation and position : colours reflected from the clouds change according to the distance of the clouds, and according to the angle they make with the eye and luminous body. Fire also communicates the sensation of pleasure at one distance, and that of pain at another. Instances of this kind are very numerous and frequent.

The conclusion drawn from them is likewise as satisfactory as can possibly be imagined. It is certain that when different impressions of the same sense arise from any object, every one of these impressions has not a resembling quality existent in the object. For as the same object cannot, at the same time, be endowed with different qualities of the same sense, and as the same quality cannot resemble impressions entirely different; it evidently follows, that many of our impressions have no external model or archetype. Now, from like effects we presume like causes. Many of the impressions of colour, sound, etc., are confessed to be nothing but internal existences, and to arise from causes which noways resemble them. These impressions are in appearance nothing different from the other impressions of colour, sound, etc. We conclude, therefore, that they are, all of them, derived from a like origin.

This principle being once admitted, all the other doctrines of that philosophy seem to follow by an easy consequence. For, upon the removal of sounds, colours, heat, cold, and other sensible qualities, from the rank of continued independent existences, we are reduced merely to what are called primary qualities, as the only *real* ones, of which we have any adequate notion. These primary qualities are extension and solidity, with their different mixtures and modifications; figure, motion, gravity, and cohesion. The generation, increase, decay, and corruption of animals and vegetables, are nothing but changes of figure and motion; as also the operations of all bodies on each other; of fire, or light, water, air, earth, and of all the elements and powers of nature. One figure and motion produces another figure and motion; nor does there remain in the material universe any other principle, either active or passive, of which we can form the most distant idea.

I believe many objections might be made to this system; but at present I shall confine myself to one, which is, in my opinion, very decisive. I assert, that instead of explaining the operations of external objects by its means, we utterly annihilate all these objects, and reduce ourselves to the opinions of the most extravagant scepticism concerning them. If colours, sounds, tastes, and smells be merely perceptions, nothing we can conceive is possessed of a real, continued, and independent existence; not even motion, extension, and solidity, which are the primary qualities chiefly insisted on.

To begin with the examination of motion; it is evident this is a quality altogether inconceivable alone, and without a reference to some other object. The idea of motion necessarily supposes that of a body moving. Now what is our idea of the moving body, without which motion is incomprehensible? It must resolve itself into the idea of extension or of solidity; and consequently the reality of motion depends upon that of these other qualities.

This opinion, which is universally acknowledged concerning motion, I have proved to be true with regard to extension;[19] and have shown that it is impossible to conceive extension but as composed of parts, endowed with colour or solidity. The idea of extension is a compound idea; but as it is not compounded of an infinite number of parts or inferior ideas, it must at last resolve itself into such as are perfectly simple and indivisible. These simple

[19] *Part* II, *Sect.* III.

and indivisible parts not being ideas of extension, must be nonentities, unless conceived as coloured or solid. Colour is excluded from any real existence. The reality therefore of our idea of extension depends upon the reality of that of solidity; nor can the former be just while the latter is chimerical. Let us then lend our attention to the examination of the idea of solidity.

The idea of solidity is that of two objects, which, being impelled by the utmost force, cannot penetrate each other, but still maintain a separate and distinct existence. Solidity therefore is perfectly incomprehensible alone, and without the conception of some bodies which are solid, and maintain this separate and distinct existence. Now what idea have we of these bodies? The ideas of colours, sounds, and other secondary qualities, are excluded. The idea of motion depends on that of extension, and the idea of extension on that of solidity. It is impossible, therefore, that the idea of solidity can depend on either of them. For that would be to run in a circle, and make one idea depend on another, while at the same time the latter depends on the former. Our modern philosophy, therefore, leaves us no just nor satisfactory idea of solidity, nor consequently of matter.

This argument will appear entirely conclusive to every one that comprehends it; but because it may seem abstruse and intricate to the generality of readers, I hope to be excused if I endeavour to render it more obvious by some variation of the expression. In order to form an idea of solidity, we must conceive two bodies pressing on each other without any penetration; and it is impossible to arrive at this idea when we confine ourselves to one object, much more without conceiving any. Two nonentities cannot exclude each other from their places, because they never possess any place, nor can be endowed with any quality. Now I ask, what idea do we form of these bodies or objects to which we suppose solidity to belong? To say that we conceive them merely as solid, is to run on *in infinitum*. To affirm that we paint them out to ourselves as extended, either resolves all into a false idea, or returns in a circle. Extension must necessarily be considered either as coloured, which is a false idea, or as solid, which brings us back to the first question. We may make the same observation concerning mobility and figure; and, upon the whole, must conclude that after the exclusion of colours, sounds, heat, and cold, from the rank of external existences, there remains nothing which can afford us a just and consistent idea of body.

Add to this, that, properly speaking, solidity or impenetrability is nothing but an impossibility of annihilation, as has been already observed:[20] for which reason it is the more necessary for us to form some distinct idea of that object whose annihilation we suppose impossible. An impossibility of being annihilated cannot exist, and can never be conceived to exist, by itself, but necessarily requires some object or real existence to which it may belong. Now the difficulty still remains how to form an idea of this object or existence, without having recourse to the secondary and sensible qualities.

Nor must we omit, on this occasion, our accustomed method of examining ideas by considering those impressions from which they are derived. The impressions which enter by the sight and hearing, the smell and taste, are affirmed by modern philosophy to be without any resembling objects; and consequently the idea of solidity, which is supposed to be real, can never be derived from any of these senses. There remains, therefore, the feeling as the only sense that can convey the impression which is original to the idea of solidity; and indeed we naturally imagine that we feel the solidity of bodies, and need but touch any object in order to perceive this quality. But this method of thinking is more popular than philosophical, as will appear from the following reflections.

First, it is easy to observe, that though bodies are felt by means of their solidity, yet the feeling is a quite different thing from the solidity, and that they have not the least

[20] Part ii, Sect. 4.

resemblance to each other. A man who has the palsy in one hand has as perfect an idea of impenetrability, when he observes that hand to be supported by the table, as when he feels the same table with the other hand. An object that presses upon any of our members meets with resistance; and that resistance, by the motion it gives to the nerves and animal spirits, conveys a certain sensation to the mind; but it does not follow that the sensation, motion, and resistance are any ways resembling.

Secondly, the impressions of touch are simple impressions, except when considered with regard to their extension; which makes nothing to the present purpose : and from this simplicity I infer that they neither represent solidity, nor any real object. For let us put two cases, viz. that of a man who presses a stone or any solid body with his hand, and that of two stones which press each other; it will readily be allowed that these two cases are not in every respect alike, but that in the former there is conjoined with the solidity a feeling or sensation of which there is no appearance in the latter. In order, therefore, to make these two cases alike, it is necessary to remove some part of the impression which the man feels by his hand, or organ of sensation; and that being impossible in a simple impression, obliges us to remove the whole, and proves that this whole impression has no archetype or model in external objects; to which we may add, that solidity necessarily supposes two bodies, along with contiguity and impulse; which being a compound object, can never be represented by a simple impression. Not to mention, that though solidity continues always invariably the same, the impressions of touch change every moment upon us, which is a clear proof that the latter are not representations of the former.

Thus there is a direct and total opposition betwixt our reason and our senses; or, more properly speaking, betwixt those conclusions we form from cause and effect, and those that persuade us of the continued and independent existence of body. When we reason from cause and effect, we conclude that neither colour, sound, taste, nor smell have a continued and independent existence. When we exclude these sensible qualities, there remains nothing in the universe which has such an existence.

SECTION V

OF THE IMMATERIALITY OF THE SOUL

Having found such contradictions and difficulties in every system concerning external objects, and in the idea of matter, which we fancy so clear and determinate, we shall naturally expect still greater difficulties and contradictions in every hypothesis concerning our internal perceptions, and the nature of the mind, which we are apt to imagine so much more obscure and uncertain. But in this we should deceive ourselves. The intellectual world, though involved in infinite obscurities, is not perplexed with any such contradictions as those we have discovered in the natural. What is known concerning it, agrees with itself; and what is unknown, we must be contented to leave so.[21]

It is true, would we hearken to certain philosophers, they promise to diminish our ignorance; but I am afraid it is at the hazard of running us into contradictions, from which the subject is itself exempted. These philosophers are the curious reasoners concerning the material or immaterial substances, in which they suppose our perceptions to inhere. In order to put a stop to these endless cavils on both sides, I know no better method than to ask these philosophers in a few words, *What they mean by substance and inhesion?* And after they have answered this question, it will then be reasonable, and not till then, to enter seriously into the dispute.

This question we have found impossible to be answered with regard to matter and body; but besides that in the

[21] *See Appendix, pp.* 330-331.

case of the mind it labours under all the same difficulties, it is burdened with some additional ones, which are peculiar to that subject. As every idea is derived from a precedent impression, had we any idea of the substance of our minds, we must also have an impression of it, which is very difficult, if not impossible, to be conceived. For how can an impression represent a substance, otherwise than by resembling it? And how can an impression resemble a substance, since, according to this philosophy, it is not a substance, and has none of the peculiar qualities or characteristics of a substance?

But leaving the question of *what may or may not be,* for that other *what actually is,* I desire those philosophers, who pretend that we have an idea of the substance of our minds, to point out the impression that produces it, and tell distinctly after what manner that impression operates, and from what object it is derived. Is it an impression of sensation or reflection? Is it pleasant, or painful, or indifferent? Does it attend us at all times, or does it only return at intervals? If at intervals, at what times principally does it return, and by what causes is it produced?

If instead of answering these questions, any one should evade the difficulty by saying that the definition of a substance is *something which may exist by itself,* and that this definition ought to satisfy us : should this be said, I should observe that this definition agrees to everything that can possibly be conceived; and never will serve to distinguish substance from accident, or the soul from its perceptions. For thus I reason. Whatever is clearly conceived may exist; and whatever is clearly conceived, after any manner, may exist after the same manner. This is one principle which has been already acknowledged. Again, everything which is different is distinguishable, and everything which is distinguishable is separable by the imagination. This is another principle. My conclusion from both is, that since all our perceptions are different from each other, and from everything else in the universe, they are also distinct and separable, and may be considered as separately existent, and may exist separately, and have no need of anything else to support their existence. They are therefore substances, as far as this definition explains a substance.

Thus, neither by considering the first origin of ideas, nor by means of a definition, are we able to arrive at any satisfactory notion of substance, which seems to me a sufficient reason for abandoning utterly that dispute concerning the materiality and immateriality of the soul, and makes me absolutely condemn even the question itself. We have no perfect idea of anything but of a perception. A substance is entirely different from a perception. We have therefore no idea of a substance. Inhesion in something is supposed to be requisite to support the existence of our perceptions. Nothing appears requisite to support the existence of a perception. We have therefore no idea of inhesion. What possibility then of answering that question, *Whether perceptions inhere in a material or immaterial substance,* when we do not so much as understand the meaning of the question?

There is one argument commonly employed for the immateriality of the soul, which seems to me remarkable. Whatever is extended consists of parts; and whatever consists of parts is divisible, if not in reality, at least in the imagination. But it is impossible anything divisible can be *conjoined* to a thought or perception, which is a being altogether inseparable and indivisible. For supposing such a conjunction, would the indivisible thought exist on the left or on the right hand of this extended divisible body? On the surface or in the middle? On the back or foreside of it? If it be conjoined with the extension, it must exist somewhere within its dimensions. If it exist within its dimensions, it must either exist in one particular part; and then that particular part is indivisible, and the perception is conjoined only with it, not with the extension : or if the thought exists in every part, it must also be extended, and separable, and divisible, as well as the body, which is utterly absurd and contradictory. For can any one conceive a passion of a yard in length, a foot in breadth, and an inch in thickness? Thought therefore and extension are qualities wholly incompatible, and never can incorporate together into one subject.

This argument affects not the question concerning the *substance* of the soul, but only that concerning its *local conjunction* with matter; and therefore it may not be improper to consider in general what objects are, or are not susceptible of a local conjunction. This is a curious question, and may lead us to some discoveries of considerable moment.

The first notion of space and extension is derived solely from the senses of sight and feeling; nor is there anything, but what is coloured or tangible, that has parts disposed after such a manner as to convey that idea. When we diminish or increase a relish, it is not after the same manner that we diminish or increase any visible object; and when several sounds strike our hearing at once, custom and reflection alone make us form an idea of the degrees of the distance and contiguity of those bodies from which they are derived. Whatever marks the place of its existence, either must be extended, or must be a mathematical point, without parts or composition. What is extended must have a particular figure, as square, round, triangular; none of which will agree to a desire, or indeed to any impression or idea, except of these two senses above mentioned. Neither ought a desire, though indivisible, to be considered as a mathematical point. For in that case it would be possible, by the addition of others, to make two, three, four desires; and these disposed and situated in such a manner as to have a determinate length, breadth, and thickness; which is evidently absurd.

It will not be surprising after this, if I deliver a maxim, which is condemned by several metaphysicians, and is esteemed contrary to the most certain principles of human reason. This maxim is, *that an object may exist, and yet be nowhere*; and I assert that this is not only possible, but that the greatest part of beings do and must exist after this manner. An object may be said to be nowhere, when its parts are not so situated with respect to each other, as to form any figure or quantity; nor the whole with respect to other bodies so as to answer to our notions of contiguity or distance. Now this is evidently the case with all our perceptions and objects, except those of the sight and feeling. A moral reflection cannot be placed on the right or on the left hand of a passion; nor can a smell or sound be either of a circular or a square figure. These objects and perceptions, so far from requiring any particular place, are absolutely incompatible with it, and even the imagination cannot attribute it to them. And as to the absurdity of supposing them to be nowhere, we may consider that if the passions and sentiments appear to the perception to have any particular place, the idea of extension might be derived from them as well as from the sight and touch; contrary to what we have already established. If they *appear* not to have any particular place, they may possibly *exist* in the same manner; since whatever we conceive is possible.

It will not now be necessary to prove, that those perceptions, which are simple, and exist nowhere, are incapable of any conjunction in place with matter or body, which is extended and divisible; since it is impossible to found a relation but on some common quality.[22] It may be better worth our while to remark, that this question of the local conjunction of objects does not only occur in metaphysical disputes concerning the nature of the soul, but that even in common life we have every moment occasion to examine it. Thus, supposing we consider a fig at one end of the table, and an olive at the other, it is evident that, in forming the complex idea of these substances, one of the most obvious is that of their different relishes; and it is as evident, that we incorporate and conjoin these qualities with such as are coloured and tangible. The bitter taste of the one, and sweet of the other, are supposed to lie in the very visible body, and to be separated from each other by the whole length of the table. This is so notable and so

22 Part I, Sect. 5.

natural an illusion, that it may be proper to consider the principles from which it is derived.

Though an extended object be incapable of a conjunction in place with another that exists without any place or extension, yet are they susceptible of many other relations. Thus the taste and smell of any fruit are inseparable from its other qualities of colour and tangibility; and whichever of them be the cause or effect, it is certain they are always co-existent. Nor are they only co-existent in general, but also contemporary in their appearance in the mind; and it is upon the application of the extended body to our senses we perceive its particular taste and smell. These relations, then, of *causation, and contiguity in the time of their appearance,* betwixt the extended object and the quality, which exists without any particular place, must have such an effect on the mind that, upon the appearance of one, it will immediately turn its thought to the conception of the other. Nor is this all. We not only turn our thought from one to the other upon account of their relation, but likewise endeavour to give them a new relation, viz. that of *a conjunction in place,* that we may render the transition more easy and natural. For it is a quality which I shall often have occasion to remark in human nature, and shall explain more fully in its proper place, that, when objects are united by any relation, we have a strong propensity to add some new relation to them, in order to complete the union. In our arrangement of bodies, we never fail to place such as are resembling in contiguity to each other, or at least in correspondent points of view : why? but because we feel a satisfaction in joining the relation of contiguity to that of resemblance, or the resemblance of situation to that of qualities. The effects of this propensity have been already observed[23] in that resemblance which we so readily suppose betwixt particular impressions and their external causes. But we shall not find a more evident effect of it than in the present instance, where from the relations of causation and contiguity in time betwixt two objects, we

[23] Sect. 2, towards the end.

feign likewise that of a conjunction in place, in order to strengthen the connection.

But whatever confused notions we may form of a union in place betwixt an extended body, as a fig, and its particular taste, it is certain that upon reflection we must observe in this union something altogether unintelligible and contradictory. For, should we ask ourselves one obvious question, viz. if the taste, which we conceive to be contained in the circumference of the body, is in every part of it, or in one only, we must quickly find ourselves at a loss, and perceive the impossibility of ever giving a satisfactory answer. We cannot reply that it is only in one part: for experience convinces us that every part has the same relish. We can as little reply that it exists in every part: for then we must suppose it figured and extended; which is absurd and incomprehensible. Here then we are influenced by two principles directly contrary to each other, viz. that *inclination* of our fancy by which we are determined to incorporate the taste with the extended object, and our *reason,* which shows us the impossibility of such a union. Being divided betwixt these opposite principles, we renounce neither one nor the other, but involve the subject in such confusion and obscurity, that we no longer perceive the opposition. We suppose that the taste exists within the circumference of the body, but in such a manner that it fills the whole without extension, and exists entire in every part without separation. In short, we use, in our most familiar way of thinking, that scholastic principle which, when crudely proposed, appears so shocking, of *totum in toto, et totum in qualibet parte:* which is much the same as if we should say, that a thing is in a certain place, and yet is not there.

All this absurdity proceeds from our endeavouring to bestow a place on what is utterly incapable of it; and that endeavour again arises from our inclination to complete a union which is founded on causation and a contiguity of time, by attributing to the objects a conjunction in place. But if ever reason be of sufficient force to overcome prejudice, it is certain, that in the present case it must prevail. For we have only this choice left, either to suppose that some beings exist without any place, or that they are figured and extended; or that when they are incorporated with extended objects, the whole is in the whole, and the whole in every part. The absurdity of the two last suppositions proves sufficiently the veracity of the first. Nor is there any fourth opinion : For as to the supposition of their existence in the manner of mathematical points, it resolves itself into the second opinion, and supposes that several passions may be placed in a circular figure, and that a certain number of smells, conjoined with a certain number of sounds, may make a body of twelve cubic inches; which appears ridiculous upon the bare mentioning of it.

But though in this view of things we cannot refuse to condemn the materialists, who conjoin all thought with extension; yet a little reflection will show us equal reason for blaming their antagonists, who conjoin all thought with a simple and indivisible substance. The most vulgar philosophy informs us that no external object can make itself known to the mind immediately, and without the interposition of an image or perception. That table, which just now appears to me, is only a perception, and all its qualities are qualities of a perception. Now the most obvious of all its qualities is extension. The perception consists of parts. These parts are so situated as to afford us the notion of distance and contiguity, of length, breadth, and thickness. The termination of these three dimensions is what we call figure. This figure is movable, separate, and divisible. Mobility and separability are the distinguishing properties of extended objects. And to cut short all disputes, the very idea of extension is copied from nothing but an impression, and consequently must perfectly agree to it. To say the idea of extension agrees to anything, is to say it is extended.

The freethinker may now triumph in his turn; and having found there are impressions and ideas really extended, may ask his antagonists how they can incorporate a simple and indivisible subject with an extended perception? All the arguments of theologians may here be retorted upon them. Is the indivisible subject or immaterial substance, if you will, on the left or on the right hand of the perception? Is it in this particular part, or in that other? Is it in every part without being extended? Or is it entire in any one part without deserting the rest? It is impossible to give any answer to these questions but what will both be absurd in itself, and will account for the union of our indivisible perceptions with an extended substance.

This gives me an occasion to take anew into consideration the question concerning the substance of the soul; and though I have condemned that question as utterly unintelligible, yet I cannot forbear proposing some further reflections concerning it. I assert that the doctrine of the immateriality, simplicity, and indivisibility of a thinking substance is a true atheism, and will serve to justify all those sentiments for which Spinoza is so universally infamous. From this topic I hope at least to reap one advantage, that my adversaries will not have any pretext to render the present doctrine odious by their declamations when they see that they can be so easily retorted on them.

The fundamental principle of the atheism of Spinoza is the doctrine of the simplicity of the universe, and the unity of that substance in which he supposes both thought and matter to inhere. There is only one substance, says he, in the world, and that substance is perfectly simple and indivisible, and exists everywhere without any local presence. Whatever we discover externally by sensation, whatever we feel internally by reflection, all these are nothing but modifications of that one simple and necessarily existent being, and are not possessed of any separate or distinct existence. Every passion of the soul, every configuration of matter however different and various, inhere in the same substance, and preserve in themselves their characters of distinction, without communicating them to that subject in which they inhere. The same *substratum,* if I may so speak, supports the most different modifications without any difference in itself, and varies them without any variation. Neither time, nor place, nor all the diversity of nature are able to produce any composition or change in its perfect simplicity and identity.

I believe this brief exposition of the principles of that famous atheist will be sufficient for the present purpose, and that without entering further into these gloomy and obscure regions, I shall be able to show, that this hideous hypothesis is almost the same with that of the immateriality of the soul, which has become so popular. To make this evident, let us remember[24] that as every idea is derived from a preceding perception, it is impossible our idea of a perception, and that of an object or external existence, can ever represent what are specifically different from each other. Whatever difference we may suppose betwixt them, it is still incomprehensible to us; and we are obliged either to conceive an external object merely as a relation without a relative, or to make it the very same with a perception or impression.

The consequence I shall draw from this may, at first sight, appear a mere sophism; but upon the least examination will be found solid and satisfactory. I say then, that since we may suppose, but never can conceive, a specific difference betwixt an object and impression, any conclusion we form concerning the connection and repugnance of impressions, will not be known certainly to be applicable to objects; but that on the other hand whatever conclusions of this kind we form concerning objects will most certainly be applicable to impressions. The reason is not difficult. As an object is supposed to be different from an impression, we cannot be sure that the circumstance, upon which we found our reasoning, is common to both, supposing we form the reasoning upon the impression. It is still possible that the object may differ from it in that particular. But when we first form our reasoning concern-

[24] Part II, Sect. 6.

ing the object, it is beyond doubt that the same reasoning must extend to the impression: and that because the quality of the object, upon which the argument is founded, must at least be conceived by the mind, and could not be conceived unless it were common to an impression; since we have no idea but what is derived from that origin. Thus we may establish it as a certain maxim, that we can never, by any principle, but by an irregular kind of reasoning from experience,[25] discover a connection or repugnance betwixt objects, which extends not to impressions; though the inverse proposition may not be equally true, that all the discoverable relations of impressions are common to objects.

To apply this to the present case; there are two different systems of beings presented, to which I suppose myself under a necessity of assigning some substance, or ground of inhesion. I observe first the universe of objects or of body: the sun, moon, and stars; the earth, seas, plants, animals, men, ships, houses, and other productions either of art or nature. Here Spinoza appears, and tells me that these are only modifications and that the subject in which they inhere is simple, uncompounded, and indivisible. After this I consider the other system of beings, viz. the universe of thought, or my impressions and ideas. There I observe another sun, moon, and stars; an earth, and seas, covered and inhabited by plants and animals; towns, houses, mountains, rivers; and in short everything I can discover or conceive in the first system. Upon my inquiring concerning these, theologians present themselves, and tell me that these also are modifications, and modifications of one simple, uncompounded, and indivisible substance. Immediately upon which I am deafened with the noise of a hundred voices, that treat the first hypothesis with detestation and scorn, and the second with applause and veneration. I turn my attention to these hypotheses to see what may be the reason of so great a partiality; and find

[25] Such as that of Sect. 2, from the coherence of our perceptions.

that they have the same fault of being unintelligible, and that as far as we can understand them, they are so much alike, that it is impossible to discover any absurdity in one, which is not common to both of them. We have no idea of any quality in an object, which does not agree to, and may not represent a quality in an impression; and that because all our ideas are derived from our impressions. We can never therefore find any repugnance betwixt an extended object as a modification, and a simple uncompounded essence, as its substance, unless that repugnance takes place equally betwixt the perception or impression of that extended object, and the same uncompounded essence. Every idea of a quality in an object passes through an impression; and therefore every *perceivable* relation, whether of connection or repugnance, must be common both to objects and impressions.

But though this argument, considered in general, seems evident beyond all doubt and contradiction, yet to make it more clear and sensible, let us survey it in detail; and see whether all the absurdities, which have been found in the system of Spinoza, may not likewise be discovered in that of theologians.[26]

First, it has been said against Spinoza, according to the scholastic way of talking, rather than thinking, that a mode, not being any distinct or separate existence, must be the very same with its substance, and consequently the extension of the universe must be in a manner identified with that simple, uncompounded essence in which the universe is supposed to inhere. But this, it may be pretended, is utterly impossible and inconceivable unless the indivisible substance expand itself, so as to correspond to the extension, or the extension contract itself, so as to answer to the indivisible substance. This argument seems just, as far as we can understand it; and it is plain nothing is required, but a change in the terms, to apply the same argument to our extended perceptions, and the simple essence of the soul; the ideas of objects and perceptions being in every

[26] See Bayle's *Dictionary,* article of Spinoza.

respect the same, only attended with the supposition of a difference, that is unknown and incomprehensible.

Secondly, it has been said that we have no idea of substance, which is not applicable to matter; nor any idea of a distinct substance, which is not applicable to every distinct portion of matter. Matter therefore is not a mode but a substance, and each part of matter is not a distinct mode, but a distinct substance. I have already proved, that we have no perfect idea of substance; but that taking it for *something that can exist by itself*, it is evident every perception is a substance, and every distinct part of a perception a distinct substance : and consequently the one hypothesis labours under the same difficulties in this respect with the other.

Thirdly, it has been objected to the system of one simple substance in the universe, that this substance, being the support or *substratum* of everything, must at the very same instant be modified into forms which are contrary and incompatible. The round and square figures are incompatible in the same substance at the same time. How then is it possible that the same substance can at once be modified into that square table, and into this round one? I ask the same question concerning the impressions of these tables; and find that the answer is no more satisfactory in one case than in the other.

It appears, then, that to whatever side we turn, the same difficulties follow us, and that we cannot advance one step towards the establishing the simplicity and immateriality of the soul, without preparing the way for a dangerous and irrecoverable atheism. It is the same case, if instead of calling thought a modification of the soul, we should give it the more ancient, and yet more modish name of an *action*. By an action we mean much the same thing as what is commonly called an abstract mode; that is, something which, properly speaking, is neither distinguishable nor separable from its substance, and is only conceived by a distinction of reason, or an abstraction. But nothing is gained by this change of the term of modification for that of action; nor do we free ourselves from one single difficulty by its means, as will appear from the two following reflections :

First, I observe that the word *action*, according to this explication of it, can never justly be applied to any perception, as derived from the mind or thinking substance. Our perceptions are all really different, and separable, and distinguishable from each other, and from everything else which we can imagine; and therefore it is impossible to conceive how they can be the action or abstract mode of any substance. The instance of motion, which is commonly made use of to show after what manner perception depends as an action upon its substance, rather confounds than instructs us. Motion to all appearance induces no real nor essential change on the body, but only varies its relation to other objects. But betwixt a person in the morning walking in a garden, with company agreeable to him; and a person in the afternoon inclosed in a dungeon, and full of terror, despair, and resentment, there seems to be a radical difference, and of quite another kind, than what is produced on a body by the change of its situation. As we conclude from the distinction and separability of their ideas, that external objects have a separate existence from each other; so, when we make these ideas themselves our objects, we must draw the same conclusion concerning *them*, according to the precedent reasoning. At least it must be confessed, that having no idea of the substance of the soul, it is impossible for us to tell how it can admit of such differences, and even contrarieties of perception, without any fundamental change; and consequently can never tell in what sense perceptions are actions of that substance. The use, therefore, of the word *action*, unaccompanied with any meaning, instead of that of modification, makes no addition to our knowledge, nor is of any advantage to the doctrine of the immateriality of the soul.

I add in the second place, that if it brings any advantage to that cause, it must bring an equal to the cause of atheism. For do our theologians pretend to make a monopoly of the word *action*, and may not the atheists likewise take possession of it, and affirm that plants, animals, men, etc., are nothing but particular actions of one simple universal substance, which exerts itself from a blind and absolute necessity? This you will say is utterly absurd. I own it is unintelligible; but at the same time assert, according to the principles above explained, that it is impossible to discover any absurdity in the supposition, that all the various objects in nature are actions of one simple substance, which absurdity will not be applicable to a like supposition concerning impressions and ideas.

From these hypotheses concerning the *substance* and *local conjunction* of our perceptions, we may pass to another, which is more intelligible than the former, and more important than the latter, viz. concerning the *cause* of our perceptions. Matter and motion, it is commonly said in the schools, however varied, are still matter and motion, and produce only a difference in the position and situation of objects. Divide a body as often as you please, it is still body. Place it in any figure, nothing ever results but figure, or the relation of parts. Move it in any manner, you still find motion or a change of relation. It is absurd to imagine that motion in a circle, for instance, should be nothing but merely motion in a circle; while motion in another direction, as in an ellipse, should also be a passion or moral reflection : that the shocking of two globular particles should become a sensation of pain, and that the meeting of two triangular ones should afford a pleasure. Now as these different shocks and variations and mixtures are the only changes of which matter is susceptible, and as these never afford us any idea of thought or perception, it is concluded to be impossible that thought can ever be caused by matter.

Few have been able to withstand the seeming evidence of this argument; and yet nothing in the world is more easy than to refute it. We need only reflect on what has been proved at large, that we are never sensible of any connection betwixt causes and effects, and that it is only by our experience of their constant conjunction we can arrive at any knowledge of this relation. Now as all objects, which are not contrary, are susceptible of a constant conjunction, and as no real objects are contrary; I have inferred from these principles,[27] that to consider the matter *a priori,* anything may produce anything, and that we shall never discover a reason why any object may or may not be the cause of any other, however great, or however little the resemblance may be betwixt them. This evidently destroys the precedent reasoning concerning the cause of thought or perception. For though there appear no manner of connection betwixt motion or thought, the case is the same with all other causes and effects. Place one body of a pound weight on one end of a lever, and another body of the same weight on another end; you will never find in these bodies any principle of motion dependent on their distances from the centre, more than of thought and perception. If you pretend, therefore, to prove *a priori* that such a position of bodies can never cause thought; because turn it which way you will, it is nothing but a position of bodies; you must by the same course of reasoning conclude that it can never produce motion; since there is no more apparent connection in the one case than in the other. But as this latter conclusion is contrary to evident experience, and as it is possible we may have a like experience in the operations of the mind, and may perceive a constant conjunction of thought and motion; you reason too hastily when, from the mere consideration of the ideas, you conclude that it is impossible motion can ever produce thought, or a different position of parts give rise to a different passion or reflection. Nay it is not only possible we may have such an experience, but it is certain we have it; since every one may perceive that the different dispositions of his body change his thoughts and sentiments. And should it be said that this depends on the union of soul and body, I would answer, that we must separate the question concerning the substance of the mind from that concerning

[27] Part III, Sect. 15.

the cause of its thought; and that, confining ourselves to
the latter question, we find by the comparing their ideas,
that thought and motion are different from each other, and
by experience, that they are constantly united; which being
all the circumstances that enter into the idea of cause and
effect, when applied to the operations of matter, we may
certainly conclude that motion may be, and actually is,
the cause of thought and perception.

There seems only this dilemma left us in the present
case; either to assert, that nothing can be the cause of
another, but where the mind can perceive the connection
in its idea of the objects : or to maintain, that all objects
which we find constantly conjoined, are upon that account
to be regarded as causes and effects. If we choose the first
part of the dilemma, these are the consequences. *First,* we
in reality affirm that there is no such thing in the universe
as a cause or productive principle, not even the Deity himself; since our idea of that Supreme Being is derived from
particular impressions, none of which contain any efficacy,
nor seem to have *any* connection with *any* other existence.
As to what may be said, that the connection betwixt the
idea of an infinitely powerful Being and that of any effect,
which he wills, is necessary and unavoidable; I answer,
that we have no idea of a Being endowed with any power,
much less of one endowed with infinite power. But if we
will change expressions, we can only define power by connection; and then in saying that the idea of an infinitely
powerful Being is connected with that of every effect
which he wills, we really do no more than assert, that a
Being, whose volition is connected with every effect, is
connected with every effect; which is an identical proposition, and gives us no insight into the nature of this power
or connection. But, *secondly,* supposing that the Deity
were the great and efficacious principle which supplies the
deficiency of all causes, this leads us into the grossest
impieties and absurdities. For upon the same account
that we have recourse to him in natural operations, and
assert that matter cannot of itself communicate motion,

or produce thought, viz. because there is no apparent connection betwixt these objects; I say, upon the very same account, we must acknowledge that the Deity is the author of all our volitions and perceptions; since they have no more apparent connection either with one another, or with the supposed but unknown substance of the soul. This agency of the Supreme Being we know to have been asserted by several philosophers[28] with relation to all the actions of the mind, except volition, or rather an inconsiderable part of volition; though it is easy to perceive that this exception is a mere pretext, to avoid the dangerous consequences of that doctrine. If nothing be active but what has an apparent power, thought is in no case any more active than matter; and if this inactivity must make us have recourse to a Deity, the Supreme Being is the real cause of all our actions, bad as well as good, vicious as well as virtuous.

Thus we are necessarily reduced to the other side of the dilemma, viz. that all objects, which are found to be constantly conjoined, are upon that account only to be regarded as causes and effects. Now as all objects which are not contrary are susceptible of a constant conjunction, and as no real objects are contrary; it follows that, for aught we can determine by the mere ideas, anything may be the cause or effect of anything; which evidently gives the advantage to the materialists above their antagonists.

To pronounce, then, the final decision upon the whole : the question concerning the substance of the soul is absolutely unintelligible : all our perceptions are not susceptible of a local union, either with what is extended or unextended; there being some of them of the one kind, and some of the other : and as the constant conjunction of objects constitutes the very essence of cause and effect, matter and motion may often be regarded as the causes of thought, as far as we have any notion of that relation.

It is certainly a kind of indignity to philosophy, whose sovereign authority ought everywhere to be acknowledged,

[28] As Father Malebranche and other Cartesians.

to oblige her on every occasion to make apologies for her conclusions, and justify herself to every particular art and science, which may be offended at her. This puts one in mind of a king arraigned for high treason against his subjects. There is only one occasion when philosophy will think it necessary and even honourable to justify herself; and that is, when religion may seem to be in the least offended; whose rights are as dear to her as her own, and are indeed the same. If any one, therefore, should imagine that the foregoing arguments are anyways dangerous to religion, I hope the following apology will remove his apprehensions.

There is no foundation for any conclusion *a priori,* either concerning the operations or duration of any object, of which it is possible for the human mind to form a conception. Any object may be imagined to become entirely inactive, or to be annihilated in a moment; and it is an evident principle, *that whatever we can imagine is possible.* Now this is no more true of matter than of spirit; of an extended compounded substance, than of a simple and unextended. In both cases the metaphysical arguments for the immortality of the soul are equally inconclusive; and in both cases the moral arguments and those derived from the analogy of nature are equally strong and convincing. If my philosophy therefore makes no addition to the arguments for religion, I have at least the satisfaction to think it takes nothing from them, but that everything remains precisely as before.†

SECTION VI

OF PERSONAL IDENTITY

There are some philosophers who imagine we are every moment intimately conscious of what we call our *self;* that we feel its existence and its continuance in existence; and are certain, beyond the evidence of a demonstration, both of its perfect identity and simplicity. The strongest sensation, the most violent passion, say they, instead of distracting us from this view, only fix it the more intensely and make us consider their influence on *self* either by their pain or pleasure. To attempt a further proof of this were to weaken its evidence; since no proof can be derived from any fact of which we are so intimately conscious; nor is there anything of which we can be certain if we doubt of this.

Unluckily all these positive assertions are contrary to that very experience which is pleaded for them; nor have we any idea of *self*, after the manner it is here explained. For from what impression could this idea be derived? This question it is impossible to answer without a manifest contradiction and absurdity; and yet it is a question which must necessarily be answered, if we would have the idea of self pass for clear and intelligible. It must be some one impression that gives rise to every real idea. But self or person is not any one impression, but that to which our several impressions and ideas are supposed to have a reference. If any impression gives rise to the idea of self, that impression must continue invariably the same, through the whole course of our lives; since self is supposed to exist after that manner. But there is no impression constant and invariable. Pain and pleasure, grief and joy, passions and sensations succeed each other, and never all exist at the same time. It cannot therefore be from any of these impressions, or from any other, that the idea of self is derived; and consequently there is no such idea.

But further, what must become of all our particular perceptions upon this hypothesis? All these are different, and distinguishable, and separable from each other, and may be separately considered, and may exist separately, and have no need of anything to support their existence. After what manner therefore do they belong to self, and how are they connected with it? For my part, when I enter most intimately into what I call *myself*, I always stumble on some particular perception or other, of heat or cold, light or shade, love or hatred, pain or pleasure. I never can catch *myself* at any time without a perception, and never can observe anything but the perception. When my perceptions are removed for any time, as by sound sleep, so long am I insensible of *myself*, and may truly be said not to exist. And were all my perceptions removed by death, and could I neither think, nor feel, nor see, nor love, nor hate, after the dissolution of my body, I should be entirely annihilated, nor do I conceive what is further requisite to make me a perfect nonentity. If any one, upon serious and unprejudiced reflection, thinks he has a different notion of *himself*, I must confess I can reason no longer with him. All I can allow him is, that he may be in the right as well as I, and that we are essentially different in this particular. He may, perhaps, perceive something simple and continued, which he calls *himself*; though I am certain there is no such principle in me.

But setting aside some metaphysicians of this kind, I may venture to affirm of the rest of mankind, that they are nothing but a bundle or collection of different perceptions, which succeed each other with an inconceivable rapidity, and are in a perpetual flux and movement. Our eyes cannot turn in their sockets without varying our perceptions. Our thought is still more variable than our sight; and all our other senses and faculties contribute to this change; nor is there any single power of the soul, which remains unalterably the same, perhaps for one moment. The mind is a kind of theatre, where several perceptions successively make their appearance; pass, repass, glide away, and mingle in an infinite variety of postures and situations. There is properly no *simplicity* in it at one time, nor *identity* in different, whatever natural propension we may have to imagine that simplicity and identity. The comparison of the theatre must not mislead us. They are the successive perceptions only, that constitute the mind; nor have we the most distant notion of the place where these scenes are represented, or of the materials of which it is composed.

What then gives us so great a propension to ascribe an identity to these successive perceptions, and to suppose ourselves possessed of an invariable and uninterrupted existence through the whole course of our lives? In order to answer this question we must distinguish betwixt personal identity, as it regards our thought or imagination, and as it regards our passions or the concern we take in ourselves. The first is our present subject; and to explain it perfectly we must take the matter pretty deep, and account for that identity, which we attribute to plants and animals; there being a great analogy betwixt it and the identity of a self or person.

We have a distinct idea of an object that remains invariable and uninterrupted through a supposed variation of time; and this idea we call that of *identity* or *sameness*. We have also a distinct idea of several different objects existing in succession, and connected together by a close relation; and this to an accurate view affords as perfect a notion of *diversity* as if there was no manner of relation among the objects. But though these two ideas of identity, and a succession of related objects, be in themselves perfectly distinct, and even contrary, yet it is certain that, in our common way of thinking, they are generally confounded with each other. That action of the imagination, by which we consider the uninterrupted and invariable object, and that by which we reflect on the succession of related objects, are almost the same to the feeling; nor is there much more effort of thought required in the latter case than in the former. The relation facilitates the transition of the mind from one object to another, and renders its passage as smooth as if it contemplated one continued object. This resemblance is the cause of the confusion and mistake, and makes us substitute the notion of identity, instead of that of related objects. However at one instant we may consider the related succession as variable or interrupted, we are sure the next to ascribe to it a perfect identity, and regard it as invariable and uninterrupted. Our propensity to this mistake is so great from the resemblance above mentioned, that we fall into it before we are aware; and though we incessantly correct ourselves by reflection, and return to a more accurate method of thinking, yet we cannot long sustain our philosophy, or take off this bias from the imagination. Our last resource is to yield to it, and boldly assert that these different related objects are in effect the same, however interrupted and variable. In order to justify to ourselves this absurdity, we often feign some new and unintelligible principle, that connects the objects together, and prevents their interruption or variation. Thus we feign the continued existence of the perceptions of our senses, to remove the interruption; and run into the notion of a *soul,* and *self,* and *substance,* to disguise the variation. But, we may further observe, that where we do not give rise to such a fiction, our propension to confound identity with relation is so great, that we are apt to imagine something unknown and mysterious,[29] connecting the parts, beside their relation; and this I take to be the case with regard to the identity we ascribe to plants and vegetables. And even when this does not take place, we still feel a propensity to confound these ideas, though we are not able fully to satisfy ourselves in that particular, nor find anything invariable aud uninterrupted to justify our notion of identity.

Thus the controversy concerning identity is not merely a dispute of words. For when we attribute identity, in an improper sense, to variable or interrupted objects, our mistake is not confined to the expression, but is commonly attended with a fiction, either of something invariable and uninterrupted, or of something mysterious and inexplicable, or at least with a propensity to such fictions. What will suffice to prove this hypothesis to the satisfaction of every fair inquirer, is to show, from daily experience and

[29] If the reader is desirous to see how a great genius may be influenced by these seemingly trivial principles of the imagination, as well as the mere vulgar, let him read my Lord Shaftesbury's reasonings concerning the uniting principle of the universe, and the identity of plants and animals. See his *Moralists,* or *Philosophical Rhapsody.*

observation, that the objects which are variable or interrupted, and yet are supposed to continue the same, are such only as consist of a succession of parts, connected together by resemblance, contiguity, or causation. For as such a succession answers evidently to our notion of diversity, it can only be by mistake we ascribe to it an identity; and as the relation of parts, which leads us into this mistake, is really nothing but a quality, which produces an association of ideas, and an easy transition of the imagination from one to another, it can only be from the resemblance, which this act of the mind bears to that by which we contemplate one continued object, that the error arises. Our chief business, then, must be to prove, that all objects, to which we ascribe identity, without observing their invariableness and uninterruptedness, are such as consist of a succession of related objects.

In order to this, suppose any mass of matter, of which the parts are contiguous and connected, to be placed before us; it is plain we must attribute a perfect identity to this mass, provided all the parts continue uninterruptedly and invariably the same, whatever motion or change of place we may observe either in the whole or in any of the parts. But supposing some very *small* or *inconsiderable* part to be added to the mass, or subtracted from it; though this absolutely destroys the identity of the whole, strictly speaking, yet as we seldom think so accurately, we scruple not to pronounce a mass of matter the same, where we find so trivial an alteration. The passage of the thought from the object before the change to the object after it, is so smooth and easy, that we scarce perceive the transition, and are apt to imagine, that it is nothing but a continued survey of the same object.

There is a very remarkable circumstance that attends this experiment; which is, that though the change of any considerable part in a mass of matter destroys the identity of the whole, yet we must measure the greatness of the part, not absolutely, but by its *proportion* to the whole. The addition or diminution of a mountain would not be sufficient to produce a diversity in a planet; though the change of a very few inches would be able to destroy the identity of some bodies. It will be impossible to account for this, but by reflecting that objects operate upon the mind, and break or interrupt the continuity of its actions, not according to their real greatness, but according to their proportion to each other; and therefore, since this interruption makes an object cease to appear the same, it must be the uninterrupted progress of the thought which constitutes the imperfect identity.

This may be confirmed by another phenomenon. A change in any considerable part of a body destroys its identity; but it is remarkable, that where the change is produced *gradually* and *insensibly,* we are less apt to ascribe to it the same effect. The reason can plainly be no other, than that the mind, in following the successive changes of the body, feels an easy passage from the surveying its condition in one moment, to the viewing of it in another, and in no particular time perceives any interruption in its actions. From which continued perception, it ascribes a continued existence and identity to the object.

But whatever precaution we may use in introducing the changes gradually, and making them proportionable to the whole, it is certain, that where the changes are at last observed to become considerable, we make a scruple of ascribing identity to such different objects. There is, however, another artifice, by which we may induce the imagination to advance a step further; and that is, by producing a reference of the parts to each other, and a combination to some *common end* or purpose. A ship, of which a considerable part has been changed by frequent reparations, is still considered as the same; nor does the difference of the materials hinder us from ascribing an identity to it. The common end, in which the parts conspire, is the same under all their variations, and affords an easy transition of the imagination from one situation of the body to another.

But this is still more remarkable, when we add a *sympathy* of parts to their *common end,* and suppose that they bear to each other the reciprocal relation of cause and effect in all their actions and operations. This is the case with all animals and vegetables; where not only the several parts have a reference to some general purpose, but also a mutual dependence on, and connection with, each other. The effect of so strong a relation is, that though every one must allow, that in a very few years both vegetables and animals endure a *total* change, yet we still attribute identity to them, while their form, size, and substance are entirely altered. An oak that grows from a small plant to a large tree is still the same oak, though there be not one particle of matter or figure of its parts the same. An infant becomes a man, and is sometimes fat, sometimes lean, without any change in his identity.

We may also consider the two following phenomena, which are remarkable in their kind. The first is, that though we commonly be able to distinguish pretty exactly betwixt numerical and specific identity, yet it sometimes happens that we confound them, and in our thinking and reasoning employ the one for the other. Thus a man, who hears a noise that is frequently interrupted and renewed, says it is still the same noise, though it is evident the sounds have only a specific identity of resemblance, and there is nothing numerically the same but the cause which produced them. In like manner it may be said, without breach of the propriety of language, that such a church, which was formerly of brick, fell to ruin, and that the parish rebuilt the same church of freestone, and according to modern architecture. Here neither the form nor materials are the same, nor is there anything common to the two objects but their relation to the inhabitants of the parish; and yet this alone is sufficient to make us denominate them the same. But we must observe, that in these cases the first object is in a manner annihilated before the second comes into existence; by which means, we are never presented, in any one point of time, with the idea of difference and multiplicity; and for that reason are less scrupulous in calling them the same.

Secondly, we may remark, that though in a succession of related objects it be in a manner requisite that the change of parts be not sudden nor entire, in order to preserve the identity, yet where the objects are in their nature changeable and inconstant, we admit of a more sudden transition than would otherwise be consistent with that relation. Thus, as the nature of a river consists in the motion and change of parts, though in less than four-and-twenty hours these be totally altered, this hinders not the river from continuing the same during several ages. What is natural and essential to anything is, in a manner, expected; and what is expected makes less impression, and appears of less moment than what is unusual and extraordinary. A considerable change of the former kind seems really less to the imagination than the most trivial alteration of the latter; and by breaking less the continuity of the thought, has less influence in destroying the identity.

We now proceed to explain the nature of *personal identity*, which has become so great a question in philosophy, especially of late years in England, where all the abstruser sciences are studied with a peculiar ardour and application. And here it is evident the same method of reasoning must be continued which has so successfully explained the identity of plants, and animals, and ships, and houses, and of all compounded and changeable productions either of art or nature. The identity which we ascribe to the mind of man is only a fictitious one, and of a like kind with that which we ascribe to vegetable and animal bodies. It cannot therefore have a different origin, but must proceed from a like operation of the imagination upon like objects.

But lest this argument should not convince the reader, though in my opinion perfectly decisive, let him weigh the following reasoning, which is still closer and more immediate. It is evident, that the identity which we attribute to the human mind, however perfect we may imagine it to be, is not able to run the several different perceptions into one, and make them lose their characters of distinction and difference, which are essential to them. It is still true that every distinct perception which enters into the composition of the mind, is a distinct existence, and is different, and distinguishable, and separable from every other perception, either contemporary or successive. But as, notwithstanding this distinction and separability, we suppose the whole train of perceptions to be united by identity, a question naturally arises concerning this relation of identity, whether it be something that really binds our several perceptions together, or only associates their ideas in the imagination; that is, in other words, whether in pronouncing concerning the identity of a person, we observe some real bond among his perceptions, or only feel one among the ideas we form of them. This question we might easily decide, if we would recollect what has been already proved at large, that the understanding never observes any real connection among objects, and that even the union of cause and effect, when strictly examined, resolves itself into a customary association of ideas. For from thence it evidently follows, that identity is nothing really belonging to these different perceptions, and uniting them together, but is merely a quality which we attribute to them, because of the union of their ideas in the imagination when we reflect upon them. Now, the only qualities which can give ideas a union in the imagination, are these three relations above mentioned. These are the uniting principles in the ideal world, and without them every distinct object is separable by the mind, and may be separately considered, and appears not to have any more connection with any other object than if disjoined by the greatest difference and remoteness. It is therefore on some of these three relations of resemblance, contiguity, and causation, that identity depends; and as the very essence of these relations consists in their producing an easy transition of ideas, it follows that our notions of personal identity proceed entirely from the smooth and uninterrupted progress of the thought along a train of connected ideas, according to the principles above explained.

The only question, therefore, which remains is, by what relations this uninterrupted progress of our thought is produced, when we consider the successive existence of a mind or thinking person. And here it is evident we must confine ourselves to resemblance and causation, and must drop contiguity, which has little or no influence in the present case.

To begin with *resemblance;* suppose we could see clearly into the breast of another, and observe that succession of perceptions which constitutes his mind or thinking principle, and suppose that he always preserves the memory of a considerable part of past perceptions, it is evident that nothing could more contribute to the bestowing a relation on this succession amidst all its variations. For what is the memory but a faculty, by which we raise up the images of past perceptions? And as an image necessarily resembles its object, must not the frequent placing of these resembling perceptions in the chain of thought, convey the imagination more easily from one link to another, and make the whole seem like the continuance of one object? In this particular, then, the memory not only discovers the identity, but also contributes to its production, by producing the relation of resemblance among the perceptions. The case is the same, whether we consider ourselves or others.

As to *causation;* we may observe that the true idea of the human mind, is to consider it as a system of different perceptions or different existences, which are linked together by the relation of cause and effect, and mutually produce, destroy, influence, and modify each other. Our impressions give rise to their correspondent ideas; and these ideas, in their turn, produce other impressions. One thought chases another, and draws after it a third, by which it is expelled in its turn. In this respect, I cannot compare the soul more properly to anything than to a republic or commonwealth, in which the several members are united by the reciprocal ties of government and subordination, and give rise to other persons who propagate the same republic in the incessant changes of its parts. And as the same individual republic may not only change its members, but also its laws and constitutions; in like manner the same person may vary his character and disposition, as well as his impressions and ideas, without losing his identity. Whatever changes he endures, his several parts are still connected by the relation of causation. And in this view our identity with regard to the passions serves to corroborate that with regard to the imagination, by the making our distant perceptions influence each other, and by giving us a present concern for our past or future pains or pleasures.

As memory alone acquaints us with the continuance and extent of this succession of perceptions, it is to be considered, upon that account chiefly, as the source of personal identity. Had we no memory, we never should have any notion of causation, nor consequently of that chain of causes and effects, which constitute our self or person. But having once acquired this notion of causation from the memory, we can extend the same chain of causes, and consequently the identity of our persons beyond our memory, and can comprehend times, and circumstances, and actions, which we have entirely forgot, but suppose in general to have existed. For how few of our past actions are there, of which we have any memory? Who can tell me, for instance, what were his thoughts and actions on the first of January 1715, the eleventh of March 1719, and the third of August 1733? Or will he affirm, because he has entirely forgot the incidents of these days, that the present self is not the same person with the self of that time; and by that means overturn all the most established notions of personal identity? In this view, therefore, memory does not so much *produce* as *discover* personal identity, by showing us the relation of cause and effect among our different perceptions. It will be incumbent on those who affirm that memory produces entirely our personal identity, to give a reason why we can thus extend our identity beyond our memory.

The whole of this doctrine leads us to a conclusion, which is of great importance in the present affair, viz. that all the nice and subtile questions concerning personal identity can never possibly be decided, and are to be regarded rather as grammatical than as philosophical difficulties. Identity depends on the relations of ideas; and these relations produce identity, by means of that easy transition they occasion. But as the relations, and the easiness of the transition may diminish by insensible degrees, we have no just standard by which we can decide any dispute concerning the time when they acquire or lose a title to the name of identity. All the disputes concerning the identity of connected objects are merely verbal, except so far as the relation of parts gives rise to some fiction or imaginary principle of union, as we have already observed.

What I have said concerning the first origin and uncertainty of our notion of identity, as applied to the human mind, may be extended with little or no variation to that of *simplicity*. An object, whose different coexistent parts are bound together by a close relation, operates upon the imagination after much the same manner as one perfectly simple and indivisible, and requires not a much greater stretch of thought in order to its conception. From this similarity of operation we attribute a simplicity to it, and feign a principle of union as the support of this simplicity, and the centre of all the different parts and qualities of the object.

Thus we have finished our examination of the several systems of philosophy, both of the intellectual and natural[30] world; and in our miscellaneous way of reasoning, have been led into several topics, which will either illustrate and confirm some preceding part of this discourse, or prepare the way for our following opinions. It is now time to return to a more close examination of our subject, and to proceed in the accurate anatomy of human nature, having fully explained the nature of our judgment and understanding.

[30] *Original edition read " moral." Corrected by Hume in the Appendix.*

CONCLUSION OF THIS BOOK

But before I launch out into those immense depths of philosophy which lie before me, I find myself inclined to stop a moment in my present station, and to ponder that voyage, which I have undertaken, and which undoubtedly requires the utmost art and industry to be brought to a happy conclusion. Methinks I am like a man, who having struck on many shoals, and having narrowly escaped shipwreck in passing a small frith, has yet the temerity to put out to sea in the same leaky weather-beaten vessel, and even carries his ambition so far as to think of compassing the globe under these disadvantageous circumstances. My memory of past errors and perplexities makes me diffident for the future. The wretched condition, weakness, and disorder of the faculties, I must employ in my inquiries, increase my apprehensions. And the impossibility of amending or correcting these faculties, reduces me almost to despair, and makes me resolve to perish on the barren rock, on which I am at present, rather than venture myself upon that boundless ocean which runs out into immensity. This sudden view of my danger strikes me with melancholy; and as it is usual for that passion, above all others, to indulge itself, I cannot forbear feeding my despair with all those desponding reflections, which the present subject furnishes me with in such abundance.

I am first affrighted and confounded with that forlorn solitude in which I am placed in my philosophy, and fancy myself some strange uncouth monster, who not being able to mingle and unite in society, has been expelled all human commerce, and left utterly abandoned and disconsolate. Fain would I run into the crowd for shelter and warmth, but cannot prevail with myself to mix with such deformity. I call upon others to join me, in order to make a company apart, but no one will hearken to me. Every one keeps at a distance, and dreads that storm, which beats upon me from every side. I have exposed myself to the enmity of all metaphysicians, logicians, mathematicians, and even theologians; and can I wonder at the insults I must suffer? I have declared my disapprobation of their systems; and can I be surprised if they should express a hatred of mine and of my person? When I look abroad, I foresee on every side dispute, contradiction, anger, calumny, and detraction. When I turn my eye inward, I find nothing but doubt and igorance. All the world conspires to oppose and contradict me; though such is my weakness, that I feel all my opinions loosen and fall of themselves, when unsupported by the approbation of others. Every step I take is with hesitation, and every new reflection makes me dread an error and absurdity in my reasoning.

For with what confidence can I venture upon such bold enterprises, when beside those numberless infirmities peculiar to myself, I find so many which are common to human nature? Can I be sure that, in leaving all established opinions, I am following the truth? and by what criterion shall I distinguish her, even if fortune should at last guide me on her footsteps? After the most accurate and exact of my reasonings, I can give no reason why I should assent to it, and feel nothing but a *strong* propensity to consider objects *strongly* in that view under which they appear to me. Experience is a principle which instructs me in the several conjunctions of objects for the past. Habit is another principle which determines me to expect the same for the future; and both of them conspiring to operate upon the imagination, make me form certain ideas in a more intense and lively manner than others, which are not attended with the same advantages. Without this quality, by which the mind enlivens some ideas beyond others (which seemingly is so trivial, and so little founded on reason), we could never assent to any argument, nor carry our view beyond those few objects which are present to our senses. Nay, even to these objects we could never attribute any existence, but what was dependent on the senses; and must comprehend them entirely in that succession of perceptions which constitutes our self or person. Nay further, even with relation to that succession, we could only admit of those perceptions which are immediately present to our consciousness, nor could those lively images, with which the memory presents us, be ever received as true pictures of past perceptions. The memory, senses, and understanding are therefore all of them founded on the imagination, or the vivacity of our ideas.

No wonder a principle so inconstant and fallacious should lead us into errors, when implicitly followed (as it must be) in all its variations. It is this principle, which makes us reason from cause and effect; and it is the same principle which convinces us of the continued existence of external objects when absent from the senses. But though these two operations be equally natural and necessary in the human mind, yet in some circumstances they are directly contrary;[31] nor is it possible for us to reason justly and regularly from causes and effects, and at the same time believe the continued existence of matter. How shall we adjust those principles together? Which of them shall we prefer? Or in case we prefer neither of them, but successively assent to both, as is usual among philosophers, with what confidence can we afterwards usurp that glorious title, when we thus knowingly embrace a manifest contradiction?

This contradiction[32] would be more excusable, were it compensated by any degree of solidity and satisfaction in the other parts of our reasoning. But the case is quite contrary. When we trace up the human understanding to its first principles, we find it to lead us into such sentiments as seem to turn into ridicule all our past pains and industry, and to discourage us from future inquiries. Nothing is more curiously inquired after by the mind of man than

[31] Sect. 4.   [32] Part III, Sect. 14.

the causes of every phenomenon; nor are we content with knowing the immediate causes, but push on our inquiries till we arrive at the original and ultimate principle. We would not willingly stop before we are acquainted with that energy in the cause by which it operates on its effect; that tie, which connects them together; and that efficacious quality on which the tie depends. This is our aim in all our studies and reflections : and how must we be disappointed when we learn that this connection, tie, or energy lies merely in ourselves, and is nothing but that determination of the mind which is acquired by custom, and causes us to make a transition from an object to its usual attendant, and from the impression of one to the lively idea of the other? Such a discovery not only cuts off all hope of ever attaining satisfaction, but even prevents our very wishes; since it appears, that when we say we desire to know the ultimate and operating principle as something which resides in the external object, we either contradict ourselves, or talk without a meaning.

This deficiency in our ideas is not, indeed, perceived in common life, nor are we sensible, that in the most usual conjunctions of cause and effect, we are as ignorant of the ultimate principle, which binds them together, as in the most unusual and extraordinary. But this proceeds merely from an illusion of the imagination; and the question is, how far we ought to yield to these illusions. This question is very difficult, and reduces us to a very dangerous dilemma, whichever way we answer it. For if we assent to every trivial suggestion of the fancy, beside that these suggestions are often contrary to each other, they lead us into such errors, absurdities, and obscurities, that we must at last become ashamed of our credulity. Nothing is more dangerous to reason than the flights of the imagination, and nothing has been the occasion of more mistakes among philosophers. Men of bright fancies may in this respect be compared to those angels, whom the Scripture represents as covering their eyes with their wings. This has already appeared in so many instances, that we may spare ourselves the trouble of enlarging upon it any further.

But on the other hand, if the consideration of these instances makes us take a resolution to reject all the trivial suggestions of the fancy, and adhere to the understanding, that is, to the general and more established properties of the imagination; even this resolution, if steadily executed, would be dangerous, and attended with the most fatal consequences. For I have already shown,[33] that the understanding, when it acts alone, and according to its most general principles, entirely subverts itself, and leaves not the lowest degree of evidence in any proposition, either in philosophy or common life. We save ourselves from this total scepticism only by means of that singular and seemingly trivial property of the fancy, by which we enter with difficulty into remote views of things, and are not able to accompany them with so sensible an impression, as we do those which are more easy and natural. Shall we, then, establish it for a general maxim, that no refined or elaborate reasoning is ever to be received? Consider well the consequences of such a principle. By this means you cut off entirely all science and philosophy : you proceed upon one singular quality of the imagination, and by a parity of reason must embrace all of them : and you expressly contradict yourself; since this maxim must be built on the preceding reasoning, which will be allowed to be sufficiently refined and metaphysical. What party, then, shall we choose among these difficulties? If we embrace this principle, and condemn all refined reasoning, we run into the most manifest absurdities. If we reject it in favour of these reasonings, we subvert entirely the human understanding. We have therefore no choice left, but betwixt a false reason and none at all. For my part, I know not what ought to be done in the present case. I can only observe what is commonly done; which is, that this difficulty is seldom or never thought of; and even where it has

[33] Sect. I.

once been present to the mind, is quickly forgot, and leaves but a small impression behind it. Very refined reflections have little or no influence upon us; and yet we do not, and cannot establish it for a rule, that they ought not to have any influence; which implies a manifest contradiction.

But what have I here said, that reflections very refined and metaphysical have little or no influence upon us? This opinion I can scarce forbear retracting, and condemning from my present feeling and experience. The *intense* view of these manifold contradictions and imperfections in human reason has so wrought upon me, and heated my brain, that I am ready to reject all belief and reasoning, and can look upon no opinion even as more probable or likely than another. Where am I, or what? From what causes do I derive my existence, and to what condition shall I return? Whose favour shall I court, and whose anger must I dread? What beings surround me? and on whom have I any influence, or who have any influence on me? I am confounded with all these questions, and begin to fancy myself in the most deplorable condition imaginable, environed with the deepest darkness, and utterly deprived of the use of every member and faculty.

Most fortunately it happens, that since reason is incapable of dispelling these clouds, Nature herself suffices to that purpose, and cures me of this philosophical melancholy and delirium, either by relaxing this bent of mind, or by some avocation, and lively impression of my senses, which obliterate all these chimeras. I dine, I play a game of backgammon, I converse, and am merry with my friends; and when, after three or four hours' amusement, I would return to these speculations, they appear so cold, and strained, and ridiculous, that I cannot find in my heart to enter into them any further.

Here then I find myself absolutely and necessarily determined to live, and talk, and act like other people in the common affairs of life. But notwithstanding that my natural propensity, and the course of my animal spirits and passions reduce me to this indolent belief in the general maxims of the world, I still feel such remains of my former disposition, that I am ready to throw all my books and papers into the fire, and resolve never more to renounce the pleasures of life for the sake of reasoning and philosophy. For those are my sentiments in that splenetic humour which governs me at present. I may, nay I must yield to the current of nature, in submitting to my senses and understanding; and in this blind submission I show most perfectly my sceptical disposition and principles. But does it follow that I must strive against the current of nature, which leads me to indolence and pleasure; that I must seclude myself in some measure, from the commerce and society of men, which is so agreeable; and that I must torture my brain with subtilties and sophistries, at the very time that I cannot satisfy myself concerning the reasonableness of so painful an application, nor have any tolerable prospect of arriving by its means at truth and certainty? Under what obligation do I lie of making such an abuse of time? And to what end can it serve, either for the service of mankind, or for my own private interest? No: if I must be a fool, as all those who reason or believe anything *certainly* are, my follies shall at least be natural and agreeable. Where I strive against my inclination, I shall have a good reason for my resistance; and will no more be led a wandering into such dreary solitudes, and rough passages, as I have hitherto met with.

These are the sentiments of my spleen and indolence; and indeed I must confess, that philosophy has nothing to oppose to them, and expects a victory more from the returns of a serious good-humoured disposition, than from the force of reason and conviction. In all the incidents of life, we ought still to preserve our scepticism. If we believe that fire warms, or water refreshes, it is only because it costs us too much pains to think otherwise. Nay, if we are philosophers, it ought only to be upon sceptical principles, and from an inclination which we feel to the employing ourselves after that manner. Where reason is lively, and mixes itself with some propensity, it ought to be assented to. Where it does not, it never can have any title to operate upon us.

At the time, therefore, that I am tired with amusement and company, and have indulged a *reverie* in my chamber, or in a solitary walk by a river side, I feel my mind all collected within itself, and am naturally *inclined* to carry my view into all those subjects, about which I have met with so many disputes in the course of my reading and conversation. I cannot forbear having a curiosity to be acquainted with the principles of moral good and evil, the nature and foundation of government, and the cause of these several passions and inclinations, which actuate and govern me. I am uneasy to think I approve of one object, and disapprove of another; call one thing beautiful, and another deformed; decide concerning truth and falsehood, reason and folly, without knowing upon what principles I proceed. I am concerned for the condition of the learned world, which lies under such a deplorable ignorance in all these particulars. I feel an ambition to arise in me of contributing to the instruction of mankind, and of acquiring a name by my inventions and discoveries. These sentiments spring up naturally in my present disposition; and should I endeavour to banish them, by attaching myself to any other business or diversion, I *feel* I should be a loser in point of pleasure; and this is the origin of my philosophy.

But even suppose this curiosity and ambition should not transport me into speculations without the sphere of common life, it would necessarily happen, that from my very weakness I must be led into such inquiries. It is certain, that superstition is much more bold in its systems and hypotheses than philosophy; and while the latter contents itself with assigning new causes and principles to the phenomena, which appear in the visible world, the former opens a world of its own, and presents us with scenes, and beings, and objects, which are altogether new. Since therefore it is almost impossible for the mind of man to rest, like those of beasts, in that narrow circle of objects, which are the subject of daily conversation and action, we ought only to deliberate concerning the choice of our guide, and ought to prefer that which is safest and most agreeable. And in this respect I make bold to recommend philosophy, and shall not scruple to give it the preference to superstition of every kind or denomination. For as superstition arises naturally and easily from the popular opinions of mankind, it seizes more strongly on the mind, and is often able to disturb us in the conduct of our lives and actions. Philosophy on the contrary, if just, can present us only with mild and moderate sentiments; and if false and extravagant, its opinions are merely the objects of a cold and general speculation, and seldom go so far as to interrupt the course of our natural propensities. The *Cynics* are an extraordinary instance of philosophers, who, from reasonings purely philosophical, ran into as great extravagancies of conduct as any *monk* or *dervise* that ever was in the world. Generally speaking, the errors in religion are dangerous; those in philosophy only ridiculous.

I am sensible, that these two cases of the strength and weakness of the mind will not comprehend all mankind, and that there are in England, in particular, many honest gentlemen, who being always employed in their domestic affairs, or amusing themselves in common recreations, have carried their thoughts very little beyond those objects, which are every day exposed to their senses. And indeed, of such as these I pretend not to make philosophers, nor do I expect them either to be associates in these researches, or auditors of these discoveries. They do well to keep themselves in their present situation; and instead of refining them into philosophers, I wish we could communicate to our founders of systems, a share of this gross earthy mixture, as an ingredient, which they commonly stand much in need of, and which would serve to temper those fiery particles, of which they are composed. While a warm imagination is allowed to enter into philosophy, and hypotheses embraced merely for being specious and agreeable, we can never have any steady principles, nor any sentiments, which will suit with common practice and experience. But were these hypotheses once removed, we might hope to establish a system or set of opinions, which if not true (for that, perhaps, is too much to be hoped for), might at least be satisfactory to the human mind, and might stand the test of the most critical examination. Nor should we despair of attaining this end, because of the many chimerical systems, which have successively arisen and decayed away among men, would we consider the shortness of that period, wherein these questions have been the subjects of inquiry and reasoning. Two thousand years with such long interruptions, and under such mighty discouragements, are a small space of time to give any tolerable perfection to the sciences; and perhaps we are still in too early an age of the world to discover any principles which will bear the examination of the latest posterity. For my part, my only hope is, that I may contribute a little to the advancement of knowledge, by giving in some particulars a different turn to the speculations of philosophers, and pointing out to them more distinctly those subjects where alone they can expect assurance and conviction. Human Nature is the only science of man; and yet has been hitherto the most neglected. It will be sufficient for me, if I can bring it a little more into fashion; and the hope of this serves to compose my temper from that spleen, and invigorate it from that indolence, which sometimes prevail upon me. If the reader finds himself in the same easy disposition, let him follow me in my future speculations. If not, let him follow his inclination, and wait the returns of application and good humour. The conduct of a man who studies philosophy in this careless manner, is more truly sceptical than that of one, who feeling in himself an inclination to it, is yet so overwhelmed with doubts and scruples, as totally to reject it. A true sceptic will be diffident of his philosophical doubts, as well as of his philosophical convictions; and will never refuse any innocent satisfaction which offers itself, upon account of either of them.

Nor is it only proper we should in general indulge our inclination in the most elaborate philosophical researches, notwithstanding our sceptical principles, but also that we should yield to that propensity, which inclines us to be positive and certain in *particular points,* according to the light in which we survey them in any *particular instant.* It is easier to forbear all examination and inquiry, than to check ourselves in so natural a propensity, and guard against that assurance, which always arises from an exact and full survey of an object. On such an occasion we are apt not only to forget our scepticism, but even our modesty too; and make use of such terms as these, *it is evident, it is certain, it is undeniable;* which a due deference to the public ought, perhaps, to prevent. I may have fallen into this fault after the example of others; but I here enter a *caveat* against any objections, which may be offered on that head; and declare that such expressions were extorted from me by the present view of the object, and imply no dogmatical spirit, nor conceited idea of my own judgment, which are sentiments that I am sensible can become nobody, and a sceptic still less than any other.

APPENDIX

There is nothing I would more willingly lay hold of than an opportunity of confessing my errors; and should esteem such a return to truth and reason to be more honourable than the most unerring judgment. A man who is free from mistakes can pretend to no praises except from the justness of his understanding; but a man who corrects his mistakes shows at once the justness of his understanding and the candour and ingenuity of his temper. I have not yet been so fortunate as to discover any very considerable mistakes in the reasonings delivered in the preceding volumes except on one article; but I have found by experience that some of my expressions have not been so well chosen as to guard against all mistakes in the readers; and it is chiefly to remedy this defect I have subjoined the following Appendix.

We can never be induced to believe any matter of fact except where its cause or its effect is present to us; but what the nature is of that belief which arises from the relation of cause and effect few have had the curiosity to ask themselves. In my opinion this dilemma is inevitable. Either the belief is some new idea such as that of *reality* or *existence*, which we join to the simple conception of an object, or it is merely a peculiar *feeling* or *sentiment*. That it is not a new idea, annexed to the simple conception, may be evinced from these two arguments. *First,* We have no abstract idea of existence distinguishable and separable from the idea of particular objects. It is impossible, therefore, that this idea of existence can be annexed to the idea of any object, or form the difference betwixt a simple conception and belief. *Secondly,* The mind has the command over all its ideas, and can separate, unite, mix, and vary them, as it pleases; so that, if belief consisted merely in a new idea annexed to the conception, it would be in a man's power to believe what he pleased. We may therefore conclude, that belief consists merely in a certain feeling or sentiment; in something that depends not on the will, but must arise from certain determinate causes and principles of which we are not masters. When we are convinced of any matter of fact, we do nothing but conceive it, along with a certain feeling, different from what attends the mere *reveries* of the imagination. And when we express our incredulity concerning any fact, we mean, that the arguments for the fact produce not that feeling. Did not the belief consist in a sentiment different from our mere conception, whatever objects were presented by the wildest imagination would be on an equal footing with the most established truths founded on history and experience. There is nothing but the feeling or sentiment to distinguish the one from the other.

This, therefore, being regarded as an undoubted truth, *that belief is nothing but a peculiar feeling, different from the simple conception,* the next question that naturally occurs is, *what is the nature of this feeling or sentiment, and whether it be analogous to any other sentiment of the human mind?* This question is important. For if it be not analogous to any other sentiment, we must despair of explaining its causes, and must consider it as an original principle of the human mind. If it be analogous, we may hope to explain its causes from analogy, and trace it up to more general principles. Now that there is a greater firmness and solidity in the conceptions, which are the objects of conviction and assurance, than in the loose and indolent *reveries* of a castle-builder, every one will readily own. They strike upon us with more force; they are more present to us; the mind has a firmer hold of them, and is more actuated and moved by them. It acquiesces in them; and, in a manner, fixes and reposes itself on them. In short, they approach nearer to the impressions, which are immediately present to us; and are therefore analogous to many other operations of the mind.

There is not, in my opinion, any possibility, of evading

this conclusion, but by asserting that belief, beside the simple conception, consists in some impression or feeling, distinguishable from the conception. It does not modify the conception, and render it more present and intense : it is only annexed to it, after the same manner that *will* and *desire* are annexed to particular conceptions of good and pleasure. But the following considerations will, I hope, be sufficient to remove this hypothesis. *First*, It is directly contrary to experience, and our immediate consciousness. All men have ever allowed reasoning to be merely an operation of our thoughts or ideas; and however those ideas may be varied to the feeling, there is nothing ever enters into our *conclusions* but ideas, or our fainter conceptions. For instance, I hear at present a person's voice with whom I am acquainted, and this sound comes from the next room. This impression of my senses immediately conveys my thoughts to the person, along with all the surrounding objects. I paint them out to myself as existent at present, with the same qualities and relations that I formerly knew them possessed of. These ideas take faster hold of my mind than the ideas of an enchanted castle. They are different to the feeling; but there is no distinct or separate impression attending them. It is the same case when I recollect the several incidents of a journey, or the events of any history. Every particular fact is there the object of belief. Its idea is modified differently from the loose *reveries* of a castle-builder : but no distinct impression attends every distinct idea, or conception of matter of fact. This is the subject of plain experience. If ever this experience can be disputed on any occasion, it is when the mind has been agitated with doubts and difficulties; and afterwards, upon taking the object in a new point of view, or being presented with a new argument, fixes and reposes itself in one settled conclusion and belief. In this case there is a feeling distinct and separate from the conception. The passage from doubt and agitation to tranquillity and repose, conveys a satisfaction and pleasure to the mind. But take any other case. Suppose I see the legs and thighs of a person in motion, while some interposed object conceals the rest of his body. Here, it is certain, the imagination spreads out the whole figure. I give him a head and shoulders, and breast and neck. These members I conceive and believe him to be possessed of. Nothing can be more evident than that this whole operation is performed by the thought or imagination alone. The transition is immediate. The ideas presently strike us. Their customary connection with the present impression varies them and modifies them in a certain manner, but produces no act of the mind distinct from this peculiarity of conception. Let any one examine his own mind, and he will evidently find this to be the truth.

Secondly, Whatever may be the case, with regard to this distinct impression, it must be allowed that the mind has a firmer hold, or more steady conception of what it takes to be matter of fact than of fictions. Why then look any further, or multiply suppositions without necessity?

Thirdly, We can explain the *causes* of the firm conception, but not those of any separate impression. And not only so, but the causes of the firm conception exhaust the whole subject, and nothing is left to produce any other effect. An inference concerning a matter of fact is nothing but the idea of an object that is frequently conjoined, or is associated with a present impression. This is the whole of it. Every part is requisite to explain, from analogy, the more steady conception; and nothing remains capable of producing any distinct impression.

Fourthly, The *effects* of belief, in influencing the passions and imagination, can all be explained from the firm conception; and there is no occasion to have recourse to any other principle. These arguments, with many others, enumerated in the foregoing volumes, sufficiently prove that belief only modifies the idea or conception; and renders it different to the feeling, without producing any distinct impression.

Thus, upon a general view of the subject, there appear to be two questions of importance, which we may venture to recommend to the consideration of philosophers, *Whether there be anything to distinguish belief from the simple conception, beside the feeling or sentiment?* And, *Whether this feeling be anything but a firmer conception, or a faster hold, that we take of the object?*

If, upon impartial inquiry, the same conclusion that I have formed be assented to by philosophers, the next business is to examine the analogy which there is betwixt belief and other acts of the mind, and find the cause of the firmness and strength of conception; and this I do not esteem a difficult task. The transition from a present impression, always enlivens and strengthens any idea. When any object is presented, the idea of its usual attendant immediately strikes us, as something real and solid. It is *felt* rather than conceived, and approaches the impression, from which it is derived, in its force and influence. This I have proved at large, and cannot add any new arguments.

I had entertained some hopes, that however deficient our theory of the intellectual world might be, it would be free from those contradictions and absurdities which seem to attend every explication that human reason can give of the material world. But upon a more strict review of the section concerning *personal identity,* I find myself involved in such a labyrinth that, I must confess, I neither know how to correct my former opinions, nor how to render them consistent. If this be not a good *general* reason for scepticism, it is at least a sufficient one (if I were not already abundantly supplied) for me to entertain a diffidence and modesty in all my decisions. I shall propose the arguments on both sides, beginning with those that induced me to deny the strict and proper identity and simplicity of a self or thinking being.

When we talk of *self* or *substance,* we must have an idea annexed to these terms, otherwise they are altogether unintelligible. Every idea is derived from preceding impressions; and we have no impression of self or substance, as something simple and individual. We have, therefore, no idea of them in that sense.

Whatever is distinct is distinguishable, and whatever is distinguishable is separable by the thought or imagination. All perceptions are distinct. They are, therefore, distinguishable, and separable, and may be conceived as separately existent, and may exist separately, without any contradiction or absurdity.

When I view this table and that chimney, nothing is present to me but particular perceptions, which are of a like nature with all the other perceptions. This is the doctrine of philosophers. But this table, which is present to me, and that chimney, may, and do exist separately. This is the doctrine of the vulgar, and implies no contradiction. There is no contradiction, therefore, in extending the same doctrine to all the perceptions.

In general, the following reasoning seems satisfactory. All ideas are borrowed from preceding perceptions. Our ideas of objects, therefore, are derived from that source. Consequently no proposition can be intelligible or consistent with regard to objects, which is not so with regard to perceptions. But it is intelligible and consistent to say, that objects exist distinct and independent, without any common *simple* substance or subject of inhesion. This proposition, therefore, can never be absurd with regard to perceptions.

When I turn my reflection on *myself,* I never can perceive this *self* without some one or more perceptions; nor can I ever perceive anything but the perceptions. It is the composition of these, therefore, which forms the self.

We can conceive a thinking being to have either many or few perceptions. Suppose the mind to be reduced even below the life of an oyster. Suppose it to have only one perception, as of thirst or hunger. Consider it in that situation. Do you conceive anything but merely that perception? Have you any notion of *self* or *substance*? If not, the addition of other perceptions can never give you that notion.

The annihilation which some people suppose to follow upon death, and which entirely destroys this self, is nothing but an extinction of all particular perceptions; love and hatred, pain and pleasure, thought and sensation. These, therefore, must be the same with self, since the one cannot survive the other.

Is *self* the same with *substance*? If it be, how can that question have place, concerning the subsistence of self, under a change of substance? If they be distinct, what is the difference betwixt them? For my part, I have a notion of neither, when conceived distinct from particular perceptions.

Philosophers begin to be reconciled to the principle, *that we have no idea of external substance, distinct from the ideas of particular qualities.* This must pave the way for a like principle with regard to the mind, *that we have no notion of it, distinct from the particular perception.*

So far I seem to be attended with sufficient evidence. But having thus loosened all our particular perceptions, when I proceed to explain the principle of connection, which binds them together, and makes us attribute to them a real simplicity and identity, I am sensible that my account is very defective, and that nothing but the seeming evidence of the precedent reasonings could have induced me to receive it. If perceptions are distinct existences, they form a whole only by being connected together. But no connections among distinct existences are ever discoverable by human understanding. We only *feel* a connection or determination of the thought to pass from one object to another. It follows, therefore, that the thought alone feels personal identity, when reflecting on the train of past perceptions that compose a mind, the ideas of them are felt to be connected together, and naturally introduce each other. However extraordinary this conclusion may seem, it need not surprise us. Most philosophers seem inclined to think, that personal identity *arises* from consciousness, and consciousness is nothing but a reflected thought or perception. The present philosophy, therefore, has so far a promising aspect. But all my hopes vanish when I come to explain the principles that unite our successive perceptions in our thought or consciousness. I cannot discover any theory which gives me satisfaction on this head.

In short, there are two principles which I cannot render consistent, nor is it in my power to renounce either of them, viz. *that all our distinct perceptions are distinct existences,* and *that the mind never perceives any real connection among distinct existences.* Did our perceptions either inhere in something simple and individual, or did the mind perceive some real connection among them, there would be no difficulty in the case. For my part, I must plead the privilege of a sceptic, and confess that this difficulty is too hard for my understanding. I pretend not, however, to pronounce it absolutely insuperable. Others, perhaps, or myself, upon more mature reflections, may discover some hypothesis that will reconcile those contradictions.

I shall also take this opportunity of confessing two other errors of less importance, which more mature reflection has discovered to me in my reasoning. The first may be found in Part II., p. 103, where I say, that the distance betwixt two bodies is known, among other things, by the angles which the rays of light flowing from the bodies make with each other. It is certain, that these angles are not known to the mind, and consequently can never discover the distance. The second error may be found in Part III., p. 143, where I say, that two ideas of the same can only be different by their different degrees of force and vivacity. I believe there are other differences among ideas, which cannot properly be comprehended under these terms. Had I said, that two ideas of the same object can only be different by their different *feeling,* I should have been nearer the truth.

APPENDICES

PREFACE

My expectations in this small performance may seem somewhat extraordinary, when I declare that my intentions are to render a larger work more intelligible to ordinary capacities, by abridging it. It is however certain, that those who are not accustomed to abstract reasoning, are apt to lose the thread of argument, where it is drawn out to a great length, and each part fortified with all the arguments, guarded against all the objections, and illustrated with all the views, which occur to a writer in the diligent survey of his subject. Such readers will more readily apprehend a chain of reasoning, that is more single and concise, where the chief propositions only are linked on to each other, illustrated by some simple examples, and confirmed by a few of the more forcible arguments. The parts lying nearer together can better be compared, and the connection be more easily traced from the first principles to the last conclusion.

The work, of which I here present the reader with an abstract, has been complained of as obscure and difficult to be comprehended, and I am apt to think, that this proceeded as much from the length as from the abstractedness of the argument. If I have remedied this inconvenience in any degree, I have attained my end. The book seemed to me to have such an air of singularity, and novelty as claimed the attention of the public; especially if it be found, as the author seems to insinuate, that were his philosophy received, we must alter from the foundation the greatest part of the sciences. Such bold attempts are always advantageous in the republic of letters, because they shake off the yoke of authority, accustom men to think for themselves, give new hints, which men of genius may carry further, and by the very opposition, illustrate points, wherein no one before suspected any difficulty.

The author must be contented to wait with patience for some time before the learned world can agree in their sentiments of his performance. It is his misfortune, that he cannot make an *appeal to the people*, who in all matters of common reason and eloquence are found so infallible a tribunal. He must be judged by the few, whose verdict is more apt to be corrupted by partiality and prejudice, especially as no one is a proper judge in these subjects, who has not often thought of them; and *such* are apt to form to themselves systems of their own, which they resolve not to relinquish. I hope the author will excuse me for intermeddling in this affair, since my aim is only to increase his auditory, by removing some difficulties, which have kept many from apprehending his meaning.

I have chosen one simple argument, which I have carefully traced from the beginning to the end. This is the only point I have taken care to finish. The rest is only hints of particular passages, which seemed to me curious and remarkable.

AN
ABSTRACT
OF
A BOOK LATELY PUBLISHED, ENTITLED,

A Treatise of Human Nature, Etc.

This book seems to be wrote upon the same plan with several other works that have had a great vogue of late years in *England*. The philosophical spirit, which has been so much improved all over *Europe* within these last fourscore years, has been carried to as great a length in this kingdom as in any other. Our writers seem even to have started a new kind of philosophy, which promises more both to the entertainment and advantage of mankind, than any other with which the world has been yet acquainted. Most of the philosophers of antiquity, who treated of human nature, have shewn more of a delicacy of sentiment, a just sense of morals, or a greatness of soul, than a depth of reasoning and reflection. They content themselves with representing the common sense of mankind in the strongest lights, and with the best turn of thought and expression, without following out steadily a chain of propositions, or forming the several truths into a regular science. But it is at least worth while to try if the science of *man* will not admit of the same accuracy which several parts of natural philosophy are found susceptible of. There seems to be all the reason in the world to imagine that it may be carried to the greatest degree of exactness. If, in examining several phenomena, we find that they resolve themselves into one common principle, and can trace this principle into another, we shall at last arrive at those few simple principles, on which all the rest depend. And though we can never arrive at the ultimate principles, it is a satisfaction to go as far as our faculties will allow us.

This seems to have been the aim of our late philosophers, and, among the rest, of this author. He proposes to anatomize human nature in a regular manner, and promises to draw no conclusions but where he is authorized by experience. He talks with contempt of hypotheses; and insinuates, that such of our countrymen as have banished them from moral philosophy, have done a more signal service to the world, than *my Lord Bacon,* whom he considers as the father of experimental physics. He mentions, on this occasion, *Mr. Locke, my Lord Shaftesbury, Dr. Mandeville, Mr. Hutchison, Dr. Butler,* who, though they differ in many points among themselves, seem all to agree in founding their accurate disquisitions of human nature entirely upon experience.

Beside the satisfaction of being acquainted with what most nearly concerns us, it may be safely affirmed, that almost all the sciences are comprehended in the science of human nature, and are dependent on it. *The sole end of logic is to explain the principles and operations of our reasoning faculty, and the nature of our ideas;* morals and criticism *regard our tastes and sentiments; and* politics *consider men as united in society, and dependent on each other.* This treatise therefore of human nature seems intended for a system of the sciences. The author has finished what regards logic, and has laid the foundation of the other parts in his account of the passions.

The celebrated *Monsieur Leibnitz* has observed it to be a defect in the common systems of logic, that they are very copious when they explain the operations of the understanding in the forming of demonstrations, but are too concise when they treat of probabilities, and those other measures of evidence on which life and action entirely depend, and which are our guides even in most of our philosophical speculations. In this censure, he comprehends *the Essay on Human Understanding, la Recherche de la Verité,* and *l'Art de Penser.* The author of the *Treatise of Human Nature* seems to have been sensible of this defect in these philosophers, and has endeavoured, as much as he can, to supply it. As his book contains a great number of speculations very new and remarkable, it will be impossible to give the reader a just notion of the whole. We shall therefore chiefly confine ourselves to his explication of our reasonings from cause and effect. If we can make this intelligible to the reader, it may serve as a specimen of the whole.

Our author begins with some definitions. He calls a *perception* whatever can be present to the mind, whether we employ our senses, or are actuated with passion, or exercise our thought and reflection. He divides our perceptions into two kinds, viz. *impressions* and *ideas*. When we feel a passion or emotion of any kind, or have the images of external objects conveyed by our senses; the perception of the mind is what he calls an *impression*, which is a word that he employs in a new sense. When we reflect on a passion or an object which is not present, this perception is an *idea*. *Impressions*, therefore, are our lively and strong perceptions; *ideas* are the fainter and weaker. This distinction is evident; as evident as that betwixt feeling and thinking.

The first proposition he advances, is, that all our ideas, or weak perceptions, are derived from our impressions, or strong perceptions, and that we can never think of any thing which we have not seen without us, or felt in our own minds. This proposition seems to be equivalent to that which *Mr. Locke* has taken such pains to establish, viz. *that no ideas are innate*. Only it may be observed, as an inaccuracy of that famous philosopher, that he comprehends all our perceptions under the term of idea, in which sense it is false, that we have no innate ideas. For it is evident our stronger perceptions or impressions are innate, and that natural affection, love of virtue, resentment, and all the other passions, arise immediately from nature. I am persuaded, whoever would take the question in this light, would be easily able to reconcile all parties. *Father Malebranche* would find himself at a loss to point out any thought of the mind, which did not represent something antecedently felt by it, either internally, or by means of the external senses, and must allow, that however we may compound, and mix, and augment, and diminish our ideas, they are all derived from these sources. *Mr. Locke*, on the other hand, would readily acknowledge, that all our passions are a kind of natural instincts, derived from nothing but the original constitution of the human mind.

Our author thinks,

that no discovery could have been made more happily for deciding all controversies concerning ideas than this, that impressions always take the precedency of them, and that every idea with which the imagination is furnished, first makes its appearance in a correspondent impression. These latter perceptions are all so clear and evident, that they admit of no controversy; though many of our ideas are so obscure, that it is almost impossible even for the mind, which forms them, to tell exactly their nature and composition.[1]

Accordingly, wherever any idea is ambiguous, he has always recourse to the impression, which must render it clear and precise. And when he suspects that any philosophical term has no idea annexed to it (as is too common) he always asks *from what impression that idea is derived*? And if no impression can be produced, he concludes that the term is altogether insignificant. It is after this manner he examines our idea of *substance* and *essence*;[2] and it were to be wished, that this rigorous method were more practised in all philosophical debates.

It is evident, that all reasonings concerning *matter of fact* are founded on the relation of cause and effect, and that we can never infer the existence of one object from another, unless they be connected together, either mediately or immediately. In order therefore to understand these reasonings, we must be perfectly acquainted with the idea of a cause; and in order to that, must look about us to find something that is the cause of another.

[1] Part II, Sect. III, p. 78.   [2] Part IV, Sect. III and V.

Here is a billiard-ball lying on the table, and another ball moving towards it with rapidity. They strike; and the ball, which was formerly at rest, now acquires a motion. This is as perfect an instance of the relation of cause and effect as any which we know, either by sensation or reflection. Let us therefore examine it. It is evident, that the two balls touched one another before the motion was communicated, and that there was no interval betwixt the shock and the motion. *Contiguity* in time and place is therefore a requisite circumstance to the operation of all causes. It is evident likewise, that the motion, which was the cause, is prior to the motion, which was the effect. Priority in time, is therefore another requisite circumstance in every cause. But this is not all. Let us try any other balls of the same kind in a like situation, and we shall always find, that the impulse of the one produces motion in the other. Here therefore is a *third* circumstance, viz. that of *a constant conjunction* betwixt the cause and effect. Every object like the cause, produces always some object like the effect. Beyond these three circumstances of contiguity, priority, and constant conjunction, I can discover nothing in this cause. The first ball is in motion; touches the second; immediately the second is in motion : and when I try the experiment with the same or like balls, in the same or like circumstances, I find, that upon the motion and touch of the one ball, motion always follows in the other. In whatever shape I turn this matter, and however I examine it, I can find nothing farther.

This is the case when both the cause and effect are present to the senses. Let us now see upon what our inference is founded, when we conclude from the one that the other has existed or will exist. Suppose I see a ball moving in a straight line towards another, I immediately conclude, that they will shock, and that the second will be in motion. This is the inference from cause to effect; and of this nature are all our reasonings in the conduct of life : on this is founded all our belief in history : and from hence is derived all philosophy, excepting only geometry and arithmetic. If we can explain the inference from the shock of two balls, we shall be able to account for this operation of the mind in all instances.

Were a man, such as *Adam,* created in the full vigour of understanding, without experience, he would never be able to infer motion in the second ball from the motion and impulse of the first. It is not any thing that reason sees in the cause, which make us *infer* the effect. Such an inference, were it possible, would amount to a demonstration, as being founded merely on the comparison of ideas. But no inference from cause to effect amounts to a demonstration. Of which there is this evident proof. The mind can always *conceive* any effect to follow from any cause, and indeed any event to follow upon another : whatever we *conceive* is possible, at least in a metaphysical sense : but wherever a demonstration takes place, the contrary is impossible, and implies a contradiction. There is no demonstration, therefore, for any conjunction of cause and effect. And this is a principle, which is generally allowed by philosophers.

It would have been necessary, therefore, for *Adam* (if he was not inspired) to have had *experience* of the effect, which followed upon the impulse of these two balls. He must have seen, in several instances, that when the one ball struck upon the other, the second always acquired motion. If he had seen a sufficient number of instances of this kind, whenever he saw the one ball moving towards the other, he would always conclude without hesitation, that the second would acquire motion. His understanding would anticipate his sight, and form a conclusion suitable to his past experience.

It follows, then, that all reasonings concerning cause and effect, are founded on experience, and that all reasonings from experience, are founded on the supposition, that the course of nature will continue uniformly the same. We conclude, that like causes, in like circumstances, will always produce like effects. It may now be worth while to consider, what determines us to form a conclusion of such infinite consequence.

It is evident, that *Adam* with all his science, would never have been able to *demonstrate*, that the course of nature must continue uniformly the same, and that the future must be conformable to the past. What is possible can never be demonstrated to be false; and it is possible the course of nature may change, since we can conceive such a change. Nay, I will go farther, and assert, that he could not so much as prove by any *probable* arguments, that the future must be conformable to the past. All probable arguments are built on the supposition, that there is this conformity betwixt the future and the past, and therefore can never prove it. This conformity is a *matter of fact,* and if it must be proved, will admit of no proof but from experience. But our experience in the past can be a proof of nothing for the future, but upon a supposition, that there is a resemblance betwixt them. This therefore is a point, which can admit of no proof at all, and which we take for granted without any proof.

We are determined by *custom* alone to suppose the future conformable to the past. When I see a billiard-ball moving towards another, my mind is immediately carried by habit to the usual effect, and anticipates my sight by conceiving the second ball in motion. There is nothing in these objects, abstractly considered, and independent of experience, which leads me to form any such conclusion : and even after I have had experience of many repeated effects of this kind, there is no argument, which determines me to suppose, that the effect will be conformable to past experience. The powers, by which bodies operate, are entirely unknown. We perceive only their sensible qualities : and what reason have we to think, that the same powers will always be conjoined with the same sensible qualities?

It is not, therefore, reason, which is the guide of life, but custom. That alone determines the mind, in all instances, to suppose the future conformable to the past. However easy this step may seem, reason would never, to all eternity, be able to make it.

This is a very curious discovery, but leads us to others, that are still more curious. *When I see a billiard-ball moving towards another, my mind is immediately carried by habit to the usual effect, and anticipate*[3] *my sight by conceiving the second ball in motion.* But is this all? Do I nothing but *conceive* the motion of the second ball? No surely. I also *believe* that it will move. What then is this *belief*? And how does it differ from the simple conception of any thing? Here is a new question unthought of by philosophers.

When a demonstration convinces me of any proposition, it not only makes me conceive the proposition, but also makes me sensible, that it is impossible to conceive any thing contrary. What is demonstratively false implies a contradiction; and what implies a contradiction cannot be conceived. But with regard to any matter of fact, however strong the proof may be from experience, I can always conceive the contrary, though I cannot always believe it. The belief, therefore, makes some difference betwixt the conception to which we assent, and that to which we do not assent.

To account for this, there are only two hypotheses. It may be said, that belief joins some new idea to those which we may conceive without assenting to them. But this hypothesis is false. For *first*, no such idea can be produced. When we simply conceive an object, we conceive it in all its parts. We conceive it as it might exist, though we do not believe it to exist. Our belief of it would discover no new qualities. We may paint out the entire object in imagination without believing it. We may set it, in a manner, before our eyes, with every circumstance of time and place. It is the very object conceived as it might exist; and when we believe it, we can do no more.

[3] *Presumably an error by Hume or his printer for " anticipates ".*

Secondly, The mind has a faculty of joining all ideas together, which involve not a contradiction; and therefore if belief consisted in some idea, which we add to the simple conception, it would be in a man's power, by adding this idea to it, to believe anything, which he can conceive.

Since therefore belief implies a conception, and yet is something more; and since it adds no new idea to the conception; it follows, that it is a different *manner* of conceiving an object; *something* that is distinguishable to the feeling, and depends not upon our will, as all our ideas do. My mind runs by habit from the visible object of one ball moving towards another, to the usual effect of motion in the second ball. It not only conceives that motion, but *feels* something different in the conception of it from a mere *reverie* of the imagination. The presence of this visible object, and the constant conjunction of that particular effect, render the idea different to the *feeling* from those loose ideas, which come into the mind without any introduction. This conclusion seems a little surprising; but we are led into it by a chain of propositions, which admit of no doubt. To ease the reader's memory I shall briefly resume them. No matter of fact can be proved but from its cause or its effect. Nothing can be known to be the cause of another but by experience. We can give no reason for extending to the future our experience of the past; but are entirely determined by custom, when we conceive an effect to follow from its usual cause. But we also believe an effect to follow, as well as conceive it. This belief joins no new idea to the conception. It only varies the manner of conceiving, and makes a difference to the feeling or sentiment. Belief, therefore, in all matters of fact arises only from custom, and is an idea conceived in a peculiar *manner.*

Our author proceeds to explain the manner or feeling, which renders belief different from a loose conception. He seems sensible, that it is impossible by words to describe this feeling, which every one must be conscious of in his own breast. He calls it sometimes a *stronger* conception, sometimes a more *lively,* a more *vivid,* a *firmer,* or a more *intense* conception. And indeed, whatever name we may give to this feeling, which constitutes belief, our author thinks it evident, that it has a more forcible effect on the mind than fiction and mere conception. This he proves by its influence on the passions and on the imagination; which are only moved by truth or what is taken for such. Poetry, with all its art, can never cause a passion, like one in real life. It fails in the original conception of its objects, which never *feel* in the same manner as those which command our belief and opinion.

Our author presuming, that he had sufficiently proved, that the ideas we assent to are different to the feeling from the other ideas, and that this feeling is more firm and lively than our common conception, endeavours in the next place to explain the cause of this lively feeling by an analogy with other acts of the mind. His reasoning seems to be curious;[4] but could scarce be rendered intelligible, or at least probable to the reader, without a long detail, which would exceed the compass I have prescribed to myself.

I have likewise omitted many arguments, which he adduces to prove that belief consists merely in a peculiar feeling or sentiment. I shall only mention one; our past experience is not always uniform. Sometimes one effect follows from a cause, sometimes another: In which case we always believe, that that will exist which is most common. I see a billiard-ball moving towards another. I cannot distinguish whether it moves upon its axis, or was struck so as to skim along the table. In the first case, I know it will not stop after the shock. In the second it may stop. The first is most common, and therefore I lay my account with that effect. But I also conceive the other effect, and conceive it as possible, and as connected with the cause. Were not the one conception different in the feeling or sentiment from the other, there would be no difference betwixt them.

[4] *See Part* III, *Sects.* VI *to* XIII.

We have confined ourselves in this whole reasoning to the relation of cause and effect, as discovered in the motions and operations of matter. But the same reasoning extends to the operations of the mind. Whether we consider the influence of the will in moving our body, or in governing our thought, it may safely be affirmed, that we could never foretell the effect, merely from the consideration of the cause, without experience. And even after we have experience of these effects, it is custom alone, not reason, which determines us to make it the standard of our future judgments. When the cause is presented, the mind, from habit, immediately passes to the conception and belief of the usual effect. This belief is something different from the conception. It does not, however, join any new idea to it. It only makes it be felt differently, and renders it stronger and more lively.

Having dispatched this material point concerning the nature of the inference from cause and effect, our author returns upon his footsteps, and examines anew the idea of that relation.[5] In the considering of motion communicated from one ball to another, we could find nothing but contiguity, priority in the cause, and constant conjunction. But, beside these circumstances, it is commonly supposed, that there is a necessary connection betwixt the cause and effect, and that the cause possesses something, which we call a *power,* or *force,* or *energy.* The question is, what idea is annexed to these terms? If all our ideas or thoughts be derived from our impressions, this power must either discover itself to our senses, or to our internal feeling. But so little does any *power* discover itself to the senses in the operations of matter, that the *Cartesians* have made no scruple to assert, that matter is utterly deprived of energy, and that all its operations are performed merely by the energy of the supreme Being. But the question still recurs, *What idea have we of energy or power even in the supreme Being?* All our idea of a Deity (according to those who deny innate ideas) is nothing but a composition of

[5] *Part* III, *Sect.* XIV.

those ideas, which we acquire from reflecting on the operations of our own minds. Now our own minds afford us no more notion of energy than matter does. When we consider our will or volition *a priori,* abstracting from experience, we should never be able to infer any effect from it. And when we take the assistance of experience, it only shows us objects contiguous, successive, and constantly conjoined.[6] Upon the whole, then, either we have no idea at all of force and energy, and these words are altogether insignificant, or they can mean nothing but that determination of the thought, acquired by habit, to pass from the cause to its usual effect. But whoever would thoroughly understand this must consult the author himself. It is sufficient, if I can make the learned world apprehend, that there is some difficulty in the case, and that whoever solves the difficulty must say something very new and extraordinary; as new as the difficulty itself.

By all that has been said the reader will easily perceive, that the philosophy contained in this book is very sceptical, and tends to give us a notion of the imperfections and narrow limits of human understanding. Almost all reasoning is there reduced to experience; and the belief, which attends experience, is explained to be nothing but a peculiar sentiment, or lively conception produced by habit. Nor is this all, when we believe any thing of *external* existence, or suppose an object to exist a moment after it is no longer perceived, this belief is nothing but a sentiment of the same kind. Our author insists upon several other sceptical topics; and upon the whole concludes, that we assent to our faculties, and employ our reason only because we cannot help it. Philosophy would render us entirely *Pyrrhonian,* were not nature too strong for it.

I shall conclude the logics of this author with an account of two opinions, which seem to be peculiar to himself, as indeed are most of his opinions. He asserts, that the soul, as far as we can conceive it, is nothing but a system or train of different perceptions, those of heat and

[6] *cf.* Part III, Sect. XIV, *p.* 211. *Note square brackets.*

cold, love and anger, thoughts and sensations; all united together, but without any perfect simplicity or identity. *Des Cartes* maintained that thought was the essence of the mind; not this thought or that thought, but thought in general. This seems to be absolutely unintelligible, since every thing, that exists, is particular : and therefore it must be our several particular perceptions, that compose the mind. I say, *compose* the mind, not *belong* to it. The mind is not a substance, in which the perceptions inhere. That notion is as unintelligible as the *Cartesian,* that thought or perception in general is the essence of the mind. We have no idea of substance of any kind, since we have no idea but what is derived from some impression, and we have no impression of any substance either material or spiritual. We know nothing but particular qualities and perceptions. As our idea of any body, a peach, for instance, is only that of a particular taste, colour, figure, size, consistence, etc. So our idea of any mind is only that of particular perceptions, without the notion of any thing we call substance, either simple or compound.

The second principle, which I proposed to take notice of, is with regard to Geometry. Having denied the infinite divisibility of extension, our author finds himself obliged to refute those mathematical arguments, which have been adduced for it; and these indeed are the only ones of any weight. This he does by denying Geometry to be a science exact enough to admit of conclusions so subtile as those which regard infinite divisibility. His arguments may be thus explained. All Geometry is founded on the notions of equality and inequality, and therefore according as we have or have not an exact standard of that relation, the science itself will or will not admit of great exactness. Now there is an exact standard of equality, if we suppose that quantity is composed of indivisible points. Two lines are equal when the numbers of the points, that compose them, are equal, and when there is a point in one corresponding to a point in the other. But though this standard be exact, it is useless; since we can never compute the number of points in any line. It is besides founded on the supposition of finite divisibility, and therefore can never afford any conclusion against it. If we reject this standard of equality, we have none that has any pretensions to exactness. I find two that are commonly made use of. Two lines above a yard, for instance, are said to be equal, when they contain any inferior quantity, as an inch, an equal number of times. But this runs in a circle. For the quantity we call an inch in the one is supposed to be *equal* to what we call an inch in the other : and the question still is, by what standard we proceed when we judge them to be equal; or, in other words, what we mean when we say they are equal. If we take still inferior quantities, we go on *in infinitum*. This therefore is no standard of equality. The greatest part of philosophers, when asked what they mean by equality, say, that the word admits of no definition, and that it is sufficient to place before us two equal bodies, such as two diameters of a circle, to make us understand that term. Now this is taking the *general appearance* of the objects for the standard of that proportion, and renders our imagination and senses the ultimate judges of it. But such a standard admits of no exactness, and can never afford any conclusion contrary to the imagination and senses. Whether this question be just or not, must be left to the learned world to judge. It were certainly to be wished, that some expedient were fallen upon to reconcile philosophy and common sense, which with regard to the question of infinite divisibility have waged most cruel wars with each other.

We must now proceed to give some account of the second volume of this work, which treats of the PASSIONS. It is of more easy comprehension than the first; but contains opinions that are altogether as new and extraordinary. The author begins with *pride* and *humility*. He observes, that the objects which excite these passions, are very numerous, and seemingly very different from each other. Pride or self-esteem may arise from the qualities of the mind; wit, good-sense, learning, courage, integrity : from those of the body; beauty, strength, agility, good mien, address in dancing, riding, fencing : from external advantages; country, family, children, relations, riches, houses, gardens, horses, dogs, clothes. He afterwards proceeds to find out that common circumstance, in which all these objects agree, and which causes them to operate on the passions. His theory likewise extends to love and hatred, and other affections. As these questions, though curious, could not be rendered intelligible without a long discourse, we shall here omit them.

It may perhaps be more acceptable to the reader to be informed of what our author says concerning *freewill*. He has laid the foundation of his doctrine in what he said concerning cause and effect, as above explained.

It is universally acknowledged, that the operations of external bodies are necessary, and that in the communication of their motion, in their attraction and mutual cohesion, there are not the least traces of indifference or liberty. . . . Whatever therefore is in this respect on the same footing with matter, must be acknowledged to be necessary. That we may know whether this be the case with the actions of the mind, we may examine matter, and consider on what the idea of a necessity in its operations are founded, and why we conclude one body or action to be the infallible cause of another.

It has been observed already, that in no single instance the ultimate connection of any object is discoverable either by our senses or reason, and that we can never penetrate so far into the essence and construction of bodies, as to perceive the principle on which their mutual influence is founded. It is their constant union alone, with which we are acquainted; and it is from the constant union the necessity arises, when the mind is determined to pass from one object to its usual attendant, and infer the existence of one from that of the other. Here then are two particulars, which we are to regard as essential to *necessity*, viz.

the constant *union* and the *inference* of the mind, and wherever we discover these we must acknowledge a necessity.[7]

Now nothing is more evident than the constant union of particular actions with particular motives. If all actions be not constantly united with their proper motives, this uncertainty is no more than what may be observed every day in the actions of matter, where by reason of the mixture and uncertainty of causes, the effect is often variable and uncertain. Thirty grains of opium will kill any man that is not accustomed to it; though thirty grains of rhubarb will not always purge him. In like manner the fear of death will always make a man go twenty paces out of his road; though it will not always make him do a bad action.

And as there is often a constant conjunction of the actions of the will with their motives, so the inference from the one to the other is often as certain as any reasoning concerning bodies : and there is always an inference proportioned to the constancy of the conjunction. On this is founded our belief in witnesses, our credit in history, and indeed all kinds of moral evidence, and almost the whole conduct of life.

Our author pretends that this reasoning puts the whole controversy in a new light, by giving a new definition of necessity. And, indeed, the most zealous advocates for freewill must allow this union and inference with regard to human actions. They will only deny, that this makes the whole of necessity. But then they must shew, that we have an idea of something else in the actions of matter; which, according to the foregoing reasoning, is impossible.

Through this whole book, there are great pretensions to new discoveries in philosophy; but if any thing can entitle the author to so glorious a name as that of an *inventor,* it is the use he makes of the principle of the association of ideas, which enters into most of his philosophy. Our imagination has a great authority over our ideas; and there are no ideas that are different from each other, which it

[7] *Book* II, *Part* III, *Sect.* I.

18

cannot separate, and join, and compose into all the varieties of fiction. But notwithstanding the empire of the imagination, there is a secret tie or union among particular ideas, which causes the mind to conjoin them more frequently together, and makes the one, upon its appearance, introduce the other. Hence arises what we call the *apropos* of discourse : hence the connection of writing : and hence that thread, or chain of thought, which a man naturally supports even in the loosest *reverie*. These principles of association are reduced to three, viz. *Resemblance;* a picture naturally makes us think of the man it was drawn for. *Contiguity;* when *St. Dennis* is mentioned, the idea of *Paris* naturally occurs. *Causation;* when we think of the son, we are apt to carry our attention to the father. It will be easy to conceive of what vast consequence these principles must be in the science of human nature, if we consider, that so far as regards the mind, these are the only links that bind the parts of the universe together, or connect us with any person or object exterior to ourselves. For as it is by means of thought only that any thing operates upon our passions, and as these are the only ties of our thoughts, they are really *to us* the cement of the universe, and all the operations of the mind must, in a great measure, depend on them.

FINIS

RELATIONS OF IDEAS AND MATTERS OF FACT IN THE ENQUIRY CONCERNING HUMAN UNDERSTANDING

All the objects of human reason or enquiry may naturally be divided into two kinds, to wit, *Relations of Ideas,* and *Matters of Fact.* Of the first kind are the sciences of Geometry, Algebra, and Arithmetic; and in short, every affirmation which is either intuitively or demonstratively certain. *That the square of the hypotenuse is equal to the square of the two sides,* is a proposition which expresses a relation between these figures. *That three times five is equal to the half of thirty,* expresses a relation between these numbers. Propositions of this kind are discoverable by the mere operation of thought, without dependence on what is anywhere existent in the universe. Though there never were a circle or triangle in nature, the truths demonstrated by Euclid would for ever retain their certainty and evidence.

Matters of fact, which are the second objects of human reason, are not ascertained in the same manner, nor is our evidence of their truth, however great, of a like nature with the foregoing. The contrary of every matter of fact is still possible; because it can never imply a contradiction, and is conceived by the mind with the same facility and distinctness, as if ever so conformable to reality. *That the sun will not rise to-morrow* is no less intelligible a proposition, and implies no more contradiction than the affirmation, *that it will rise.* We should in vain, therefore, attempt to demonstrate its falsehood. Were it demonstratively false, it would imply a contradiction, and could never be distinctly conceived by the mind. (*Sect* IV, *Part I*)

EDITOR'S NOTES

BIBLIOGRAPHY

CHRONOLOGICAL
TABLE

INDEX

p. 72. This proposition is true, not because, as Hume thinks, the number of parts into which the idea can be divided is less than twenty, but because it does not make sense to talk of dividing ideas into parts at all. This mistake vitiates the whole section. Hume's admission that we may be able to "imagine" the grain of sand divided into tiny invisible parts, suggests that something is wrong with the doctrine of impressions and ideas.

p. 73. The mistake here is to suppose that ideas can be compared in size with physical objects, as painted portraits can with their subjects. We can of course compare the size things look with the size they are; and Hume oddly suggests that a mite looks to the naked eye much smaller than it is, but through an ideal microscope would look the size it is.

p. 74 (2). The reader need not puzzle himself about this ancient dispute, in which three distinct questions are hopelessly confused :

1. Is there any limit to the size of fractions of which formal mathematics can treat? The answer is no.
2. Is there any limit to the exactness with which scientists can in practice measure small quantities? Answer, yes, though it varies with technical progress.
3. What are the smallest units into which material particles can be split by physical processes? This is a question for the experimental physicist.

For detailed discussions of the ensuing arguments consult N. Kemp Smith *The Philosophy of David Hume* and J. Laird *Hume's Philosophy of Human Nature*.

p. 76 : The wild goose chase for units that are both real

constituents of the world and ideal in their indivisibility dates from ancient Greek philosophy, and Hume's simple impressions are in this respect the successors of Plato's forms. In fact "one" is neither a real nor a fictitious denomination, it is an incomplete denomination. We must always ask, "one what?" One *platoon*, consisting of 20 *men* each consisting of n million *atoms*, is a perfectly real unit, and can be handled mathematically as such.

Each kind of thing that is countable has its own proper criteria of identity and diversity, and hence of unity and plurality. (Compare Hume on the identity of a river, *Treatise*, Bk. 1, p. 308.)

The reference at the beginning of the paragraph is to *Elémens de Géometrie de Monseigneur le Duc de Bourgogne*, presumed to be almost verbally inspired by his tutor Nicolas de Malezieu. Kemp Smith and Laird both quote the relevant passage.

p. 79. This proposition seems to the editor to be false, though some painters have painted as though it seemed to them to be true.

p. 86 (1). Hume has a good point here. The impenetrability of matter is a postulate necessary for the use of our ordinary criterion for the identity of material things, viz. spatio-temporal continuity.

p. 86 (2). There remains the difficulty that the red spot must touch only one side of the blue spot. So the spots must have distinguishable sides.

p. 99 (1) Hume does not appear to be arguing, as some have thought, that the propositions of geometry are empirical. He always regards them as statements of relations of ideas, not of matters of fact (Part III, Sec. 1, para. 1). What he is denying is that ideal exactitude which mathematicians claim for these relations. His position would perhaps be stronger if he had said that the more exact our standards of measurement, the nearer these propositions approach to exact truth. For instance, given two lines with identical terminations, if one can be found to be straighter than the other, then it will also be found to be shorter, if any difference in length can be detected.

p. 99 (2). Hume's discussion of this question is needlessly lengthened by his theory that an idea is a mental image. Of course we have no mental image of a vacuum, i.e. of nothing. His real point is simply that there is an empirical difference between two things which have nothing between them because they are in contact, and two things which have nothing between them because the interval is unoccupied. The difference is simply that in the latter case they are perceptibly related in the same way as objects which have other objects between them, whereas in the former case they are not.

p. 101. The reader may find it interesting to consider by what tests the truth or falsehood of this proposition could be decided.

p. 112. In this important section Hume in effect advances three propositions :—

(1) Existence is not a predicate, i.e. is not an attribute which we can suppose a thing either to have or to lack. Compare Kant, *Critique of Pure Reason* (Transcendental Dialectic, Bk. II, Ch. III, Sect. 4), and G. E. Moore, *Proceedings of the Aristotelian Society Supp.* Vol. XV (1936). See also *Treatise* Bk. I, Part III, Section VII. This proposition is true, and, as Kant saw, refutes the ontological argument for the existence of God.

(2) We can form no conception of things as they really are, which is altogether independent of how they appear to us. Our ordinary criterion for the real, as opposed to the apparent, characteristics of objects is how they would appear in other, usually more " favourable," circumstances.

(3) We are never aware of anything except the sensations, feelings and images in our own minds.
Propositions (1) and (2) are true. Proposition (3) is
false.

p. 122. Hume probably means that, according to his theory,
it is the *constancy* of the relationship between two kinds
of object which makes us pronounce them causally related
and infer the existence of one from that of the other.
Whether such constant relationships hold only between
contiguous and successive objects is a question of secondary importance. As a matter of fact the law of gravity
appears to establish constant relations between the movements of objects very *distant* from one another in space,
and most scientific laws take the form of equations representing the values of one variable as a function of the
contemporary values of another. Compare Russell, *Mys-
ticism and Logic,* ch. IX. It is true, however, that it is often
proper to speak of earlier events causing later events, but
never of later events causing earlier events. See Ayer,
The Problem of Knowledge, ch. IV, Sect. VII.

p. 131. Hume is not saying that we can tell from their coherence or incoherence whether our perceptions are true
or false, but that the truth or falsehood of an observation
is irrelevant to the validity of an inference from it (though
not irrelevant of course to the truth of the conclusion of
the inference).

p. 133. The unsatisfactory nature of Hume's account of
memory is noticed by nearly all his commentators. It is a
fault however which he shares with nearly all other philosophers.

p. 138. Hume usually speaks as if he thought it made sense
to talk of some ultimate connection between causes and
effects, some ultimate principles by which natural things
operate, but that these ultimate principles lie for ever

beyond our ken. But his most developed view, in part III, sect. XIV, is that our only idea of a connection, a power, a principle of operation, is the idea of a constant conjunction observed and expected to be repeated, and that talk of unobservable powers and connections is meaningless (compare Part IV, sect. VII, p. 316). Many philosophers, e.g. Stout in *Mind and Matter*, reject Hume's more developed view, and assert that we can perceive or infer the "active tendencies" of things. Such philosophers have still to face Hume's argument in the preceding paragraph, which shows that no such knowledge of tendencies can enable reason to anticipate experience.

p. 146 (1). Hume's reasons for adding this passage are given in his Appendix. He there says in the final paragraph that ideas of the same object may differ otherwise than in their force and vivacity. But I do not think he wishes to substitute one of these other differences (whatever they may be) for vivacity as the distinguishing mark of belief. His considered position seems to be that belief is distinguished by *one* peculiar manner of conception, which is known to consciousness by its feeling, and for which, on second thoughts, he offers a wider variety of descriptions. Hume is attempting the impossible in trying to catch by a word the introspectible character of a feeling. Words are public instruments and their meanings must be fixed by public criteria, in the case of words like "joy", "belief", etc., by the causes and manifestations of the states they refer to. The introspectible characteristics of feelings are, as it were, private signs, by which each of us learns to distinguish in himself the states these words refer to.

p. 146 (2). The arguments of sections VIII to x are very intricate and difficult. Hume is maintaining three propositions, which he has some difficulty in reconciling with one another.

(1) Any association of an idea with a present impression has some tendency to enliven that idea, by trans-

ferring to it a share of the vivacity of the impression.

(2) The vivacity so conferred upon an idea by an impression associated with it by constant conjunction *is* the belief we have in objects inferred from their causes or effects. Causal inference is a special case of the psychological tendency described in proposition (1).

(3) Belief in objects not observed or remembered arises from constant conjunction, i.e. causation, and from no other relationship.

The difficulty is, why are ideas enlivened by relations other than causation not beliefs?

Hume's first point is that other relations do not enliven our ideas very much *unless we already believe them*. In the *Enquiry* (Sect. v, Part II, para. 44 in Selby-Bigge), he says they do not enliven them at all. Watching the " mummeries " of Roman Catholics did not, we may presume, much enliven Hume's ideas of the objects of their faith. Therefore, if belief is an enlivenment of an idea by an associated impression, it can only occur when there is such an association based on constant conjunction; for the other relations only enliven ideas, if belief is already present. But the fact that they do so enliven them, given prior belief, confirms, Hume thinks, the general principle of transfer of vivacity along associative channels, under which he wishes to subsume his account of causal inference and belief.

Hume then proceeds to explain why the other relations fail to enliven ideas, unless they are already beliefs.

The enlivenment of an idea is essentially something involuntary. If I find that I can at will bestow an association with a present impression on either of two incompatible ideas, the enlivenment fails. This is the case, for instance, where, not knowing whom a portrait represents, I can suppose it to be a portrait of either one person or another.

Hume then maintains that the relation of cause and

effect is the only one which a single non-arbitrary system of ideas can acquire to our impressions of sense and our memories. This system we call "*reality*". Hume has a good point here. If we ask why sensible men are guided by experience rather than the vaticinations of prophets or the presages of astrology, one good answer is that by the latter methods a man can vary his conclusions as he pleases by changing his prophet or altering the significations of the various stars. But what has happened cannot be altered.

But men are not always sensible. They believe what they are told, especially if they are told it repeatedly. Real belief does arise from credulity and education, as well as from experience. Hume proceeds to accommodate these facts with his theory, by maintaining two propositions :—

(1) There is some good empirical warrant for believing what we are told. What we have been told has often turned out to be true. Indeed, though Hume does not say this, unless we had normally been told the truth, we could not have learned the use of language; deception is parasitic on veracity.

(2) Our tendency to believe what we are told is increased beyond the degree experience warrants by two factors :

(a) The *resemblance* between the ideas suggested by the words we hear and the alleged facts they represent. This is the essence of *credulity*.

(b) By the frequent *repetition* of statements, which sets up a *customary* association between the ideas involved. This is the essence of *education*.

Finally Hume considers the effect of poetry on the imagination. Here he is really in difficulties. For it is hard to deny that "poetical fervour" can greatly enliven ideas in whose objects we do not believe at all. Hume does not at all save his thesis by pointing out that an admixture of real places and persons, and some degree of verisimilitude, assist the effect. For the fact remains that we do not believe in Odysseus' visit to Hades, but imagine it very vividly when we read Homer. He is therefore driven to distinguish the vivacity of poetic imagination from belief not in terms of its feebleness, uncertainty or dependence on prior belief, but in terms of its difference to the feeling.

> But how great soever the pitch may be to which this vivacity rise, it is evident, that in poetry it never has the same *feeling* with that which arises in the mind, when we reason, though even upon the lowest species of probability. (Sect. x, p. 172.)

This statement, from one of the improvement-insertions recommended in the Appendix, is quite incompatible with the vivacity theory of belief, which Hume nevertheless retained in the Appendix, in the *Abstract*, and in the *Enquiry*.

To attempt an assessment of these arguments, I would say that Hume is right in thinking that genuine belief is distinguished by some feature which *normally* or *primarily* arises only from experience, but wrong in identifying this feature with either vivacity or a special feeling. Hume himself comes near to a correct identification when he says that belief "renders them (sc. ideas believed in) the governing principles of all our actions" (Sect. vii, p. 146.) To see what a person really thinks, watch how he acts.

Following this clue, we can see in Hume's picture of the vivacity of an impression "diffusing itself along the relations . . . as by so many pipes or canals to every idea that has any communication with the primary one" (Sect. x, p. 171), a prophetic analogue of the more modern picture of the nervous energy generated by the stimulation of receptor nerves diffusing itself to all the motor nerves concerned with responses and preparations for responses connected by the processes of learning with the original stimulus.

p. 148. In reading this paragraph and the next we are reminded that Hume was writing in France.

p. 151. Hume here seems to forget that demonstrative

arguments can also occur in philosophy. Compare Part II, Sect. II, p. 76.

p. 153. Compart Part III, Sect. XII, p. 183.

p. 155. This explanation is far from satisfactory. The "je ne scai quoi", the impression of having an idea, is a very odd sort of impression. And how does memory represent an idea as of the past rather than the future?

p. 180. The reader may wonder what Hume would say if the die had its sides inscribed with the numbers from one to six, and the question were, will it turn up a number greater than two? There would then be no "one figure" in which the four impulses could unite. I think he would have to say they unite in the abstract idea of a number greater than two and less than seven, but it is difficult to see just how, according to his theory of abstract ideas, this could happen.

p. 182. This paragraph gives Hume's account of the reasons we have for accepting the uniformity of nature. It is simply an induction from the success of natural science.

p. 185. And, as with the die, Hume fails to explain how a number of differing images, in this case of ships of various sizes and rigs, can concur into one image.

p. 200. Hume seems to have several quite distinct things in mind, which he does not sufficiently distinguish, and all of which he calls "general rules".
  (1) Unreflective habits of judging set up by accidental conjunctions and vague resemblances.
  (2) Very wide generalisations, such as that for every difference in the effect there is a corresponding difference in the cause.
  (3) Generalisations about the effectiveness of various

kinds of inference in attaining consistency and making true predictions.

(4) Generalisations, such as Hume himself is seeking, about the way the human mind works.

(5) Rules, in the normative sense, based on generalisations of types (2), (3) and (4), telling us how we *ought* to think.

p. 212. These arguments are more fully elaborated in the *Enquiry concerning Human Understanding* (Sect. VII, part 1).

p. 213. In this extremely perceptive passage we have an anticipation of the modern view that metaphysical problems and paradoxes arise from using common words in contexts where they cannot retain their common meaning, and fail to acquire a new one. See Ryle and Wittgenstein *passim*.

We may also note that, according to this argument, Hume's frequent suggestions that the ultimate connections of causes and effects lie beyond our ken, are as nonsensical as the statement that power belongs to God alone.

p. 217. Hume should not be understood to be denying any difference between these two kinds of necessity. His meaning is, two and two *must* make four, because it is impossible to *conceive* their making any other number, so long as the ideas of two, addition and four remain unchanged. Flames *must* be hot, because experience will not suffer us to *believe* in a flame that is not hot.

p. 220. This passage in effect provides the answer Hume would give to critics who have accused his argument of circularity. They say that, when Hume speaks of repeated conjunction as *producing* a customary transition, of the mind being *necessarily determined* etc., he ascribes to impressions and ideas the very sort of necessary connection of which he denies that we have any idea.

p. 222 (1). Mr. J. M. Rogers has pointed out to me that this appears at first sight to be a rejection of the indispensable distinction between necessary and sufficient conditions, which indeed Hume never clearly draws. But Hume is talking of *causes*, not conditions. From Section xv it is clear that he means by a cause a necessary *and* sufficient condition. His point here is that if, given (a), (b) always follows, and (b) is always preceded by (a), there can be no possible ground for saying that (a) is a cause *sine qua non*, and not the efficient cause, of (b). He has in mind philosophers like the Cartesians and Berkeley, who insist that only God can be the true and efficient cause of a phenomenon, however invariable its natural antecedent may be.

Hume's point regarding formal, final, material and exemplary causes is that, however distinct these types of cause may be from one another, they must not be distinguished from efficient causes. For unless they are constantly conjoined with their effects, they are not causes, and if they are, they are efficient causes, in the only intelligible sense of that term. All causes are efficient. The distinctions in question may be illustrated by an example. The front wheel of an aeroplane rolls evenly because it is round (formal cause), is light because it is made of aluminium (material cause), is there to support the nose of the plane when not in flight (final cause), and is there because specified in the design (exemplary cause). The term " exemplary cause " was in fact used by Christian Platonists for features of Divine rather than human designs.

p. 222 (2). Moral necessity is supposed to be that sort of rational necessity which guides a will free from physical necessity. (cf. *Treatise* Book ii, Part iii, Sect. i.)

p. 222 (3). Hume need not be taken to mean that we are never able to do things which we do not in fact do. He means that the power or ability is nothing distinct from the fact that we do the action when we want to and have the opportunity.

p. 228. I fear this "touchstone" could be applied with damaging effects to Hume's theory of perception (Part IV, Sect. II). It is certain that a dog sees a rabbit, in the same sense of "see" as we see it, and that he attributes a continued existence to his bone; but it is quite unnecessary to suppose that his imagination goes through all the processes which Hume ascribes to ours in such cases.

p. 240. It is extremely difficult to pinpoint and correct the mistakes in the following seven paragraphs. But unless this is done it is impossible to devise any theory of perception much less fantastic than Hume's. The underlying confusion is between the perception of objects (cf. my definition of "seeing" in note to p. 250) and awareness of the private sensations and experiences by which we are conscious that we are perceiving (cf. note to p. 146).

p. 249. The parallel may be put thus; just as the supposition of ideally exact units of length enables us to suppose geometrical theorems exactly true, which by any practical standards of measurement are only approximately true, so the supposition of perfectly continuous objects enables us to suppose natural laws to be exactly true, which, as far as any practicable observations go, are only approximately true.

p. 250. In these pages Hume recognises that the permanence of identifiable objects and the existence of casual uniformities are presuppositions of experience. They are not conclusions from observation and inductive inference, but prior conditions without which observation and inference are impossible. For this reason Kant called substance and cause "categories". But both Hume and Kant made the same mistake of supposing that this prior condition is satisfied because our imaginations build causality and per-

manence into the picture of the world which is our perception of it; though they give very different accounts of
how we do it. As Kant clearly saw, such a view makes the
empirical world a world of appearances, not of things in
themselves. It is still idealistic. This consequence can be
avoided if we regard causality and permanence not as
imaginatively built into a constructed picture, but as
logically built into the concepts of observation and learning. To see something is to be able, as a largely learned
response to optical stimulation, to adapt one's behaviour
to its proximate source. This could not conceivably happen
in a world of total irregularity and flux.

p. 252. It is now possible to give a far simpler solution
to this problem. We often use two different descriptions,
by each of which we refer to one individual thing, e.g.
" The man who is now talking to you " and " the man you
see reflected in yonder mirror." The question may then
arise whether there are two things, one of which is referred to by the first description and the other by the
second, or whether there is only one thing to which they
both refer. In the latter case the man reflected in the
mirror is identical with the speaker. Note that in this
instance the two terms identified are contemporary. Compare Frege *Sense and Reference* (*Philosophical Writings of
Gottlob Frege*, Tr. by P. Geach and M. Black).

p. 253. This has been Hume's practice throughout
Part III. And thereby he in effect concealed what in this
section he confesses, that our actual *impressions* never
display the complete regularity of which he says scientists
constantly find examples; for a well timed closing of the
eyes can produce an exception to any law of nature, if
stated in terms of impressions.

p. 258. This view has more recently been known as
" neutral monism ". Compare Russell, *Analysis of Mind*,
chs. VI and VII.

p. 300. A book could be written on the insights and mistakes contained in this remarkable chapter. Two points however stand out and can be briefly summarised.

First, Hume would appear to many modern philosophers to be dead right in saying that because something is the sort of thing that " exists but exists nowhere ", it does not follow that it must be a state of mind, still less that it must be a state of an immaterial substance. The taste of the fig is commonly regarded, as Hume points out, as in the fig. Descartes would say that because it has no shape and size, it cannot be an attribute of a material substance, therefore it must be an attribute of an immaterial substance, i.e. taste is a secondary quality, exists in the mind. To see the absurdity of this line of argument, let the reader consider whether he would regard any of the following as having shape, size, position and motion, and if not, whether he would regard them as states of mind : an attack of indigestion, New Year's Day, the reliability of a motor car, the negative charge on an electron, the French Revolution.

Secondly, Hume's ingenious attempt to convict the immaterialists of the same error as Spinoza is fallacious. It depends on the representative theory of perception, which regards our sensible knowledge of the material world as the possession of a comprehensive mental picture which resembles that world; so that the perception of a round penny must be itself round (or at least elliptical), and could not, says Hume, according to the immaterialist's way of reasoning, inhere in an unextended substance. But the perception of a round penny is not round, or any other shape. For if it were, and the idea of a pound note, being the copy of an impression of it, were oblong, we would have to ask whether the impression of the penny is to the right or to the left of the idea of the pound note which we wish we had instead.

p. 319. Hume's sceptical bent appears to have been largely due to French writers such as Boyle, who, following Montaigne, deployed the ancient sceptical arguments preserved in Sextus Empiricus. (Consult R. H. Popkin, *History of Scepticism from Erasmus to Descartes*.)

pp. 126-7 The passages referred to in Hume's footnotes are generally thought to be as follows: Hobbes, *Of Liberty and Necessity*, Works, ed. Molesworth, Vol. IV, p. 276; Clarke, *Demonstration of the Being and Attributes of God*, Propositions I and II; Locke, *An Essay Concerning Human Understanding*, IV, 10, 3 and 8.

Mr E. J. Rhamara has pointed out to me that though Hobbes is here fairly represented and criticised by Hume, Locke and Clarke are not. Clarke was concerned to show that whether the physical world had a beginning in time, or whether it has always existed, there must have existed as its cause a necessary being (i.e. a being the grounds of whose existence lies wholly within itself). Otherwise, he argues, the world must either have sprung into existence out of nothing, that is without a cause, or it must be self-caused, i.e. a necessary being. But even if it has existed for Eternity it cannot be a necessary being, for each of its parts depends on foregoing parts and "where no part is necessary . . . the whole cannot be necessary". It must therefore depend on something else. Locke uses the same argument as Clarke with regard to the hypothesis of a beginning in time. These arguments are not circular; they assume, but they do not pretend to prove, the principle of universal causation, for which both philosophers produce other reasons. Locke (*First Letter to Stillingfleet*) says that the idea of beginning to be is necessarily connected with the idea of some operation, and the idea of operation with the idea of something operating, i.e. a cause. The former connection is, of course, denied by Hume. Clarke (loc. cit.) says that it is a contradiction to suppose that what *is* is effected by *nothing*, i.e. *not effected* at all. Here he is plainly guilty of the fallacy of the fourth argument, criticised by Hume (p. 127). What is effected must indeed be effected by something, but it does not follow that everything that *is* is *effected*.

BIBLIOGRAPHY

PRINCIPAL WORKS

A Treatise of Human Nature (1739). ed. L. A. Selby-Bigge 1888 and 1896, Everyman, No. 548).

An Abstract of a Treatise of Human Nature (1740). (ed. J. M. Keynes & P. Sraffa (1938).

Essays, Moral and Political (1741-1742).

Three Essays (of Natural Character, the Original Contract, Passive Obedience), (1748).

Inquiry concerning Human Understanding (1748), and

Inquiry concerning the Principles of Morals (1751) ("Hume's Enquiries", ed. L. A. Selby-Bigge, 1894).

Political Discourses (1752).

Four Dissertations (The Natural History of Religion, The Passions, Tragedy, The Standard of Taste), (1757).

Two Essays (on Suicide and the Immortality of the Soul). (1777).

Autobiography (1777). (Printed as Appendix A in Mossner's Life of David Hume).

Dialogues Concerning Natural Religion. (Published after his death).

(All above, except the *Abstract*, in "Hume's Philosophical Works", ed. T. H. Green and T. H. Grose, 1895).

History of England (1754-1762).

CORRESPONDENCE

The Letters of David Hume, ed. J. Y. T. Greig. Oxford, 1932.

New Letters of David Hume, ed. R. Klibansky & E. C. Mossner. Oxford, 1954.

PRINCIPAL BIOGRAPHIES

J. Y. T. Greig, *David Hume*. London, 1931.
E. C. Mossner, *The Life of David Hume*. Nelson, 1954.

CRITICAL BOOKS

C. W. Hendel, *Studies in the Philosophy of David Hume*. Princeton, 1925.
R. W. Church, *Hume's Theory of the Understanding*.
J. Laird, *Hume's Philosophy of Human Nature*. Methuen, 1932.
N. Kemp Smith, *The Philosophy of David Hume*. Macmillan, 1941.
H. H. Price, *Hume's Theory of the External World*. Oxford University Press, 1940.
J. A. Passmore, *Hume's Intentions*. Cambridge University Press, 1952.
D. G. C. Macnabb, *David Hume, his Theory of Knowledge and Morality*. Hutchinsons University Library, 1951.
B. M. Laing, *David Hume*. London, 1932.
A. Flew, *Hume's Philosophy of Belief*. Routledge and Kegan Paul, 1961.

CHRONOLOGICAL TABLE

1687 Newton's *Principia*

1690 Locke's *Essay Concerning Human Understanding*

1710 Berkeley's *Principles of Human Knowledge*

1711 Hume born in Edinburgh

1723 to 1725 or '26 At Edinburgh University

1726 to 1734 At Ninewells, studying

1729 Francis Hutcheson appointed Professor of Moral Philosophy at Glasgow

1734 to 1737 In France, principally La Flèche, writing the *Treatise*

1737 to 1739 In London arranging publication

1739 *Treatise,* Books I and II published

1740 The *Abstract* published
Treatise, Book III, with Appendix, published

1739 to 1745 At Ninewells and Edinburgh

1744 Unsuccessful candidate for Chair of Ethics and Pneumatical Philosophy at Edinburgh

1745 to 1746 Tutor to Marquis of Annandale, near St. Albans

1746 to 1749 Secretary to General St. Clair on military expedition to Brittany and diplomatic mission to Vienna and Turin

1748 *Philosophical Essays* (later called *Enquiry*) *Concerning Human Understanding* published

1751 Unsuccessful candidate for Chair of Logic at Glasgow

1751 *Enquiry Concerning the Principles of Morals* published

1752 to 1757 Keeper of Advocates' Library, Edinburgh
Writing *History of Great Britain*

1763 to 1766 Private Secretary to Lord Hertford
Secretary and for a time *chargé d'affaires* at the British Embassy in Paris

1766   Returns to London, bringing Rousseau
       Quarrel with Rousseau. Publication of correspon-
           dence with Rousseau
1767 to 1769 In London. Under-Secretary of State, North-
           ern Dept., till 1768
1769 to 1776 In Edinburgh
1776   Visits London and Bath
1776   Died 25th August in Edinburgh
1779   *Dialogues Concerning Natural Religion* published

INDEX

Abstraction, 61ff., 79-80, 212

Accidents (distinguished from substance), 27, 272

Action, 294-5, 296

Adam, instance of, 342

Adam, Robert, 29

Analytical propositions, 26

Annihilation, hypothetical, 100, 108, 160, 224, 280

Aristotle, 15; *see also* Peripatetics

Association of ideas, 13, 54ff., 139-40, 160-1, 218, 253, 309, 352-3, 361-2

Atheism, 290, 295-6

Ayer, A. J., 360

Bacon, Francis, 12, 42, 338

Barrow, Isaac, 91n.

Bayle's *Dictionary*, 293n.

Belief, 11, 14, 29, 133, 140, 141, 144-6, 149-52, 154, 159, 192, 203-4, 234, 237, 344, 347, 361, 363-4; effect of, 167ff., 171

Belief, and external existence, 258ff., 260, 324ff.

Berkeley, G., 10, 13-14, 17, 61n., 102n., 367

Body (human), relation to mind, 10, 242

Body (i.e. matter), idea of, 160, 243, 260, 270, 349; existence of, 238-9, 244, 249, 250, 281; qualities of, 278, 280-2, 331

Boufflers, Comtesse de, 28

Butler, Bp. J., 13, 42n., 338

Cæsar (as historical example), 129, 142, 195

Cartesians, 25, 209-10, 299n., 347, 367

Categories, 23, 368-9

Causation, 10, 11, 18, 27, 246, 309; analysis of, 21, 121-8, 133ff., 140ff., 156, 158, 205ff., 213ff., 296-7, 298-9, 316, 339; and personal identity, 310-11; in association of ideas, 54, 55, 106, 107, 139, 149, 275, 315, 353; as philosophical relation, 59, 115, 119, 221; and probability, 175ff., 186-7; and belief, 204, 262-3, 281-2, 324, 327; and perception, 296

Cause, 9, 42, 56-7, 206-7; as a " category ", 23, 368; idea of, 16, 17, 22, 273-4

Chance, and probability, 175ff., 222

Change, relation to idea of time, 81-2, 85; and identity, 306

Children, 227, 228, 275

Christianity, 159, 163, 196, 367

Clarke, Dr., 126n.

Coherence and truth, 130-1; and perception, 246, 248ff., 259-60, 268, 292n.

Cohesion, 278

Colour, 94, 143, 278ff.

Conception, 143-4n., 283

Congruity, 140

Conjunction, constant, in causation, 134, 138, 140, 215, 224-5, 298-9, 341; frequent but not constant, 183

Consciousness, 30, 330-1

Constancy of impressions, 245-6, 250, 255, 259-60, 268

Contiguity, in association of

Fontana Philosophy Classics

This series of texts and anthologies, with substantial introductions, was originated by G. J. Warnock and is being continued under the editorship of A. M. Quinton.